$2.50

FEAR AND TREMBLING

AND

THE SICKNESS UNTO DEATH

———————

BY SØREN KIERKEGAARD

Translated with Introductions and Notes by

WALTER LOWRIE

PRINCETON UNIVERSITY PRESS

PRINCETON, NEW JERSEY

Printed in the United States of America
by Princeton University Press, Princeton, New Jersey

The two books comprised in this volume are in greater demand than any other works of Kierkegaard. This preference is a credit to the public taste, for Kierkegaard himself called them "the most perfect books I have written," though in this commendation he included *The Concept of Dread*, and later stretched it to include *Training in Christianity*.

To improve this new edition, which marks a milestone in the popularization of S.K., my friend Howard A. Johnson, Fellow of St. Augustine's College at Canterbury, who knows Danish thoroughly, and knows Kierkegaard better than any other man now living, has taken infinite pains, even to the point of consulting about difficult passages, which abound in S.K.'s works, with Niels Thulstrup, Secretary of the Kierkegaard Society of Denmark. Such co-operation, prompted by love for S.K. (and for me too), has resulted in nearly 200 major and minor corrections of the text published in 1941 by the Princeton University Press. Humiliating as it is to me that my translation should stand in need of so many corrections, I am cheered by the hope that the text of this edition is perhaps the only example of an impeccable translation.

In the individual introductions to *Fear and Trembling* and *The Sickness unto Death*, reprinted, with a few changes, from the original Princeton University Press editions, I have quoted enough from Kierkegaard's journals to inform the reader of the situation in which these poetical books were produced. When *Fear and Trembling* was first published in Denmark, no one could have the least suspicion that it depicted a crisis in the author's life. Such a book may be interesting, even enthralling, when the reader is unaware how serious it is and how personal; but it gains immensely in pathos when one knows that it is a transcription, however poetical, of the author's agonizing reflections upon a problem which was gnawing at his viscera.

Princeton
1953

WALTER LOWRIE

CONTENTS

FEAR AND TREMBLING

It is a strange fact that Kierkegaard's very full *Journal* furnishes hardly any hint of preparation for *Fear and Trembling*. Here, as in the case of all the "aesthetic" works, the most essential introduction is a knowledge of S.K.'s story, in this case especially the story of his engagement and the tragic breach of it, which can be read in my *Kierkegaard*, pp. 193–271. I need give here only a dry list of dates, which, coming so close together as they do, serve to reveal the prodigious speed of S.K.'s literary production. October 11, 1841, was the date of his final rupture with Regina. Thereupon he fled to Berlin, ostensibly to pursue the study of philosophy. But he was away from home only from October 25, 1841, to March 6, 1842, and on February 20, 1843, appeared in two volumes his first great work, *Either/Or*, which he boasted of writing in eight months. This work was "accompanied" rather tardily by *Three Edifying Discourses*, which were through the hands of the printer on May 6 (to be published ten days later), and on the 8th S.K. again departed for Berlin. He was there barely two months, for we have evidence that he was back in Copenhagen sometime in July. Incredible as it seems, he began and finished in this brief period both *Fear and Trembling* and *Repetition*, which were published on October 16 of that year and, in spite of the haste with which they were written, are his most perfect poetical productions. They both recount his desperate struggle in renouncing every hope of earthly happiness when he gave up the prospect of marriage with the woman he loved. We know that while he was writing these two works the struggle to attain resignation was complicated by the hope that he might yet make Regina his wife. This was so evident in *Repetition* that the text had to be altered when, on his return to Copenhagen, S.K. learned that Regina was already engaged to another. *Fear and Trembling*, being a "dialectical lyric," maintained itself throughout on so sublime a plane that no change had to be made in it; for it never was the chief point in the story that he might get Regina back as Abraham received Isaac alive.

Even while he hoped, he was hoping against hope. He says in the *Journal* of that time (IV A 108):*

"Faith therefore hopes also for this life, but, be it noted, by virtue of the absurd, not by virtue of human understanding, otherwise it is only practical wisdom, not faith. Faith is therefore what the Greeks called the divine madness. This is not merely a witty remark but is a thought which can be clearly developed."

An entry in the *Journal* of this period shows that before publishing these books, which not only were drawn from his own experience but involved also his lady-love, S.K. reflected upon the possible impropriety of such a thing (IV A 161):

"The law of delicacy, according to which an author has a right to use what he himself has experienced, is that he is never to utter verity but is to keep verity for himself and only let it be refracted in various ways."

One may perhaps doubt whether in *Repetition* this canon of good taste was strictly observed, but certainly in *Fear and Trembling* there was no risk that anybody else might recognize Regina under the figure of Isaac, and even she might have had difficulty in recognizing herself as Agnes who was carried off by the merman. The white light of truth is here so thoroughly refracted that even the reader who has such acquaintance with S.K.'s story as his contemporaries did not have may need to be told that Abraham's sacrifice of Isaac is a symbol of S.K.'s sacrifice of the dearest thing he had on earth. And the reader who is not acquainted with this story must be told that in order to liberate Regina from her attachment and to "set her afloat" S.K. felt obliged to be cruel enough to make her believe he was a scoundrel who had merely been trifling with her affections.

Apart from one entry in the *Journal* which suggested the possibility of remodeling the familiar story of Agnes and the

*These references are to the twenty-volume edition (in Danish) of S.K.'s papers.

merman (IV A 113), there is only one passage which suggests the plan of *Fear and Trembling*. I quote it in full because it is profoundly characteristic that the idea of a whole work often came to S.K. in a flash (IV A 76, early in May 1843):

"Let us assume (as neither the Old Testament nor the Koran reports) that Isaac knew that the object of the journey he had to make with his father to Mount Moria was that he should be offered as a sacrifice.—If there were living now a poet in our generation, he would be able to relate what these two men talked about on the way. One might also suppose that Abraham's previous life was not blameless, and might let him now mumble under his breath that it was God's punishment, one might even perhaps let him get the melancholy idea that he must assist God in making the punishment as heavy as possible. I suppose that at first Abraham looked upon Isaac with all his fatherly love; his venerable countenance, his broken heart, has made his speech the more impressive, he exhorts him to bear his fate with patience, he has let him darkly understand that he the father suffered from it still more. However, that was of no avail.—Then I think that Abraham has for an instant turned away from him, and when again he turned toward him he was unrecognizable to Isaac, his eyes were wild, his venerable locks had risen like the locks of furies above his head. He seized Isaac by the throat, he drew the knife, he said: 'Thou didst believe it was for God's sake I would do this, thou art mistaken, I am an idolater, this desire has again awakened in my soul, I want to murder thee, this is my desire, I am worse than any cannibal; despair thou foolish boy who didst imagine that I was thy father, I am thy murderer, and this is my desire.' And Isaac fell upon his knees and cried to heaven, 'Merciful God, have mercy upon me!' But then said Abraham softly to himself, 'Thus it must be, for it is better after all that he believes I am a monster, that he curses me for being his father, rather than he should know it was God who imposed the temptation, for then he would lose his reason and perhaps curse God.'

"But where indeed is there a poet in our age who has a

presentiment of such collisions! And yet Abraham's conduct was genuinely poetic, magnanimous, more magnanimous than anything I have read of in tragedies.

"When the child has to be weaned the mother blackens her breast, but her eyes rest just as lovingly upon the child. The child believes it is the breast that has changed, but that the mother is unchanged. And why does she blacken her breast? Because, she says, it would be a shame that it should seem delicious when the child must not get it.—This collision is easily resolved, for the breast is only a part of the mother herself. Happy is he who has not experienced more dreadful collisions, who did not need to blacken *himself*, who did not need to go to hell in order to see what the devil looks like, so that he might paint himself accordingly and in that way if possible save another person in that person's God-relationship at least. This would be Abraham's collision.

"—He who has explained this riddle has explained my life. Yet who was there among my contemporaries that understood this?"

S.K. did not expect this to be understood, he did not wish it to be. Accordingly the pseudonymous author of *Repetition* says at the end of the book that "like Clement Alexandrinus he writes in such a way that the heretics cannot understand him"; in *Fear and Trembling* the very name of the pseudonym, Johannes *de silentio*, suggests mystery, and the motto on the back of the title page, which he got from Hamann, recalls the well-known story of old Rome, which relates that when the son of Tarquinius Superbus had craftily gained the confidence of the people of Gabii he secretly sent a messenger to his father in Rome, asking what he should do next. The father, not willing to trust the messenger, took him into the field where as he walked he struck off with his cane the heads of the tallest poppies. The son understood that he was to bring about the death of the most eminent men in the city and proceeded to do so. S.K. says in his *Journal* that the motto he first thought of was a saying which originated with Herder, though this too he got directly from Hamann in the form (almost) in which he uses it here (III A 203, IV A 126, IV B 961 b and c):

"Write."—"For whom?"—"Write for the dead whom
thou didst love in the past."—"Will they read me?"—"Yea,
for they return as posterity." S.K. made a melancholy correction, for instead of the last reply he wrote simply, "Nay." In
a more optimistic mood he thought of using as a motto the
title of Shakespeare's play, "All's Well that Ends Well."
Again, more tragically, he thought of using the motto he
actually used for that part of the *Stages* which tells his love-
story: *Periisem nisi periisem*, "I had perished had I not perished." This too he got from Hamann, who in turn ascribed
it to "a Greek."

The penury of the *Journal* with respect to allusions to *Fear
and Trembling* seems all the more remarkable when we note
that precisely at the time when he was writing this book and
Repetition, and because of this preoccupation made few entries in the *Journal*, at the most forty-nine, among these there
were fifteen entries which show that his mind was teeming
with thoughts which were to be developed in later works,
and with as many more which were stillborn. Six of them
adumbrate striking themes which the following year appeared
in the *Stages*. The figure of the Fashion Tailor who spoke
at the Banquet is here sketched in five entries. Of the remarkable stories told in Quidam's Diary in place of the entry for
the fifth of each month at midnight four are suggested here:
A Leper's Soliloquy; Solomon's Dream; The Mad Accountant
(Possibility); and Nebuchadnezzar. In addition we find an
adaptation to his case of the story of Abélard and Héloïse,
which strangely enough was not used to fill the place left
vacant on the date of July 5. There is also a plan for "my
Antigone," which had been treated in *Either/Or* but never
was further developed, and for a book to be entitled "Conic
Sections," a study of life in Copenhagen at different hours of
the day when different classes were most in evidence. Not far
separated from these entries in the *Journal*, though they
probably are of a somewhat later date, are suggestions for The
Banquet; for a "Diary of Seducer No. 2," a study in the demoniacal, which perhaps eventuated in the speech of the

Seducer at the Banquet; and the study of a female seducer which was to have been called "The Diary of a Hetaera."

That a man's mind should at one moment be teeming with so many thoughts is certainly abnormal. It perhaps justifies S.K. in saying at this time in the *Journal* (IV A 107): "I am living through within myself more poetry than there is in all novels put together." Soon after his arrival in Berlin he wrote to his friend Boesen: "I have finished one work which I regard as important and am in full swing with a new one. At the beginning I was ill, now I am comparatively well, that is to say, my spirit expands and presumably is killing my body. I never have worked so hard as now. I go out a little while in the morning. Then I come home and sit in my room uninterruptedly until about 3 o'clock. I am hardly able to see out of my eyes. Then I shuffle with my cane to the restaurant, but am so weak that I believe if one were to call my name aloud I should fall over and die. Then I go home and begin again. During the past months [in Copenhagen] I had been indolently pumping up a thorough shower-bath, now I have pulled the cord, and the ideas stream down upon me—healthy, joyful, thriving, merry, blessed children, easily brought to birth, and yet all of them bearing the birthmarks of my personality. Otherwise, as I have said, I am weak, my legs tremble, my knees give under me."

The joys and the sorrows of genuis could hardly be more tellingly described. S.K. was aware that he was a genius, and sadly aware also how much he had to suffer for it. It is significant that at this very time he quoted in his *Journal* with qualified assent a Latin saying that "there never existed great genius without some madness": "*Nullum exstitit magnum ingenium sine aliqua dementia*. This is the worldly expression for the religious affirmation that him whom God blesses He *eo ipso* curses in a worldly sense. Thus it must be. The first is due to the limitations of nature, the second to its duplicity."

Here I have introduced several observations which, though they may seem extraneous to this book, cast much light upon the author of it, for S.K.'s genius was nowhere more evident than in *Fear and Trembling*.

The following account of *Fear and Trembling* was written

by Professor David F. Swenson for the "Philosophical Review," and I am glad to have Swenson's permission to use it here because I believe it to be the clearest exposition of the purport of this book that has ever been written:

"Having in an earlier work (*Either/Or*) delineated the ethical consciousness with a universal religious background, Kierkegaard is in this volume concerned with some of the distinctive traits of the religious concept of faith, taken in the more specific sense in which it is fundamental to the Christian consciousness. It is here depicted as a major human passion, affecting daily life at every point, its content being the entire essential reality of the individual's existence. By reason of its transcendence of the calculations of worldly wisdom and of the naïve illusions of immediacy, in consequence of the firmness of its grasp of the finite life as distinct from the withdrawal from it which ensues when resignation is the final word, and in view of its struggles with and victory over that fear and trembling which its sense of responsibility makes it feel, faith becomes the highest of human passions. It is here presented as heroic and is poetically apprehended with an authentic aesthetic pathos deriving from the realities of Kierkegaard's personal life. The pseudonym places himself admiringly outside, assigning to himself the lower plane of infinite resignation.

"The chief categorical determinants assigned to faith and developed in the essay are: (1) the *particularity* of its relationship to God, dispensing with every form of universal intermediary—community, state, humanity, tradition—so that the individual sustains qua individual an absolute relation to the Absolute; (2) the infinite *resignation* with respect to finite goods which it psychologically presupposes, thus dissociating itself *toto coelo* from those dreams of wish-fulfilment with which the inexperienced confuse it; (3) the *double movement* of the spirit, by which after the infinite resignation it again lives in the finite, but only in virtue of a God-relationship which has no dependence upon calculations of the understanding; (4) the fearful *teleological suspension of the ethical* as exemplified in Abraham, whom the poetic imagination of the author makes to live vividly in the present.

"This suspension of the ethical consciousness finds a more essential and universal expression in the Christian consciousness of sin and its forgiveness, though the treatment of this *motif* is here withheld and given a place in a later volume, *The Concept of Dread*. Other aspects of faith are dealt with in a companion volume, *Repetition*.

"The various determinants of faith are by Kierkegaard concentrated in the single category of the *absurd*, since the movement of faith seems paradoxical to the ordinary consciousness from which faith emerges. The paradoxical is Kierkegaard's careful and precise development of a thought which the Greeks dimly shadowed forth as the divine madness (Plato's *Phaedrus*). Since even thoughtful readers may misunderstand this category when they approach it too exclusively through the traditional and imperfect contrast between faith and reason, I may perhaps be pardoned a word of comment. This category has nothing whatever to do with the supposed antithesis between intellect and will. Kierkegaard did indeed hold that any individual who permits his life to culminate in unutilized thought, speculation, or knowledge, is to be apprehended as essentially comical in his absentmindedness, and to be condemned ethically for attempting to evade the essential task of human existence, which in his view consists in realizing a *decisiveness of spirit* which forms and establishes the personality. But this involves no positing of an antithesis between intellect and will; on the contrary, it protests against leaving incomplete a movement in which intellect, feeling and will normally play their several rôles.

"The paradoxical is rooted in an entirely different antithesis, namely, that between God and man, between God's understanding of what human life ought to be, and man's. It makes its appearance only when the individual has become ethically mature, when he has been developed ethically and religiously to the point where there can be some question of his submitting himself to the divine in order to be radically transformed by the discipline of the relationship. In this conflict the individual's strength consists in his weakness, his victory in his defeat. The human, all-too-human understanding of life which he thus comes to renounce is no abstract intellectual function, but a concrete consciousness involving intellect, feeling and will. In other words, it is his *reason* as the expression for what he initially *is*, in contradistinction to what he strives in faith to *become*. Hence there exists indeed no paradox for faith in its perfection, but for the human individual who is in process of becoming the paradoxical cannot be avoided without arbitrarily limiting the spiritual process. Kierkegaard's insistence upon the paradoxical is a consequence of his deep-seated predilection for apprehending the spiritual life in process, and hence ethically, rather than aesthetically, in a foreshortened perspective, or altogether in static terms.

"Most writers on the philosophy of religion display no inkling of the existence of such a conflict, and much less do they reveal any sympathetic apprehension of its significance. Their descriptions of spiritual attitudes are much like those naïve paintings which depict a landscape in general, fitting everything and nothing. To describe religion as devotion to an ideal, without distinguishing *inter et inter*, and without expending a single word upon the all-important question of the 'how' of this devotion, is about as illuminating as to describe iron as a physical element. For those whose religious experience has been concrete enough to need a more precise intellectual orientation, Kierkegaard offers a rich and concrete psychology of the varied aspects of the life of the spirit; and his categories are sharply enough defined to satisfy the intellectually ambitious."

In my book on *Kierkegaard* (pp. 254ff.) I ventured to express the opinion (which, as I learned later, Professor Emanuel Hirsch, in his *Kierkegaard Studien*, supports by additional arguments) that *Repetition* was written first, *Fear and Trembling* second. That, however, is a question of no great importance, for essentially the plan of both was in S.K.'s mind at the same time, and both books were published on the same day. Following as they did very soon after the two volumes in which *Either/Or* first appeared on February 20, 1843 (nothing being published in the meanwhile except the *Three Edifying Discourses* of May 16), these two little volumes are to be regarded as a second either/or addressed to Regina, and I believe with Hirsch that what prompted S.K. to repeat the question in a different form was the profound disturbance he experienced at seeing Regina twice nod to him in church at evensong on Easter Day (April 16, 1843). Doubtless it was this which prompted him again to take refuge in Berlin, and there he wrote these two books, as a year earlier he had written there a large part of *Either/Or*.

We are not left in doubt as to whether Regina read the books which were meant for her, for we read in Meyer's *Forlovelsen* (Preface, p. iv) that she read all his books—but she read them aloud with her husband. The question put to her by these four volumes, was answered, alas, before it was finally put.

Hirsch rightly insists that the brute fact of Regina's engagement, revealing as it did to S.K. the vanity of all his poetical production, and compelling him to recognize that his life up to this point, including his religious thought and experience, had no better foundation than "possibility," was the occasion of his deepest religious conversion.

From the aesthetic point of view S.K. accounted these two books the most perfect he ever wrote, in spite of the mutilation which *Repetition* had to undergo. Six years later (X²A 15, cf. Dru's translation, No. 965) he wrote in his *Journal*: "Oh, when once I am dead—then *Fear and Trembling* alone will be enough to give me the name of an immortal author. Then it will be read, then too it will be translated into foreign tongues. People will almost shudder at the frightful pathos of the book. But at the time when it was written, when the man who was regarded as the author went about in the incognito of a flâneur and seemed to be nothing but wantonness and wit and frivolity—then nobody could well comprehend the seriousness of it. O ye fools, never was the book so serious as then. Just that appearance was the genuine expression of the horror. If the author had appeared serious, the horror would have been less. Reduplication is the monstrous thing in this horror. But when I am dead people will make of me an imaginary figure, a gloomy figure—and then the book will be terrifying.

"But one true word was already uttered in it, when attention was directed to the difference between the poet and the hero. In me there is a predominant poetic tendency, and yet the mystification was essentially this, that *Fear and Trembling* reproduced my own life. It was in this sense also the theme was first suggested in the earliest journal." He refers here to the entry which has already been quoted.

But from a religious point of view these two books were antiquated before they were published. In view of his profounder experience S.K. could no longer rest satisfied with the easy position of a poet somewhere between the "knight of infinite resignation" and the "knight of faith." In fact these categories never again cropped up in his writings. They were plainly inadequate. His deeper apprehension of what it is to be a Christian is revealed in the *Three Edifying Discourses* which were published on the same date, October 16, but were written after the "thunderstorm," which cleared the air much more thoroughly than he knew when he rewrote the last pages of *Repetition*.

From his new point of view he perceived that not only the first either/or but the second also failed to state the case adequately. I agree with Professor Hirsch in surmising that he therefore felt impelled to restate it in the big book which he called *Stages on Life's Way*. The long "passion story" in that book may be understood as a rectification of *Repetition*, and the concluding remarks of Frater Taciturnus as a rectification of *Fear and Trembling*. Till this work was done S.K. was not free to go on to the *Postscript*, the belated sequel of the *Fragments*, and then to his decisive religious works.

FEAR AND TREMBLING

A DIALECTICAL LYRIC

By *Johannes* DE SILENTIO

COPENHAGEN 1843
[October 16]

Was Tarquinius Superbus in seinem Garten mit den
Mohnköpfen sprach, verstand der Sohn, aber nicht
der Bote. (*What Tarquinius Superbus spoke in his
garden with the poppies was understood by his son,
but not by the messenger.*)[1]

Hamann.

Not merely in the realm of commerce but in the world of ideas as well our age is organizing a regular clearance sale. Everything is to be had at such a bargain that it is questionable whether in the end there is anybody who will want to bid. Every speculative price-fixer who conscientiously directs attention to the significant march of modern philosophy, every *Privatdocent*, tutor, and student, every crofter and cottar in philosophy, is not content with doubting everything but goes further. Perhaps it would be untimely and ill-timed to ask them where they are going, but surely it is courteous and unobtrusive to regard it as certain that they have doubted everything, since otherwise it would be a queer thing for them to be going further. This preliminary movement they have therefore all of them made, and presumably with such ease that they do not find it necessary to let drop a word about the how; for not even he who anxiously and with deep concern sought a little enlightenment was able to find any such thing, any guiding sign, any little dietetic prescription, as to how one was to comport oneself in supporting this prodigious task. "But Descartes[3] did it." Descartes, a venerable, humble and honest thinker, whose writings surely no one can read without the deepest emotion, did what he said and said what he did. Alas, alack, that is a great rarity in our times! Descartes, as he repeatedly affirmed, did not doubt in matters of faith. "*Memores tamen, ut jam dictum est, huic lumini naturali tamdiu tantum esse credendum, quamdiu nihil contrarium a Deo ipso revelatur. . . . Praeter caetera autem, memoriae nostrae pro summa regula est infigendum, ea quae nobis a Deo revelata sunt, ut omnium certissima esse credenda; et quamvis forte lumen rationis, quam maxime clarum et evidens, aliud quid nobis suggerere videretur, soli tamen auctoritati divinae potius quam proprio nostro judicio fidem esse adhibendam.*"[4] He did not cry, "Fire!" nor did he make it a duty for everyone to doubt; for Descartes was a quiet and solitary thinker, not a bellowing night-watchman; he modestly admitted that his method had importance for him alone and was justified in part by the bungled knowledge of his earlier years. "*Ne quis igitur putet me hic traditurum aliquam methodum quam unusquisque sequi debeat ad recte regendum rationem; illam enim tantum quam ipsemet secutus sum exponere decrevi. . . . Sed simul ac illud studiorum curriculum absolvi (sc. juventutis), quo decurso mos est in eruditorum numerum cooptari, plane aliud coepi cogitare. Tot enim me dubiis totque erroribus implicatum esse animadverti, ut omnes discendi conatus nihil aliud mihi profuisse judicarem, quam quod ignorantiam meam magis magisque detexissem.*"[5]

What those ancient Greeks (who also had some understanding of philosophy) regarded as a task for a whole lifetime, seeing that dexterity in doubting is not acquired in a few days or weeks, what the veteran combatant attained when he had preserved the equilibrium of doubt through all the pitfalls he encountered, who intrepidly denied the certainty of sense-perception and the certainty of the processes of thought, incorruptibly defied the apprehensions of self-love and the insinuations of sympathy—that is where everybody begins in our time.

In our time nobody is content to stop with faith but wants to go further. It would perhaps be rash to ask where these people are going, but it is surely a sign of breeding and culture for me to assume that everybody has faith, for otherwise it would be queer for them to be . . . going further. In those old days it was different, then faith was a task for a whole lifetime, because it was assumed that dexterity in faith is not acquired in a few days or weeks. When the tried oldster drew near to his last hour, having fought the good fight and kept the faith, his heart was still young enough not to have forgotten that fear and trembling which chastened the youth, which the man indeed held in check, but which no man quite outgrows . . . except as he might succeed at the earliest opportunity in going further. Where these revered figures arrived, that is the point where everybody in our day begins to go further.

The present writer is nothing of a philosopher, he has not understood the System, does not know whether it actually exists, whether it is completed; already he has enough for his weak head in the thought of what a prodigious head everybody in our day must have, since everybody has such a prodigious thought. Even though one were capable of converting the whole content of faith into the form of a concept, it does not follow that one has adequately conceived faith and understands how one got into it, or how it got into one. The present writer is nothing of a philosopher; he is, *poetice et eleganter*, an amateur writer who neither writes the System nor *promises*[6] of the System, who neither subscribes to the System nor ascribes anything to it. He writes because for him it is a luxury which becomes the more agreeable and more evident, the fewer there are who buy and read what he writes. He can easily foresee his fate in an age when passion has been obliterated in favor of learning, in an age when an author who wants to have readers must take care to write in such a way that the book can easily be perused during the afternoon nap, and take care to fashion his outward deportment in likeness to the picture of that polite young gardener in the advertisement sheet,[7] who with hat in hand, and with a good certificate from the place where he last served, recommends himself to the esteemed public. He foresees his fate—that he will be entirely ignored. He has a presentiment of the dreadful event, that a jealous criticism will many a time let him feel the birch; he trembles at the still more dreadful thought that one or another enterprising scribe, a gulper of paragraphs, who to rescue learning is always willing to do with other peoples' writings what Trop[8] "to preserve good taste" magnanimously resolved to do with a book called *The Destruction of the Human Race*—that is, he will slice the author into paragraphs, and will do it with the same inflexibility as the man who in the interest of the science of punctuation divided his discourse by counting the words, so that there were fifty words for a period and thirty-five for a semicolon.

I prostrate myself with the profoundest deference before every systematic "bag-peerer" at the custom house, protesting, "This is not the System, it has nothing whatever to do with the System." I call down every blessing upon the System and upon the Danish shareholders in this omnibus[9]—for a tower it is hardly likely to become. I wish them all and sundry good luck and all prosperity.

Respectfully,

Johannes DE SILENTIO

Once upon a time there was a man who as a child had heard the beautiful story[11] about how God tempted Abraham, and how he endured temptation, kept the faith, and a second time received again a son contrary to expectation. When the child became older he read the same story with even greater admiration, for life had separated what was united in the pious simplicity of the child. The older he became, the more frequently his mind reverted to that story, his enthusiasm became greater and greater, and yet he was less and less able to understand the story. At last in his interest for that he forgot everything else; his soul had only one wish, to see Abraham, one longing, to have been witness to that event. His desire was not to behold the beautiful countries of the Orient, or the earthly glory of the Promised Land, or that godfearing couple whose old age God had blessed, or the venerable figure of the aged patriarch, or the vigorous young manhood of Isaac whom God had bestowed upon Abraham —he saw no reason why the same thing might not have taken place on a barren heath in Denmark. His yearning was to accompany them on the three days' journey when Abraham rode with sorrow before him and with Isaac by his side. His only wish was to be present at the time when Abraham lifted up his eyes and saw Mount Moriah afar off, at the time when he left the asses behind and went alone with Isaac up unto the mountain; for what his mind was intent upon was not the ingenious web of imagination but the shudder of thought.

That man was not a thinker, he felt no need of getting beyond faith; he deemed it the most glorious thing to be remembered as the father of it, an enviable lot to possess it, even though no one else were to know it.

That man was not a learned exegete, he didn't know Hebrew, if he had known Hebrew, he perhaps would easily have understood the story and Abraham.

I

"And God tempted Abraham and said unto him, Take Isaac, thine only son, whom thou lovest, and get thee into the land of Moriah, and offer him there for a burnt offering upon the mountain which I will show thee."

It was early in the morning, Abraham arose betimes, he had the asses saddled, left his tent, and Isaac with him, but Sarah looked out of the window after them until they had passed down the valley and she could see them no more.[12] They rode in silence for three days. On the morning of the fourth day Abraham said never a word, but he lifted up his eyes and saw Mount Moriah afar off. He left the young men behind and went on alone with Isaac beside him up to the mountain. But Abraham said to himself, "I will not conceal from Isaac whither this course leads him." He stood still, he laid his hand upon the head of Isaac in benediction, and Isaac bowed to receive the blessing. And Abraham's face was fatherliness, his look was mild, his speech encouraging. But Isaac was unable to understand him, his soul could not be exalted; he embraced Abraham's knees, he fell at his feet imploringly, he begged for his young life, for the fair hope of his future, he called to mind the joy in Abraham's house, he called to mind the sorrow and loneliness. Then Abraham lifted up the boy, he walked with him by his side, and his talk was full of comfort and exhortation. But Isaac could not understand him. He climbed Mount Moriah, but Isaac understood him not. Then for an instant he turned away from him, and when Isaac again saw Abraham's face it was changed, his glance was wild, his form was horror. He seized Isaac by the throat, threw him to the ground, and said, "Stupid boy, dost thou then suppose that I am thy father? I am an idolater. Dost thou suppose that this is God's bidding? No, it is my desire." Then Isaac trembled and cried out in his terror, "O God in heaven, have compassion upon me. God of Abraham, have compassion upon me. If I have no father upon earth, be Thou my father!" But Abraham in a low voice said to himself, "O Lord in heaven, I thank Thee. After all it is better for him to believe that I am a monster, rather than that he should lose faith in Thee."

When the child must be weaned, the mother blackens her breast, it would indeed be a shame that the breast should look delicious when the child must not have it. So the child believes that the breast has changed, but the mother is the same, her glance is as loving and tender as ever. Happy the person who had no need of more dreadful expedients for weaning the child!

II

It was early in the morning, Abraham arose betimes, he embraced Sarah, the bride of his old age, and Sarah kissed Isaac, who had taken away her reproach, who was her pride, her hope for all time. So they rode on in silence along the way, and Abraham's glance was fixed upon the ground until the fourth day when he lifted up his eyes and saw afar off Mount Moriah, but his glance turned again to the ground. Silently he laid the wood in order, he bound Isaac, in silence he drew the knife —then he saw the ram which God had prepared. Then he offered that and returned home. . . . From that time on Abraham became old, he could not forget that God had required this of him. Isaac throve as before, but Abraham's eyes were darkened, and he knew joy no more.

When the child has grown big and must be weaned, the mother virginally hides her breast, so the child has no more a mother. Happy the child which did not in another way lose its mother.

III

It was early in the morning, Abraham arose betimes, he kissed Sarah, the young mother, and Sarah kissed Isaac, her delight, her joy at all times. And Abraham rode pensively along the way, he thought of Hagar and of the son whom he drove out into the wilderness, he climbed Mount Moriah, he drew the knife.

It was a quiet evening when Abraham rode out alone, and he rode to Mount Moriah; he threw himself upon his face, he prayed God to forgive him his sin, that he had been willing to offer Isaac, that the father had forgotten his duty toward the son. Often he rode his lonely way, but he found no rest. He could not comprehend that it was a sin to be willing to offer to God the best thing he possessed, that for which he would many times have given his life; and if it was a sin, if he had not loved Isaac as he did, then he could not understand that it might be forgiven. For what sin could be more dreadful?

When the child must be weaned, the mother too is not without sorrow at the thought that she and the child are separated more and more, that the child which first lay under her heart and later reposed upon her breast will be so near to her no more. So they mourn together for the brief period of mourning. Happy the person who has kept the child as near and needed not to sorrow any more!

IV

It was early in the morning, everything was prepared for the journey in Abraham's house. He bade Sarah farewell, and Eleazar, the faithful servant, followed him along the way, until he turned back. They rode together in harmony, Abraham and Isaac, until they came to Mount Moriah. But Abraham prepared everything for the sacrifice, calmly and quietly; but when he turned and drew the knife, Isaac saw that his left hand was clenched in despair, that a tremor passed through his body—but Abraham drew the knife.

Then they returned again home, and Sarah hastened to meet them, but Isaac had lost his faith. No word of this had ever been spoken in the world, and Isaac never talked to anyone about what he had seen, and Abraham did not suspect that anyone had seen it.

When the child must be weaned, the mother has stronger food in readiness, lest the child should perish. Happy the person who has stronger food in readiness!

Thus and in many like ways that man of whom we are speaking thought concerning this event. Every time he returned home after wandering to Mount Moriah, he sank down with weariness, he folded his hands and said, "No one is so great as Abraham! Who is capable of understanding him?"

If there were no eternal consciousness in a man, if at the foundation of all there lay only a wildly seething power which writhing with obscure passions produced everything that is great and everything that is insignificant, if a bottomless void never satiated lay hidden beneath all—what then would life be but despair? If such were the case, if there were no sacred bond which united mankind, if one generation arose after another like the leafage in the forest, if the one generation replaced the other like the song of birds in the forest, if the human race passed through the world as the ship goes through the sea, like the wind through the desert, a thoughtless and fruitless activity, if an eternal oblivion were always lurking hungrily for its prey and there was no power strong enough to wrest it from its maw—how empty then and comfortless life would be! But therefore it is not thus, but as God created man and woman, so too He fashioned the hero and the poet or orator. The poet cannot do what that other does, he can only admire, love and rejoice in the hero. Yet he too is happy, and not less so, for the hero is as it were his better nature, with which he is in love, rejoicing in the fact that this after all is not himself, that his love can be admiration. He is the genius of recollection, can do nothing except call to mind what has been done, do nothing but admire what has been done; he contributes nothing of his own, but is jealous of the intrusted treasure. He follows the option of his heart, but when he has found what he sought, he wanders before every man's door with his song and with his oration, that all may admire the hero as he does, be proud of the hero as he is. This is his achievement, his humble work, this is his faithful service in the house of the hero. If he thus remains true to his love, he strives day and night against the cunning of oblivion which would trick him out of his hero, then he has completed his work, then he is gathered to the hero, who has loved him just as faithfully, for the poet is as it were the hero's better nature, powerless it may be as a memory is, but also transfigured as a memory is. Hence no one shall be forgotten who was great, and though time tarries long, though a cloud[18] of misunderstanding takes the hero away, his lover comes nevertheless, and the longer the time that has passed, the more faithfully will he cling to him.

No, not one shall be forgotten who was great in the world. But each was great in his own way, and each in proportion to the greatness of that which he *loved*. For he who loved himself became great by himself, and he who loved other men became great by his selfless devotion, but he who loved God became greater than all. Everyone shall be remembered, but each became great in proportion to his *expectation*. One became great by expecting the possible, another by expecting the eternal, but he who expected the impossible became greater than all. Everyone shall be remembered, but each was great in proportion to the greatness of that with which he *strove*. For he who strove with the world became great by overcoming the world, and he who strove with himself became great by overcoming himself, but he who strove with God became greater than all. So there was strife in the world, man against man, one against a thousand, but he who strove with God was greater than all. So there was strife upon earth: there was one who overcame all by his power, and there was one who overcame God by his impotence. There was one who relied upon himself and gained all, there was one who secure in his strength sacrificed all, but he who believed God was greater than all. There was one who was great by reason of his power, and one who was great by reason of his wisdom, and one who was great by reason of his hope, and one who was great by reason of his love; but Abraham was greater than all, great by reason of his power whose strength is impotence, great by reason of his wisdom whose secret is foolishness, great by reason of his hope whose form is madness, great by reason of the love which is hatred of oneself.

By faith Abraham went out from the land of his fathers and became a sojourner in the land of promise. He left one thing behind, took one thing with him: he left his earthly understanding behind and took faith with him—otherwise he would not have wandered forth but would have thought this unreasonable. By faith he was a stranger in the land of promise, and there was nothing to recall what was dear to him, but by its novelty everything tempted his soul to melancholy yearning —and yet he was God's elect, in whom the Lord was well pleased! Yea, if he had been disowned, cast off from God's grace, he could have comprehended it better; but now it was like a mockery of him and of his faith. There was in the world one too who lived in banishment[14] from the fatherland he loved. He is not forgotten, nor his Lamentations when he sorrowfully sought and found what he had lost. There is no song of Lamentations by Abraham. It is human to lament, human to weep with them that weep, but it is greater to believe, more blessed to contemplate the believer.

By faith Abraham received the promise that in his seed all races of the world would be blessed. Time passed, the possibility was there, Abraham believed; time passed, it became unreasonable, Abraham believed. There was in the world one who had an expectation, time passed, the evening drew nigh, he was not paltry enough to have forgotten his expectation, therefore he too shall not be forgotten. Then he sorrowed, and sorrow did not deceive him as life had done, it did for him all it could, in the sweetness of sorrow he possessed his delusive expectation. It is human to sorrow, human to sorrow with them that sorrow, but it is greater to believe, more blessed to contemplate the believer. There is no song of Lamentations by Abraham. He did not mournfully count the days while time passed, he did not look at Sarah with a suspicious glance, wondering whether she were growing old, he did not arrest the course of the sun, that Sarah might not grow old, and his expectation with her. He did not sing lullingly before Sarah his mournful lay. Abraham became old, Sarah became a laughing-stock in the land, and yet he was God's elect and inheritor of the promise that in his seed all the races of the world would be blessed. So were it not better if he had not been God's elect? What is it to be God's elect? It is to be denied in youth the wishes of youth, so as with great pains to get them fulfilled in old age. But Abraham believed and held fast the expectation. If Abraham had wavered, he would have given it up. If he had said to God, "Then perhaps it is not after all Thy will that it should come to pass, so I will give up the wish. It was my only wish, it was my bliss. My soul is sincere, I hide no secret malice because Thou didst deny it to me"—he would not have been forgotten, he would have saved many by his example, yet he would not be the father of faith. For it is great to give up one's wish, but it is greater to hold it fast after having given it up, it is great to grasp the eternal, but it is greater to hold fast to the temporal after having given it up.[15]

Then came the fulness of time. If Abraham had not believed, Sarah surely would have been dead of sorrow, and Abraham, dulled by grief, would not have understood the fulfilment but would have smiled at it as at a dream of youth. But Abraham believed, therefore he was young; for he who always hopes for the best becomes old, and he who is always prepared for the worst grows old early, but he who believes preserves an eternal youth. Praise therefore to that story! For Sarah, though stricken in years, was young enough to desire the pleasure of motherhood, and Abraham, though gray-haired, was young enough to wish to be a father. In an outward respect the marvel consists in the fact that it came to pass according to their expectation, in a deeper sense the miracle of faith consists in the fact that Abraham and Sarah were young enough to wish, and that faith had preserved their wish and therewith their youth. He accepted the fulfilment of the promise, he accepted it by faith, and it came to pass according to the promise and according to his faith—for Moses smote the rock with his rod, but he did not believe.

Then there was joy in Abraham's house, when Sarah became a bride on the day of their golden wedding.

But it was not to remain thus. Still once more Abraham was to be tried. He had fought with that cunning power which invents everything, with that alert enemy which never slumbers, with that old man who outlives all things—he had fought with Time and preserved his faith. Now all the terror of the strife was concentrated in one instant. "And God tempted Abraham and said unto him, Take Isaac, thine only son, whom thou lovest, and get thee into the land of Moriah, and offer him there for a burnt offering upon the mountain which I will show thee."

So all was lost—more dreadfully than if it had never come

to pass! So the Lord was only making sport of Abraham! He made miraculously the preposterous actual, and now in turn He would annihilate it. It was indeed foolishness, but Abraham did not laugh at it like Sarah when the promise was announced. All was lost! Seventy years of faithful expectation, the brief joy at the fulfilment of faith. Who then is he that plucks away the old man's staff, who is it that requires that he himself shall break it? Who is he that would make a man's gray hairs comfortless, who is it that requires that he himself shall do it? Is there no compassion for the venerable oldling, none for the innocent child? And yet Abraham was God's elect, and it was the Lord who imposed the trial. All would now be lost. The glorious memory to be preserved by the human race, the promise in Abraham's seed—this was only a whim, a fleeting thought which the Lord had had, which Abraham should now obliterate. That glorious treasure which was just as old as faith in Abraham's heart, many, many years older than Isaac, the fruit of Abraham's life, sanctified by prayers, matured in conflict—the blessing upon Abraham's lips, this fruit was now to be plucked prematurely and remain without significance. For what significance had it when Isaac was to be sacrificed? That sad and yet blissful hour when Abraham was to take leave of all that was dear to him, when yet once more he was to lift up his head, when his countenance would shine like that of the Lord, when he would concentrate his whole soul in a blessing which was potent to make Isaac blessed all his days—this time would not come! For he would indeed take leave of Isaac, but in such a way that he himself would remain behind; death would separate them, but in such a way that Isaac remained its prey. The old man would not be joyful in death as he laid his hands in blessing upon Isaac, but he would be weary of life as he laid violent hands upon Isaac. And it was God who tried him. Yea, woe, woe unto the messenger who had come before Abraham with such tidings! Who would have ventured to be the emissary of this sorrow? But it was God who tried Abraham.

Yet Abraham believed, and believed for this life. Yea, if his faith had been only for a future life, he surely would have cast everything away in order to hasten out of this world to which he did not belong. But Abraham's faith was not of this sort, if there be such a faith; for really this is not faith but the furthest possibility of faith which has a presentiment of its object at the extremest limit of the horizon, yet is separated from it by a yawning abyss within which despair carries on its game. But Abraham believed precisely for this life, that he was to grow old in the land, honored by the people, blessed in his generation, remembered forever in Isaac, his dearest thing in life, whom he embraced with a love for which it would be a poor expression to say that he loyally fulfilled the father's duty of loving the son, as indeed is evinced in the words of the summons, "the son whom thou lovest." Jacob had twelve sons, and one of them he loved; Abraham had only one, the son whom he loved.

Yet Abraham believed and did not doubt, he believed the preposterous. If Abraham had doubted—then he would have done something else, something glorious; for how could Abraham do anything but what is great and glorious! He would have marched up to Mount Moriah, he would have cleft the fire-wood, lit the pyre, drawn the knife—he would have cried out to God, "Despise not this sacrifice, it is not the best thing I possess, that I know well, for what is an old man in compari-son with the child of promise; but it is the best I am able to give Thee. Let Isaac never come to know this, that he may console himself with his youth." He would have plunged the knife into his own breast. He would have been admired in the world, and his name would not have been forgotten; but it is one thing to be admired, and another to be the guiding star which saves the anguished.

But Abraham believed. He did not pray for himself, with the hope of moving the Lord—it was only when the righteous punishment was decreed upon Sodom and Gomorrha that Abraham came forward with his prayers.

We read in those holy books: "And God tempted Abraham, and said unto him, Abraham, Abraham, where art thou? And he said, Here am I." Thou to whom my speech is addressed, was such the case with thee? When afar off thou didst see the heavy dispensation of providence approaching thee, didst thou not say to the mountains, Fall on me, and to the hills, Cover me? Or if thou wast stronger, did not thy foot move slowly along the way, longing as it were for the old path? When a call was issued to thee, didst thou answer, or didst thou not answer perhaps in a low voice, whisperingly? Not so Abraham: joyfully, buoyantly, confidently, with a loud voice, he answered, "Here am I." We read further: "And Abraham rose early in the morning"—as though it were to a festival, so he hastened, and early in the morning he had come to the place spoken of, to Mount Moriah. He said nothing to Sarah, nothing to Eleazar. Indeed who could understand him? Had not the temptation by its very nature exacted of him an oath of silence? He cleft the wood, he bound Isaac, he lit the pyre, he drew the knife. My hearer, there was many a father who believed that with his son he lost everything that was dearest to him in the world, that he was deprived of every hope for the future, but yet there was none that was the child of promise in the sense that Isaac was for Abraham. There was many a father who lost his child; but then it was God, it was the unalterable, the unsearchable will of the Almighty, it was His hand took the child. Not so with Abraham. For him was reserved a harder trial, and Isaac's fate was laid along with the knife in Abraham's hand. And there he stood, the old man, with his only hope! But he did not doubt, he did not look anxiously to the right or to the left, he did not challenge heaven with his prayers. He knew that it was God the Almighty who was trying him, he knew that it was the hardest sacrifice that could be required of him; but he knew also that no sacrifice was too hard when God required it—and he drew the knife.

Who gave strength to Abraham's arm? Who held his right hand up so that it did not fall limp at his side? He who gazes at this becomes paralyzed. Who gave strength to Abraham's soul, so that his eyes did not grow dim, so that he saw neither Isaac nor the ram? He who gazes at this becomes blind.—And yet rare enough perhaps is the man who becomes paralyzed and blind, still more rare one who worthily recounts what happened. We all know it—it was only a trial.

If Abraham when he stood upon Mount Moriah had doubted, if he had gazed about him irresolutely, if before he drew the knife he had by chance discovered the ram, if God had permitted him to offer it instead of Isaac—then he would have betaken himself home, everything would have been the same, he has Sarah, he retained Isaac, and yet how changed! For his retreat would have been a flight, his salvation an accident, his reward dishonor, his future perhaps perdition. Then he would have borne witness neither to his faith nor to God's grace, but would have testified only how dreadful it is to march out to Mount Moriah. Then Abraham would not have been forgotten, nor would Mount Moriah, this mountain would then be mentioned, not like Ararat where the Ark landed, but would be spoken of as a consternation, because it was here that Abraham doubted.

Venerable Father Abraham! In marching home from Mount Moriah thou hadst no need of a panegyric which might console thee for thy loss; for thou didst gain all and didst retain Isaac. Was it not so? Never again did the Lord take him from thee, but thou didst sit at table joyfully with him in thy tent, as thou dost in the beyond to all eternity. Venerable Father Abraham! Thousands of years have run their course since those days, but thou hast need of no tardy lover to snatch the memorial of thee from the power of oblivion, for every language calls thee to remembrance—and yet thou dost reward thy lover more gloriously than does any other; hereafter thou dost make him blessed in thy bosom; here thou dost enthral his eyes and his heart by the marvel of thy deed. Venerable Father Abraham! Second Father of the human race! Thou who first wast sensible of and didst first bear witness to that prodigious passion which disdains the dreadful conflict with the rage of the elements and with the powers of creation in order to strive with God; thou who first didst know that highest passion, the holy, pure and humble expression of the divine madness[16] which the pagans admired—forgive him who would speak in praise of thee, if he does not do it fittingly. He spoke humbly, as if it were the desire of his own heart, he spoke briefly, as it becomes him to do, but he will never forget that thou hadst need of a hundred years to obtain a son of old age against expectation, that thou didst have to draw the knife before retaining Isaac; he will never forget that in a hundred and thirty years thou didst not get further than to faith.

An old proverb fetched from the outward and visible world says: "Only the man that works gets the bread." Strangely enough this proverb does not aptly apply in that world to which it expressly belongs. For the outward world is subjected to the law of imperfection, and again and again the experience is repeated that he too who does not work gets the bread, and that he who sleeps gets it more abundantly than the man who works. In the outward world everything is made payable to the bearer, this world is in bondage to the law of indifference, and to him who has the ring, the spirit of the ring is obedient, whether he be Noureddin or Aladdin,[17] and he who has the world's treasure, has it, however he got it. It is different in the world of spirit. Here an eternal divine order prevails, here it does not rain both upon the just and upon the unjust, here the sun does not shine both upon the good and upon the evil, here it holds good that only he who works gets the bread, only he who was in anguish finds repose, only he who descends into the underworld rescues the beloved, only he who draws the knife gets Isaac. He who will not work does not get the bread but remains deluded, as the gods deluded Orpheus with an airy figure in place of the loved one, deluded him because he was effeminate, not courageous, because he was a cithara-player, not a man. Here it is of no use to have Abraham for one's father, nor to have seventeen ancestors— he who will not work must take note of what is written about the maidens of Israel,[18] for he gives birth to wind, but he who is willing to work gives birth to his own father.

There is a knowledge which would presumptuously introduce into the world of spirit the same law of indifference under which the external world sighs. It counts it enough to think the great—other work is not necessary. But therefore it doesn't get the bread, it perishes of hunger, while everything is transformed into gold. And what does it really know? There were many thousands of Greek contemporaries, and countless numbers in subsequent generations, who knew all the triumphs of Miltiades, but only one[19] was made sleepless by them. There were countless generations which knew by rote, word for word, the story of Abraham—how many were made sleepless by it?

Now the story of Abraham has the remarkable property that it is always glorious, however poorly one may understand it; yet here again the proverb applies, that all depends upon whether one is willing to labor and be heavy laden. But they will not labor, and yet they would understand the story. They exalt Abraham—but how? They express the whole thing in perfectly general terms: "The great thing was that he loved God so much that he was willing to sacrifice to Him the best." That is very true, but "the best" is an indefinite expression. In the course of thought, as the tongue wags on, Isaac and "the best" are confidently identified, and he who meditates can very well smoke his pipe during the meditation, and the auditor can very well stretch out his legs in comfort. In case that rich young man whom Christ encountered on the road had sold all his goods and given to the poor, we should extol him, as we do all that is great, though without labor we would not understand him—and yet he would not have become an Abraham, in spite of the fact that he offered his best. What they leave out of Abraham's history is dread;[20] for to money I have no ethical obligation, but to the son the father has the highest and most sacred obligation. Dread, however, is a perilous thing for effeminate natures, hence they forget it, and in spite of that they want to talk about Abraham. So they talk— in the course of the oration they use indifferently the two terms, Isaac and "the best." All goes famously. However, if it chanced that among the auditors there was one who suffered from insomnia—then the most dreadful, the profoundest tragic and comic misunderstanding lies very close. He went home, he would do as Abraham did, for the son is indeed "the best."

If the orator got to know of it, he perhaps went to him, he summoned all his clerical dignity, he shouted, "O abominable man, offscouring of society, what devil possessed thee to want to murder thy son?" And the parson, who had not been conscious of warmth or perspiration in preaching about Abraham, is astonished at himself, at the earnest wrath which he thundered down upon that poor man. He was delighted with himself, for he had never spoken with such verve and unction. He said to himself and to his wife, "I am an orator. What I lacked was the occasion. When I talked about Abraham on Sunday I did not feel moved in the least." In case the same orator had a little superabundance of reason which might be lost, I think he would have lost it if the sinner were to say calmly and with dignity, "That in fact is what you yourself preached on Sunday." How could the parson be able to get into his head such a consequence? And yet it was so, and the mistake was merely that he didn't know what he was saying. Would there were a poet who might resolve to prefer such situations, rather than the stuff and nonsense with which comedies and novels are filled! The comic and the tragic here touch one another at the absolute point of infinity. The parson's speech was perhaps in itself ludicrous enough, but it became infinitely ludicrous by its effect, and yet this consequence was quite natural. Or if the sinner, without raising any objection, were to be converted by the parson's severe lecture, if the zealous clergyman were to go joyfully home, rejoicing in the consciousness that he not only was effective in the pulpit, but above all by his irresistible power as a pastor of souls, who on Sunday roused the congregation to enthusiasm, and on Monday like a cherub with a flaming sword placed himself before the man who by his action wanted to put to shame the old proverb, that "things don't go on in the world as the parson preaches."*

If on the other hand the sinner was not convinced, his situation is pretty tragic. Presumably he would be executed or sent to the lunatic asylum, in short, he would have become unhappy in relation to so-called reality—in another sense I can

---

*In the old days they said, "What a pity things don't go on in the world as the parson preaches"—perhaps the time is coming, especially with the help of philosophy, when they will say, "Fortunately things don't go on as the parson preaches; for after all there is some sense in life, but none at all in his preaching."

well think that Abraham made him happy, for he that labors
does not perish.

How is one to explain the contradiction illustrated by that
orator? Is it because Abraham had a prescriptive right to be a
great man, so that what he did is great, and when another does
the same it is sin, a heinous sin? In that case I do not wish
to participate in such thoughtless eulogy. If faith does not
make it a holy act to be willing to murder one's son, then let
the same condemnation be pronounced upon Abraham as upon
every other man. If a man perhaps lacks courage to carry his
thought through, and to say that Abraham was a murderer,
then it is surely better to acquire this courage, rather than
waste time upon undeserved eulogies. The ethical expression
for what Abraham did is, that he would murder Isaac; the
religious expression is, that he would sacrifice Isaac; but precisely in this contradiction consists the dread which can well
make a man sleepless, and yet Abraham is not what he is without this dread. Or perhaps he did not do at all what is related,
but something altogether different, which is accounted for by
the circumstances of his times—then let us forget him, for it
is not worth while to remember *that* past which cannot become a present. Or had perhaps that orator forgotten something which corresponds to the ethical forgetfulness of the
fact that Isaac was the son? For when faith is eliminated by
becoming null or nothing, then there only remains the crude
fact that Abraham wanted to murder Isaac—which is easy
enough for anyone to imitate who has not faith, the faith, that
is to say, which makes it hard for him.

For my part I do not lack the courage to think a thought
whole. Hitherto there has been no thought I have been afraid
of; if I should run across such a thought, I hope that I have
at least the sincerity to say, "I am afraid of this thought, it
stirs up something else in me, and therefore I will not think
it. If in this I do wrong, the punishment will not fail to
follow." If I had recognized that it was the verdict of truth that
Abraham was a murderer, I do not know whether I would have
been able to silence my pious veneration for him. However, if
I had thought that, I presumably would have kept silent about
it, for one should not initiate others into such thoughts. But

Abraham is no dazzling illusion, he did not sleep into renown, it was not a whim of fate.

Can one then speak plainly about Abraham without incurring the danger that an individual might in bewilderment go ahead and do likewise? If I do not dare to speak freely, I will be completely silent about Abraham, above all I will not disparage him in such a way that precisely thereby he becomes a pitfall for the weak. For if one makes faith everything, that is, makes it what it is, then, according to my way of thinking, one may speak of it without danger in our age, which hardly extravagates in the matter of faith, and it is only by faith one attains likeness to Abraham, not by murder. If one makes love a transitory mood, a voluptuous emotion in a man, then one only lays pitfalls for the weak when one would talk about the exploits of love. Transient emotions every man surely has, but if as a consequence of such emotions one would do the terrible thing which love has sanctified as an immortal exploit, then all is lost, including the exploit and the bewildered doer of it.

So one surely can talk about Abraham, for the great can never do harm when it is apprehended in its greatness; it is like a two-edged sword which slays and saves. If it should fall to my lot to talk on the subject, I would begin by showing what a pious and God-fearing man Abraham was, worthy to be called God's elect. Only upon such a man is imposed such a test. But where is there such a man? Next I would describe how Abraham loved Isaac. To this end I would pray all good spirits to come to my aid, that my speech might be as glowing as paternal love is. I hope that I should be able to describe it in such a way that there would not be many a father in the realms and territories of the King who would dare to affirm that he loved his son in such a way. But if he does not love like Abraham, then every thought of offering Isaac would be not a trial but a base temptation [Anfechtung]. On this theme one could talk for several Sundays, one need be in no haste. The consequence would be that, if one spoke rightly, some few of the fathers would not require to hear more, but for the time being they would be joyful if they really succeeded in loving their sons as Abraham loved. If there was one who, after having heard about the greatness, but also about the dreadfulness of Abraham's deed, ventured to go forth upon that road, I would saddle my horse and ride with him. At every stopping place till we came to Mount Moriah I would explain to him that he still could turn back, could repent the misunderstanding that he was called to be tried in such a conflict, that he could confess his lack of courage, so that God Himself must take Isaac, if He would have him. It is my conviction that such a man is not repudiated but may become blessed like all the others. But in time he does not become blessed. Would they not, even in the great ages of faith, have passed this judgment upon such a man? I knew a person who on one occasion could have saved my life if he[21] had been magnanimous. He said, "I see well enough what I could do, but I do not dare to. I am afraid that later I might lack strength and that I should regret it." He was not magnanimous, but who for this cause would not continue to love him?

Having spoken thus and moved the audience so that at least they had sensed the dialectical conflict of faith and its gigantic passion, I would not give rise to the error on the part of the audience that "he then has faith in such a high degree that it is enough for us to hold on to his skirts." For I would add, "I have no faith at all, I am by nature a shrewd pate, and every such person always has great difficulty in making the movements of faith—not that I attach, however, in and for itself, any value to this difficulty which through the overcoming of it brought the clever head further than the point which the simplest and most ordinary man reaches more easily."

After all, in the poets love has its priests, and sometimes one hears a voice which knows how to defend it; but of faith one hears never a word. Who speaks in honor of this passion? Philosophy goes further. Theology sits rouged at the window and courts its favor, offering to sell her charms to philosophy. It is supposed to be difficult to understand Hegel, but to understand Abraham is a trifle. To go beyond Hegel[22] is a miracle, but to get beyond Abraham is the easiest thing of all. I for my part have devoted a good deal of time to the understanding of the Hegelian philosophy, I believe also that I understand it tolerably well, but when in spite of the trouble

I have taken there are certain passages I cannot understand, I am foolhardy enough to think that he himself has not been quite clear. All this I do easily and naturally, my head does not suffer from it. But on the other hand when I have to think of Abraham, I am as though annihilated. I catch sight every moment of that enormous paradox which is the substance of Abraham's life, every moment I am repelled, and my thought in spite of all its passion cannot get a hairs-breadth further. I strain every muscle to get a view of it—that very instant I am paralyzed.

I am not unacquainted with what has been admired as great and noble in the world, my soul feels affinity with it, being convinced in all humility that it was in my cause the hero contended, and the instant I contemplate his deed I cry out to myself, *jam tua res agitur*.[23] I *think* myself *into* the hero, but into Abraham I cannot think myself; when I reach the height I fall down, for what I encounter there is the paradox. I do not however mean in any sense to say that faith is something lowly, but on the contrary that it is the highest thing, and that it is dishonest of philosophy to give something else instead of it and to make light of faith. Philosophy cannot and should not give faith, but it should understand itself and know what it has to offer and take nothing away, and least of all should fool people out of something as if it were nothing. I am not unacquainted with the perplexities and dangers of life, I do not fear them, and I encounter them buoyantly. I am not unacquainted with the dreadful, my memory is a faithful wife, and my imagination is (as I myself am not) a diligent little maiden who all day sits quietly at her work, and in the evening knows how to chat to me about it so prettily that I must look at it, though not always, I must say, is it landscapes, or flowers, or pastoral idyls she paints. I have seen the dreadful before my own eyes, I do not flee from it timorously, but I know very well that, although I advance to meet it, my courage is not the courage of faith, nor anything comparable to it. I am unable to make the movements of faith, I cannot shut my eyes and plunge confidently into the absurd, for me that is an impossibility . . . but I do not boast of it. I am convinced that God is love,[24] this thought has for me a primitive lyrical validity. When it is present to me, I am unspeakably blissful, when it is absent, I long for it more vehemently than does the lover for his object; but I do not believe, this courage I lack. For me the love of God is, both in a direct and in an inverse sense, incommensurable with the whole of reality. I am not cowardly enough to whimper and complain, but neither am I deceitful enough to deny that faith is something much higher. I can well endure living in my way, I am joyful and content, but my joy is not that of faith, and in comparison with that it is unhappy. I do not trouble God with my petty sorrows, the particular does not trouble me, I gaze only at my love, and I keep its virginal flame pure and clear. Faith is convinced that God is concerned about the least things. I am content in this life with being married to the left hand, faith is humble enough to demand the right hand—for that this is humility I do not deny and shall never deny.

But really is everyone in my generation capable of making the movements of faith, I wonder? Unless I am very much mistaken, this generation is rather inclined to be proud of making what they do not even believe I am capable of making, viz. incomplete movements. It is repugnant to me to do as so often is done, namely, to speak inhumanly about a great deed, as though some thousands of years were an immense distance; I would rather speak humanly about it, as though it had occurred yesterday, letting only the greatness be the distance, which either exalts or condemns. So if (*in the quality of a tragic hero*, for I can get no higher) I had been summoned to undertake such a royal progress to Mount Moriah, I know well what I would have done. I would not have been cowardly enough to stay at home, neither would I have laid down or sauntered along the way, nor have forgotten the knife, so that there might be a little delay—I am pretty well convinced that I would have been there on the stroke of the clock and would have had everything in order, perhaps I would have arrived too early in order to get through with it sooner. But I also know what else I would have done. The very instant I mounted the horse I would have said to myself, "Now all is lost. God requires Isaac, I sacrifice him, and with him my joy—yet God is love and continues to be that for me; for in the temporal world God and I cannot talk together, we have no language in common." Perhaps one or another in our age will be foolish enough, or envious enough of the great, to want to make himself and me believe that if I really had done this, I would have done even a greater deed than Abraham; for my prodigious resignation was far more ideal and poetic than Abraham's narrow-mindedness. And yet this is the greatest falsehood, for my prodigious resignation was the surrogate for faith, nor could I do more than make the infinite movement, in order to find myself and again repose in myself. In that case I would not have loved Isaac as Abraham loved. That I was resolute in making the movement might prove my courage, humanly speaking; that I loved him with all my soul is the presumption apart from which the whole thing becomes a crime, but yet I did not love like Abraham, for in that case I would have held back even at the last minute, though not for this would I have arrived too late at Mount Moriah. Besides, by my behavior I would have spoiled the whole story; for if I had got Isaac back again, I would have been in embarrassment. What Abraham found easiest, I would have found hard, namely to be joyful again with Isaac; for he who with all the infinity of his soul, *propio motu et propiis auspiciis* [by his own power and on his own responsibility], has performed the infinite movement [of resignation] and cannot do more, only retains Isaac with pain.

But what did Abraham do? He arrived neither too soon nor too late. He mounted the ass, he rode slowly along the way. All that time he believed—he believed that God would not require Isaac of him, whereas he was willing nevertheless to sacrifice him if it was required. He believed by virtue of the absurd; for there could be no question of human calculation, and it was indeed the absurd that God who required it of him should the next instant recall the requirement. He climbed the mountain, even at the instant when the knife glittered he believed . . . that God would not require Isaac. He was indeed astonished at the outcome, but by a double-movement he had reached his first position, and therefore he received Isaac more gladly than the first time. Let us go further. We let Isaac be really sacrificed. Abraham believed. He did not believe that some day he would be blessed in the beyond, but that he would be happy here in the world. God could give him a new Isaac, could recall to life him who had been sacrificed. He believed by virtue of the absurd; for all human reckoning had long since ceased to function. That sorrow can derange a man's mind, that we see, and it is sad enough. That there is such a thing as strength of will which is able to haul up so exceedingly close to the wind that it saves a man's reason, even though he remains a little queer,[25] that too one sees. I have no intention of disparaging this; but to be able to lose one's reason, and therefore the whole of finiteness of which reason is the broker, and then by virtue of the absurd to gain precisely the same finiteness—that appalls my soul, but I do not for this cause say that it is something lowly, since on the contrary it is the only prodigy. Generally people are of the opinion that what faith produces is not a work of art, that it is coarse and common work, only for the more clumsy natures; but in fact this is far from the truth. The dialectic of faith is the finest and most remarkable of all; it possesses an elevation, of which indeed I can form a conception, but nothing more. I am able to make from the springboard the great leap whereby I pass into infinity, my back is like that of a tight-rope dancer, having been twisted in my childhood,[26] hence I find this easy; with a one-two-three! I can walk about existence on my head; but the next thing I cannot do, for I cannot perform the miraculous, but can only be astonished by it. Yes, if Abraham the instant he swung his leg over the ass's back had said to himself, "Now, since Isaac is lost, I might just as well sacrifice him here at home, rather than ride the long way to Moriah"—then I should have no need of Abraham, whereas now I bow seven times before his name and seventy times before his deed. For this indeed he did not do, as I can prove by the fact that he was glad at receiving Isaac, heartily glad, that he needed no preparation, no time to concentrate upon the finite and its joy. If this had not been the case with Abraham, then perhaps he might have loved God but not believed; for he who loves God without faith reflects upon himself, he who loves God believingly reflects upon God.

Upon this pinnacle stands Abraham. The last stage he loses

sight of is the infinite resignation. He really goes further, and reaches faith; for all these caricatures of faith, the miserable lukewarm indolence which thinks, "There surely is no instant need, it is not worth while sorrowing before the time," the pitiful hope which says, "One cannot know what is going to happen . . . it might possibly be after all"—these caricatures of faith are part and parcel of life's wretchedness, and the infinite resignation has already consigned them to infinite contempt.

Abraham I cannot understand,[27] in a certain sense there is nothing I can learn from him but astonishment. If people fancy that by considering the outcome of this story they might let themselves be moved to believe, they deceive themselves and want to swindle God out of the first movement of faith, the infinite resignation. They would suck worldly wisdom out of the paradox. Perhaps one or another may succeed in that, for our age is not willing to stop with faith, with its miracle of turning water into wine, it goes further, it turns wine into water.

Would it not be better to stop with faith, and is it not re-volting that everybody wants to go further? When in our age (as indeed is proclaimed in various ways) they will not stop with love, where then are they going? To earthy wisdom, to petty calculation, to paltriness and wretchedness, to everything which can make man's divine origin doubtful. Would it not be better that they should stand still at faith, and that he who stands should take heed lest he fall? For the movements of faith must constantly be made by virtue of the absurd, yet in such a way, be it observed, that one does not lose the finite but gains it every inch. For my part I can well describe the move-ments of faith, but I cannot make them. When one would learn to make the motions of swimming one can let oneself be hung by a swimming-belt from the ceiling and go through the motions (describe them, so to speak, as we speak of describing a circle), but one is not swimming. In that way I can describe the movements of faith, but when I am thrown into the water, I swim, it is true (for I don't belong to the beach-waders), but I make other movements, I make the movements of infinity, whereas faith does the opposite: after having made the move-ments of infinity, it makes those of finiteness. Hail to him who can make those movements, he performs the marvellous, and I shall never grow tired of admiring him, whether he be Abraham or a slave in Abraham's house; whether he be a professor of philosophy or a servant-girl, I look only at the movements. But at them I do look, and do not let myself be fooled, either by myself or by any other man. The knights of the infinite resignation are easily recognized: their gait is gliding and assured. Those on the other hand who carry the jewel of faith are likely to be delusive, because their outward appearance bears a striking resemblance to that which both the infinite resignation and faith profoundly despise . . . to Philistinism.

I candidly admit that in my practice I have not found any reliable example of the knight of faith, though I would not therefore deny that every second man may be such an example. I have been trying, however, for several years to get on the track of this, and all in vain. People commonly travel around the world to see rivers and mountains, new stars, birds of rare plumage, queerly deformed fishes, ridiculous breeds of men— they abandon themselves to the bestial stupor which gapes at existence, and they think they have seen something. This does not interest me. But if I knew where there was such a knight of faith, I would make a pilgrimage to him on foot, for this prodigy interests me absolutely. I would not let go of him for an instant, every moment I would watch to see how he managed to make the movements, I would regard myself as secured for life, and would divide my time between looking at him and practising the exercises myself, and thus would spend all my time admiring him. As was said, I have not found any such person, but I can well think him. Here he is. Acquaintance made, I am introduced to him. The moment I set eyes on him I instantly push him from me, I myself leap backwards, I clasp my hands and say half aloud, "Good Lord, is this the man? Is it really he? Why, he looks like a tax-collector!" However, it is the man after all. I draw closer to him, watching his least movements to see whether there might not be visible a little heterogeneous fractional telegraphic message from the infinite, a glance, a look, a gesture, a note of sadness, a smile, which betrayed the infinite in its heterogeneity with the finite. No! I examine his figure from tip to toe to see if there might not be a cranny through which the infinite was peeping. No! He is solid through and through. His tread? It is vigorous, belonging entirely to finiteness; no smartly dressed townsman who walks out to Fresberg on a Sunday afternoon treads the ground more firmly, he belongs entirely to the world, no Philistine more so. One can discover nothing of that aloof and superior nature whereby one recognizes the knight of the infinite. He takes delight in everything, and whenever one sees him taking part in a particular pleasure, he does it with the persistence which is the mark of the earthly man whose soul is absorbed in such things. He tends to his work. So when one looks at him one might suppose that he was a clerk who had lost his soul in an intricate system of book-keeping, so precise is he. He takes a holiday on Sunday. He goes to church. No heavenly glance or any other token of the incommensurable betrays him; if one did not know him, it would be impossible to distinguish him from the rest of the congregation, for his healthy and vigorous hymn-singing proves at the most that he has a good chest. In the afternoon he walks to the forest. He takes delight in everything he sees, in the human swarm, in the new omnibuses,[28] in the water of the Sound; when one meets him on the Beach Road one might suppose he was a shopkeeper taking his fling, that's just the way he disports himself, for he is not a poet, and I have sought in vain to detect in him the poetic incommensurability. Toward evening he walks home, his gait is as indefatigable as that of the postman. On his way he reflects that his wife has surely a special little warm dish prepared for him, e.g. a calf's head roasted, garnished with vegetables. If he were to meet a man like-minded, he could continue as far as East Gate to discourse with him about that dish, with a passion befitting a hotel chef. As it happens, he hasn't four pence to his name, and yet he fully and firmly believes that his wife has that dainty dish for him. If she had it, it would then be an invidious sight for superior people and an inspiring one for the plain man, to see him eat; for his appetite is greater than Esau's. His wife hasn't it—strangely enough, it is quite the same to him. On the way he comes past a building site and runs across another man. They talk together for a moment. In the twinkling of an eye he erects a new building, he has at his disposition all the powers necessary for it. The stranger leaves him with the thought that he certainly was a capitalist, while my admired knight thinks, "Yes, if the money were needed, I dare say I could get it." He lounges at an open window and looks out on the square on which he lives; he is interested in everything that goes on, in a rat which slips under the curb, in the children's play, and this with the nonchalance of a girl of sixteen. And yet he is no genius, for in vain I have sought in him the incommensurability of genius. In the evening he smokes his pipe; to look at him one would swear that it was the grocer over the way vegetating in the twilight. He lives as carefree as a ne'er-do-well, and yet he buys up the acceptable time at the dearest price, for he does not do the least thing except by virtue of the absurd. And yet, and yet—actually I could become furious over it, for envy if for no other reason— this man has made and every instant is making the movements of infinity. With infinite resignation he has drained the cup of life's profound sadness, he knows the bliss of the infinite, he senses the pain of renouncing everything, the dearest things he possesses in the world, and yet finiteness tastes to him just as good as to one who never knew anything higher, for his continuance in the finite did not bear a trace of the cowed and fearful spirit produced by the process of training; and yet he has this sense of security in enjoying it, as though the finite life were the surest thing of all. And yet, and yet the whole earthly form he exhibits is a new creation by virtue of the absurd. He resigned everything infinitely, and then he grasped everything again by virtue of the absurd. He constantly makes the movements of infinity, but he does this with such correctness and assurance that he constantly gets the finite out of it, and there is not a second when one has a notion of anything else. It is supposed to be the most difficult task for a dancer to leap into a definite posture in such a way that there is not a second when he is grasping after the posture, but by the leap itself he stands fixed in that posture. Perhaps no dancer can do it—that is what this knight does. Most people live dejectedly in worldly sorrow and joy; they are the ones who sit along the wall and do not join in the dance. The knights of infinity are dancers and possess elevation. They make the movements upward, and fall down again; and this too is no mean pastime, nor ungraceful to behold. But whenever they fall down they are not able at once to assume the posture, they vacillate an instant, and this vacillation shows that after all they are strangers in the world. This is more or less strikingly evident in proportion to the art they possess, but even the most artistic knights cannot altogether conceal this vacillation. One need not look at them when they are up in the air, but only the instant they touch or have touched the ground—then one recognizes them. But to be able to fall down in such a way that the same second it looks as if one were standing and walking, to transform the leap of life into a walk, absolutely to express the sublime in the pedestrian—that only the knight of faith can do—and this is the one and only prodigy.

But since the prodigy is so likely to be delusive, I will describe the movements in a definite instance which will serve to illustrate their relation to reality, for upon this everything turns. A young swain falls in love with a princess,[29] and the whole content of his life consists in this love, and yet the situation is such that it is impossible for it to be realized, impossible for it to be translated from ideality into reality.* The slaves of paltriness, the frogs in life's swamp, will naturally cry out, "Such a love is foolishness. The rich brewer's widow is a match fully as good and respectable." Let them croak in the swamp undisturbed. It is not so with the knight of infinite resignation, he does not give up his love, not for all the glory of the world. He is no fool. First he makes sure that this really is the content of his life, and his soul is too healthy and too proud to squander the least thing upon an inebriation. He is not cowardly, he is not afraid of letting love creep into his most secret, his most hidden thoughts, to let it twine in innumerable coils about every ligament of his consciousness—if

*Of course any other instance whatsoever in which the individual finds that for him the whole reality of actual existence is concentrated, may, when it is seen to be unrealizable, be an occasion for the movement of resignation. However, I have chosen a love experience to make the movement visible, because this interest is doubtless easier to understand, and so relieves me from the necessity of making preliminary observations which in a deeper sense could be of interest only to a few.

the love becomes an unhappy love, he will never be able to tear himself loose from it. He feels a blissful rapture in letting love tingle through every nerve, and yet his soul is as solemn as that of the man who has drained the poisoned goblet and feels how the juice permeates every drop of blood—for this instant is life and death.[30] So when he has thus sucked into himself the whole of love and absorbed himself in it, he does not lack courage to make trial of everything and to venture everything. He surveys the situation of his life, he convokes the swift thoughts, which like tame doves obey his every bidding, he waves his wand over them, and they dart off in all directions. But when they all return, all as messengers of sorrow, and declare to him that it is an impossibility, then he becomes quiet, he dismisses them, he remains alone, and then he performs the movements. If what I am saying is to have any significance, it is requisite that the movement come about normally.* So for the first thing, the knight will have power to concentrate the whole content of life and the whole significance of reality in one single wish. If a man lacks this concentration, this intensity, if his soul from the beginning is dispersed in the multifarious, he never comes to the point of making the movement, he will deal shrewdly in life like the capitalists who invest their money in all sorts of securities, so as to gain on the one what they lose on the other—in short, he is not a knight. In the next place the knight will have the power to concentrate the whole result of the operations of

*To this end passion is necessary. Every movement of infinity comes about by passion, and no reflection can bring a movement about. This is the continual leap in existence which explains the movement, whereas mediation is a chimera which according to Hegel is supposed to explain everything, and at the same time this is the only thing he has never tried to explain. Even to make the well-known Socratic distinction between what one understands and what one does not understand, passion is required, and of course even more to make the characteristic Socratic movement, the movement, namely, of ignorance. What our age lacks, however, is not reflection but passion. Hence in a sense our age is too tenacious of life to die, for dying is one of the most remarkable leaps, and a little verse of a poet has always attracted me much, because, after having expressed prettily and simply in five or six preceding lines his wish for good things in life, he concludes thus:[31]

Ein seliger Sprung in die Ewigkeit.

thought in one act of consciousness. If he lacks this intensity, if his soul from the beginning is dispersed in the multifarious, he will never get time to make the movements, he will be constantly running errands in life, never enter into eternity, for even at the instant when he is closest to it he will suddenly discover that he has forgotten something for which he must go back. He will think that to enter eternity is possible the next instant, and that also is perfectly true, but by such considerations one never reaches the point of making the movements, but by their aid one sinks deeper and deeper into the mire.

So the knight makes the movement—but what movement? Will he forget the whole thing? (For in this too there is indeed a kind of concentration.) No! For the knight does not contradict himself, and it is a contradiction to forget the whole content of one's life and yet remain the same man. To become another man he feels no inclination, nor does he by any means regard this as greatness. Only the lower natures forget themselves and become something new. Thus the butterfly has entirely forgotten that it was a caterpillar, perhaps it may in turn so entirely forget it was a butterfly that it becomes a fish. The deeper natures never forget themselves and never become anything else than what they were. So the knight remembers everything, but precisely this remembrance is pain, and yet by the infinite resignation he is reconciled with existence. Love for that princess became for him the expression for an eternal love, assumed a religious character, was transfigured into a love for the Eternal Being, which did to be sure deny him the fulfilment of his love, yet reconciled him again by the eternal consciousness of its validity in the form of eternity, which no reality can take from him. Fools and young men prate about everything being possible for a man. That, however, is a great error. Spiritually speaking, everything is possible, but in the world of the finite there is much which is not possible. This impossible, however, the knight makes possible by expressing it spiritually, but he expresses it spiritually by waiving his claim to it. The wish which would carry him out into reality, but was wrecked upon the impossibility, is now bent inward, but it is not therefore lost, neither is it forgotten. At one moment it is the obscure emotion of the wish within him which awakens recollections, at another moment he awakens them himself; for he is too proud to be willing that what was the whole content of his life should be the thing of a fleeting moment. He keeps this love young, and along with him it increases in years and in beauty. On the other hand, he has no need of the intervention of the finite for the further growth of his love. From the instant he made the movement the princess is lost to him. He has no need of those erotic tinglings in the nerves at the sight of the beloved etc., nor does he need to be constantly taking leave of her in a finite sense, because he recollects her in an eternal sense,[32] and he knows very well that the lovers who are so bent upon seeing "her" yet once again, to say farefell for the last time, are right in being bent upon it, are right in thinking that it is the last time, for they forget one another the soonest. He has comprehended the deep secret that also in loving another person one must be sufficient unto oneself. He no longer takes a finite interest in what the princess is doing, and precisely this is proof that he has made the movement infinitely. Here one may have an opportunity to see whether the movement on the part of a particular person is true or fictitious. There was one who also believed that he had made the movement; but lo, time passed, the princess did something else, she married[33]—a prince, let us say—then his soul lost the elasticity of resignation. Thereby he knew that he had not made the movement rightly; for he who has made the act of resignation infinitely is sufficient unto himself. The knight does not annul his resignation, he preserves his love just as young as it was in its first moment, he never lets it go from him, precisely because he makes the movements infinitely. What the princess does, cannot disturb him, it is only the lower natures which find in other people the law for their actions, which find the premises for their actions outside themselves. If on the other hand the princess is like-minded, the beautiful consequence will be apparent. She will introduce herself into that order of knighthood into which one is not received by balloting, but of which everyone is a member who has courage to introduce himself, that order of knighthood which proves its immortality by the fact that it makes no distinction between man and woman. The two will preserve their love young and sound, she also will have triumphed over her pains, even though she does not, as it is said in the ballad, "lie every night beside her lord." These two will to all eternity remain in agreement with one another, with a well-timed *harmonia praestabilita*,[34] so that if ever the moment were to come, the moment which does not, however, concern them finitely (for then they would be growing older), if ever the moment were to come which offered to give love its expression in time, then they will be capable of beginning precisely at the point where they would have begun if originally they had been united. He who understands this, be he man or woman, can never be deceived, for it is only the lower natures which imagine they were deceived. No girl who is not so proud really knows how to love; but if she is so proud, then the cunning and shrewdness of all the world cannot deceive her.

In the infinite resignation there is peace and rest; every man who wills it, who has not abased himself by scorning himself (which is still more dreadful than being proud), can train himself to make this movement which in its pain reconciles one with existence. Infinite resignation is that shirt we read about in the old fable.[35] The thread is spun under tears, the cloth bleached with tears, the shirt sewn with tears; but then too it is a better protection than iron and steel. The imperfection in the fable is that a third party can manufacture this shirt. The secret in life is that everyone must sew it for himself, and the astonishing thing is that a man can sew it fully as well as a woman. In the infinite resignation there is peace and rest and comfort in sorrow—that is, if the movement is made normally. It would not be difficult for me, however, to write a whole book, were I to examine the various misunderstandings, the preposterous attitudes, the deceptive movements, which I have encountered in my brief practice. People believe very little in spirit, and yet making this movement depends upon spirit, it depends upon whether this is or is not a one-sided result of a *dira necessitas*, and if this is present, the more dubious it always is whether the movement is normal. If one means by this that the cold, unfruitful necessity must necessarily be present, one thereby affirms that no one can experience death before he actually dies, and that appears to me a crass materialism. However, in our time people concern themselves rather little about making pure movements. In case one who was about to learn to dance were to say, "For centuries now one generation after another has been learning positions, it is high time I drew some advantage out of this and began straightway with the French dances"—then people would laugh at him; but in the world of spirit they find this exceedingly plausible. What is education? I should suppose that education was the curriculum one had to run through in order to catch up with oneself, and he who will not pass through this curriculum is helped very little by the fact that he was born in the most enlightened age.

The infinite resignation is the last stage prior to faith, so that one who has not made this movement has not faith; for only in the infinite resignation do I become clear to myself with respect to my eternal validity, and only then can there be any question of grasping existence by virtue of faith.

Now we will let the knight of faith appear in the rôle just described. He makes exactly the same movements as the other knight, infinitely renounces claim to the love which is the content of his life, he is reconciled in pain; but then occurs the prodigy, he makes still another movement more wonderful than all, for he says, "I believe nevertheless that I shall get her, in virtue, that is, of the absurd, in virtue of the fact that with God all things are possible."[36] The absurd is not one of the factors which can be discriminated within the proper compass of the understanding: it is not identical with the improbable, the unexpected, the unforeseen. At the moment when the knight made the act of resignation,[37] he was convinced, humanly speaking, of the impossibility. This was the result reached by the understanding, and he had sufficient energy to think it. On the other hand, in an infinite sense it was possible, namely, by renouncing it; but this sort of possessing is at the same time a relinquishing, and yet there is no absurdity in this for the understanding, for the understanding continued to be in the right in affirming that in the world of the finite where it holds sway this was and remained an impossibility. This is quite as clear to the knight of faith, so the only thing that can save him is the absurd, and this he grasps by faith. So he recognizes the impossibility, and that very instant he believes the absurd; for, if without recognizing the impossibility with all the passion of his soul and with all his heart, he should wish to imagine that he has faith, he deceives himself, and his testimony has no bearing, since he has not even reached the infinite resignation.

Faith therefore is not an aesthetic emotion but something far higher, precisely because it has resignation as its presupposition; it is not an immediate instinct of the heart, but is the paradox of life and existence. So when in spite of all difficulties a young girl still remains convinced that her wish will surely be fulfilled, this conviction is not the assurance of faith, even if she was brought up by Christian parents, and for a whole year perhaps has been catechized by the parson. She is convinced in all her childish naïveté and innocence, this conviction also ennobles her nature and imparts to her a preternatural greatness, so that like a thaumaturge she is able to conjure the finite powers of existence and make the very stones weep, while on the other hand in her flurry she may just as well run to Herod as to Pilate and move the whole world by her tears. Her conviction is very lovable, and one can learn much from her, but one thing is not to be learned from her, one does not learn the movements, for her conviction does not dare in the pain of resignation to face the impossibility.

So I can perceive that it requires strength and energy and freedom of spirit to make the infinite movement of resignation, I can also perceive that it is feasible. But the next thing astonishes me, it makes my head swim, for after having made the movement of resignation, then by virtue of the absurd to get everything, to get the wish whole and uncurtailed—that is beyond human power, it is a prodigy. But this I can perceive, that the young girl's conviction is mere levity in comparison with the firmness faith displays notwithstanding it has perceived the impossibility. Whenever I essay to make this movement, I turn giddy, the very instant I am admiring it absolutely a prodigious dread grips my soul—for what is it to tempt God? And yet this movement is the movement of faith and remains such, even though philosophy, in order to confuse the concepts, would make us believe that it has faith, and even though theology would sell out faith at a bargain price.

For the act of resignation faith is not required, for what I gain by resignation is my eternal consciousness, and this is a purely philosophical movement which I dare say I am able to make if it is required, and which I can train myself to make, for whenever any finiteness would get the mastery over me, I starve myself until I can make the movement, for my eternal consciousness is my love to God, and for me this is higher than everything. For the act of resignation faith is not required, but it is needed when it is the case of acquiring the very least thing more than my eternal consciousness, for this is the paradoxical. The movements are frequently confounded, for it is said that one needs faith to renounce the claim to everything, yea, a stranger thing than this may be heard, when a man laments the loss of his faith, and when one looks at the scale to see where he is, one sees, strangely enough, that he has only reached the point where he should make the infinite movement of resignation. In resignation I make renunciation of everything, this movement I make by myself, and if I do not make it, it is because I am cowardly and effeminate and without enthusiasm and do not feel the significance of the lofty dignity which is assigned to every man, that of being his own censor, which is a far prouder title than that of Censor General to the whole Roman Republic. This movement I make by myself, and what I gain is myself in my eternal consciousness, in blissful agreement with my love for the Eternal Being. By faith I make renunciation of nothing, on the contrary, by faith I acquire everything, precisely in the sense in which it is said that he who has faith like a grain of mustard can remove mountains. A purely human courage is required to renounce the whole of the temporal to gain the eternal; but this I gain, and to all eternity I cannot renounce it—that is a self-contradiction. But a paradoxical and humble courage is required to grasp the whole of the temporal by virtue of the absurd, and this is the courage of faith. By faith Abraham did not renounce his claim upon Isaac, but by faith he got Isaac. By virtue of resignation that rich young man should have given away everything, but then when he had done that, the knight of faith should have said to him, "By virtue of the absurd thou shalt get every penny back again. Canst thou believe that?"

And this speech ought by no means to have been indifferent to the aforesaid rich young man, for in case he gave away his goods because he was tired of them, his resignation was not much to boast of.

It is about the temporal, the finite, everything turns in this case. I am able by my own strength to renounce everything, and then to find peace and repose in pain. I can stand everything—even though that horrible demon, more dreadful than death, the king of terrors, even though madness were to hold up before my eyes the motley of the fool, and I understood by its look that it was I who must put it on, I still am able to save my soul, if only it is more to me than my earthly happiness that my love to God should triumph in me. A man may still be able at the last instant to concentrate his whole soul in a single glance toward that heaven from which cometh every good gift, and his glance will be intelligible to himself and also to Him whom it seeks as a sign that he nevertheless remained true to his love. Then he will calmly put on the motley garb. He whose soul has not this romantic enthusiasm has sold his soul, whether he got a kingdom for it or a paltry piece of silver. But by my own strength I am not able to get the least of the things which belong to finiteness, for I am constantly using my strength to renounce everything. By my own strength I am able to give up the princess, and I shall not become a grumbler, but shall find joy and repose in my pain; but by my own strength I am not able to get her again, for I am employing all my strength to be resigned. But by faith, says that marvellous knight, by faith I shall get her in virtue of the absurd.

So this movement I am unable to make. As soon as I would begin to make it everything turns around dizzily, and I flee back to the pain of resignation. I can swim in existence, but for this mystical soaring I am too heavy. To exist in such a way that my opposition to existence is expressed as the most beautiful and assured harmony with it, is something I cannot do. And yet it must be glorious to get the princess, that is what I say every instant, and the knight of resignation who does not say it is a deceiver, he has not had one only wish, and he has not kept the wish young by his pain. Perhaps there was one who thought it fitting enough that the wish was no longer vivid, that the barb of pain was dulled, but such a man is no knight. A free-born soul who caught himself entertaining such thoughts would despise himself and begin over again, above all he would not permit his soul to be deceived by itself. And yet it must be glorious to get the princess, and yet the knight of faith is the only happy one, the heir apparent to the finite, whereas the knight of resignation is a stranger and a foreigner. Thus to get the princess, to live with her joyfully and happily day in and day out (for it is also conceivable that the knight of resignation might get the princess, but that his soul had discerned the impossibility of their future happiness), thus to live joyfully and happily every instant by virtue of the absurd, every instant to see the sword hanging over the head of the beloved, and yet not to find repose in the pain of resignation, but joy by virtue of the absurd—this is marvellous. He who does it is great, the only great man. The thought of it stirs my soul, which never was niggardly in the admiration of greatness.

In case then everyone in my generation who will not stop at faith is really a man who has comprehended life's horror, who has understood what Daub[38] means when he says that a soldier who stands alone at his post with a loaded gun in a stormy night beside a powder-magazine . . . will get strange thoughts into his head—in case then everyone who will not stop at faith is a man who had strength of soul to comprehend that the wish was an impossibility, and thereupon gave himself time to remain alone with this thought, in case everyone who will not stop at faith is a man who is reconciled in pain and is reconciled to pain, in case everyone who will not stop at faith is a man who in the next place (and if he has not done all the foregoing, there is no need of his troubling himself about faith)—in the next place did the marvellous thing, grasped the whole of existence by virtue of the absurd . . . then what I write is the highest eulogy of my contemporaries by one of the lowliest among them, who was able only to make the movement of resignation. But why will they not stop at faith, why does one sometimes hear that people are ashamed to acknowledge that they have faith? This I cannot comprehend. If ever I contrive to be able to make this movement, I shall in the future ride in a coach and four.

If it is really true that all the Philistinism I behold in life (which I do not permit my word but my actions to condemn) is not what it seems to be—is it the miracle? That is conceivable, for the hero of faith had in fact a striking resemblance to it—for that hero of faith was not so much an ironist or a humorist, but something far higher. Much is said in our age about irony and humor, especially by people who have never been capable of engaging in the practice of these arts, but who neverthless know how to explain everything. I am not entirely unacquainted with these two passions,[39] I know a little more about them than what is to be found in German and German-Danish compendiums. I know therefore that these two passions are essentially different from the passion of faith. Irony and humor reflect also upon themselves, and therefore belong within the sphere of the infinite resignation, their elasticity is due to the fact that the individual is incommensurable with reality.

The last movement, the paradoxical movement of faith, I cannot make (be that a duty or whatever it may be), in spite of the fact that I would do it more than gladly. Whether a man has a right to make this affirmation, must be left to him, it is a question between him and the Eternal Being who is the object of faith whether in this respect he can hit upon an amicable compromise. What every man can do is to make the movement of infinite resignation, and I for my part would not hesitate to pronounce everyone cowardly who wishes to make himself believe he can not do it. With faith it is a diffcrent matter. But what every man has not a right to do, is to make others believe that faith is something lowly, or that it is an easy thing, whereas it is the greatest and the hardest.

People construe the story of Abraham in another way. They extol God's grace in bestowing Isaac upon him again—the whole thing was only a trial. A trial—that word may say much or little, and yet the whole thing is over as quickly as it is said. One mounts a winged horse, the same instant one is at Mount Moriah, the same instant one sees the ram; one forgets that Abraham rode only upon an ass, which walks slowly along the road, that he had a journey of three days, that he needed some time to cleave the wood, to bind Isaac, and to sharpen the knife.

And yet they extol Abraham. He who is to deliver the discourse can very well sleep till a quarter of an hour before he has to preach, the auditor can well take a nap during the discourse, for all goes smoothly, without the least trouble from any quarter. If there was a man present who suffered from insomnia, perhaps he then went home and sat in a corner and thought: "It's an affair of a moment, this whole thing; if only you wait a minute, you see the ram, and the trial is over." If the orator were to encounter him in this condition, he would, I think, confront him with all his dignity and say, "Wretched man, that thou couldst let thy soul sink into such foolishness! No miracle occurs. The whole of life is a trial." In proportion as the orator proceeds with his outpouring, he would get more and more excited, would become more and more delighted with himself, and whereas he had noticed no congestion of the blood while he talked about Abraham, he now felt how the vein swelled in his forehead. Perhaps he would have lost his breath as well as his tongue if the sinner had answered calmly and with dignity, "But it was about this you preached last Sunday."

Let us then either consign Abraham to oblivion, or let us learn to be dismayed by the tremendous paradox which constitutes the significance of Abraham's life, that we may understand that our age, like every age, can be joyful if it has faith. In case Abraham is not a nullity, a phantom, a show one employs for a pastime, then the fault can never consist in the fact that the sinner wants to do likewise, but the point is to see how great a thing it was that Abraham did, in order that man may judge for himself whether he has the call and the courage to be subjected to such a test. The comic contradiction in the behavior of the orator is that he reduced Abraham to an insignificance, and yet would admonish the other to behave in the same way.

Should not one dare then to talk about Abraham? I think one should. If I were to talk about him, I would first depict the pain of his trial. To that end I would like a leech suck all the dread and distress and torture out of a father's sufferings, so that I might describe what Abraham suffered, whereas all the while he nevertheless believed. I would remind the audience that the journey lasted three days and a good part of the fourth, yea, that these three and a half days were infinitely longer than the few thousand years which separate me from Abraham. Then I would remind them that, in my opinion, every man dare still turn around ere he begins such an undertaking, and every instant he can repentantly turn back. If one does this, I fear no danger, nor am I afraid of awakening in people an inclination to be tried like Abraham. But if one would dispose of a cheap edition of Abraham, and yet admonish everyone to do likewise, then it is ludicrous.

It is now my intention to draw out from the story of Abraham the dialectical consequences inherent in it, expressing them in the form of *problemata*, in order to see what a tremendous paradox faith is, a paradox which is capable of transforming a murder into a holy act well-pleasing to God, a paradox which gives Isaac back to Abraham, which no thought can master, because faith begins precisely there where thinking leaves off.

PROBLEM I

Is there such a thing as a teleological suspension of the ethical?

The ethical as such is the universal, and as the universal it applies to everyone, which may be expressed from another point of view by saying that it applies every instant. It reposes immanently in itself, it has nothing without itself which is its *telos*,[40] but is itself *telos* for everything outside it, and when this has been incorporated by the ethical it can go no further. Conceived immediately as physical and psychical, the particular individual is the individual who has his *telos* in the universal, and his ethical task is to express himself constantly in it, to abolish his particularity in order to become the universal. As soon as the individual would assert himself in his particularity over against the universal he sins, and only by recognizing this can he again reconcile himself with the universal. Whenever the individual after he has entered the universal feels an impulse to assert himself as the particular, he is in temptation (*Anfechtung*), and he can labor himself out of this only by penitently abandoning himself as the particular in the universal. If this be the highest thing that can be said of man and of his existence, then the ethical has the same character as man's eternal blessedness, which to all eternity and at every instant is his *telos*, since it would be a contradiction to say that this might be abandoned (i.e. teleologically suspended), inasmuch as this is no sooner suspended than it is forfeited, whereas in other cases what is suspended is not forfeited but is preserved precisely in that higher thing which is its *telos*.[41]

If such be the case, then Hegel is right when in his chapter on "The Good and the Conscience,"[42] he characterizes man merely as the particular and regards this character as "a moral form of evil" which is to be annulled in the teleology of the moral, so that the individual who remains in this stage is either sinning or subjected to temptation (*Anfechtung*). On the other hand, Hegel is wrong in talking of faith, wrong in not protesting loudly and clearly against the fact that Abraham enjoys honor and glory as the father of faith, whereas he ought to be prosecuted and convicted of murder.

For faith is this paradox, that the particular is higher than the universal—yet in such a way, be it observed, that the movement repeats itself, and that consequently the individual, after having been in the universal, now as the particular isolates himself as higher than the universal. If this be not faith, then Abraham is lost, then faith has never existed in the world . . . because it has always existed. For if the ethical (i.e. the moral) is the highest thing, and if nothing incommensurable remains in man in any other way but as the evil (i.e. the particular which has to be expressed in the universal), then one needs no other categories besides those which the Greeks possessed or which by consistent thinking can be derived from them. This fact Hegel ought not to have concealed, for after all he was acquainted with Greek thought.

One not infrequently hears it said by men who for lack of losing themselves in studies are absorbed in phrases that a light shines upon the Christian world whereas a darkness broods over paganism. This utterance has always seemed strange to me, inasmuch as every profound thinker and every serious artist is even in our day rejuvenated by the eternal youth of the Greek race. Such an utterance may be explained by the consideration that people do not know what they ought to say but only that they must say something. It is quite right for one to say that paganism did not possess faith, but if with this one is to have said something, one must be a little clearer about what one understands by faith, since otherwise one falls back into such phrases. To explain the whole of existence and faith along with it, without having a conception of what faith is, is easy, and that man does not make the poorest calculation in life who reckons upon admiration when he possesses such an explanation; for, as Boileau says, "*un sot trouve toujours un plus sot qui l'admire.*"

Faith is precisely this paradox, that the individual as the particular is higher than the universal, is justified over against it, is not subordinate but superior—yet in such a way, be it observed, that it is the particular individual who, after he has been subordinated as the particular to the universal, now through the universal becomes the individual who as the particular is superior to the universal, for the fact that the individual as the particular stands in an absolute relation to the absolute. This position cannot be mediated, for all mediation comes about precisely by virtue of the universal; it is and remains to all eternity a paradox, inaccessible to thought. And yet faith is this paradox—or else (these are the logical deductions which I would beg the reader to have *in mente* at every point, though it would be too prolix for me to reiterate them on every occasion)—or else there never has been faith . . . precisely because it always has been. In other words, Abraham is lost.

That for the particular individual this paradox may easily be mistaken for a temptation (*Anfechtung*) is indeed true, but one ought not for this reason to conceal it. That the whole constitution of many persons may be such that this paradox repels them is indeed true, but one ought not for this reason to make faith something different in order to be able to possess it, but ought rather to admit that one does not possess it, whereas those who possess faith should take care to set up certain criteria so that one might distinguish the paradox from a temptation (*Anfechtung*).

Now the story of Abraham contains such a teleological suspension of the ethical. There have not been lacking clever pates and profound investigators who have found analogies to it. Their wisdom is derived from the pretty proposition that at bottom everything is the same. If one will look a little more closely, I have not much doubt that in the whole world one will not find a single analogy (except a later instance which proves nothing), if it stands fast that Abraham is the representative of faith, and that faith is normally expressed in him whose life is not merely the most paradoxical that can be thought but so paradoxical that it cannot be thought at all. He acts by virtue of the absurd, for it is precisely absurd that he as the particular is higher than the universal. This paradox cannot be mediated; for as soon as he begins to do this he has to admit that he was in temptation (*Anfechtung*), and if such was the case, he never gets to the point of sacrificing Isaac, or, if he has sacrificed Isaac, he must turn back repentantly to the universal. By virtue of the absurd he gets Isaac again. Abraham is therefore at no instant a tragic hero but something quite different, either a murderer or a believer. The middle term which saves the tragic hero, Abraham has not. Hence it is that I can understand the tragic hero but cannot understand Abraham, though in a certain crazy sense I admire him more than all other men.

Abraham's relation to Isaac, ethically speaking, is quite simply expressed by saying that a father shall love his son more dearly than himself. Yet within its own compass the ethical has various gradations. Let us see whether in this story there is to be found any higher expression for the ethical such as would ethically explain his conduct, ethically justify him in suspending the ethical obligation toward his son, without in this search going beyond the teleology of the ethical.

When an undertaking in which a whole nation is concerned is hindered,[43] when such an enterprise is brought to a standstill by the disfavor of heaven, when the angry deity sends a calm which mocks all efforts, when the seer performs his heavy task and proclaims that the deity demands a young maiden as a sacrifice—then will the father heroically make the sacrifice. He will magnanimously conceal his pain, even though he might wish that he were "the lowly man who dares to weep,"[44] not the king who must act royally. And though solitary pain forces its way into his breast, he has only three confidants among the people, yet soon the whole nation will be cognizant of his pain, but also cognizant of his exploit, that for the welfare of the whole he was willing to sacrifice her, his daughter, the lovely young maiden. O charming bosom! O beautiful cheeks! O bright golden hair! (v.687). And the daughter will affect him by her tears, and the father will turn his face away, but the hero will raise the knife.— When the report of this reaches the ancestral home, then will the beautiful maidens of Greece blush with enthusiasm, and if the daughter was betrothed, her true love will not be angry but be proud of sharing in the father's deed, because the maiden belonged to him more feelingly than to the father.

When the intrepid judge[45] who saved Israel in the hour of need in one breath binds himself and God by the same vow, then heroically the young maiden's jubilation, the beloved daughter's joy, he will turn to sorrow, and with her all Israel will lament her maiden youth; but every free-born man will understand, and every stout-hearted woman will admire Jephtha, and every maiden in Israel will wish to act as did his daughter. For what good would it do if Jephtha were victorious by reason of his vow if he did not keep it? Would not the victory again be taken from the nation?

When a son is forgetful of his duty,[46] when the state entrusts the father with the sword of justice, when the laws require punishment at the hand of the father, then will the father heroically forget that the guilty one is his son, he will magnanimously conceal his pain, but there will not be a single one among the people, not even the son, who will not admire the father, and whenever the law of Rome is interpreted, it will be remembered that many interpreted it more learnedly, but none so gloriously as Brutus.

If, on the other hand, while a favorable wind bore the fleet on with swelling sails to its goal, Agamemnon had sent that messenger who fetched Iphigenia in order to be sacrificed; if Jephtha, without being bound by any vow which decided the fate of the nation, had said to his daughter, "Bewail now thy virginity for the space of two months, for I will sacrifice thee"; if Brutus had had a righteous son and yet would have ordered the lictors to execute him—who would have understood them? If these three men had replied to the query why they did it by saying, "It is a trial in which we are tested," would people have understood them better?

When Agamemnon, Jephtha, Brutus at the decisive moment heroically overcome their pain, have heroically lost the beloved and have merely to accomplish the outward sacrifice, then there never will be a noble soul in the world who will not shed tears of compassion for their pain and of admiration for their exploit. If, on the other hand, these three men at the decisive moment were to adjoin to their heroic conduct this little word, "But for all that it will not come to pass," who then would understand them? If as an explanation they added, "This we believe by virtue of the absurd," who would understand them better? For who would not easily understand that it was absurd, but who would understand that one could then believe it?

The difference between the tragic hero and Abraham is clearly evident. The tragic hero still remains within the ethical. He lets one expression of the ethical find its *telos* in a higher expression of the ethical; the ethical relation between father and son, or daughter and father, he reduces to a sentiment which has its dialectic in its relation to the idea of morality. Here there can be no question of a teleological suspension of the ethical itself.

With Abraham the situation was different. By his act he overstepped the ethical entirely and possessed a higher *telos* outside of it, in relation to which he suspended the former. For I should very much like to know how one would bring Abraham's act into relation with the universal, and whether it is possible to discover any connection whatever between what Abraham did and the universal . . . except the fact that he transgressed it. It was not for the sake of saving a people, not to maintain the idea of the state, that Abraham did this, and not in order to reconcile angry deities. If there could be a question of the deity being angry, he was angry only with Abraham, and Abraham's whole action stands in no relation to the universal, is a purely private undertaking. Therefore, whereas the tragic hero is great by reason of his moral virtue, Abraham is great by reason of a purely personal virtue. In Abraham's life there is no higher expression for the ethical than this, that the father shall love his son. Of the ethical in the sense of morality there can be no question in this instance. In so far as the universal was present, it was indeed cryptically present in Isaac, hidden as it were in Isaac's loins, and must therefore cry out with Isaac's mouth, "Do it not! Thou art bringing everything to naught."

Why then did Abraham do it? For God's sake, and (in complete identity with this) for his own sake. He did it for God's sake because God required this proof of his faith; for his own sake he did it in order that he might furnish the proof. The unity of these two points of view is perfectly expressed by the word which has always been used to characterize this situation: it is a trial, a temptation (*Fristelse*).[47] A temptation—but what does that mean? What ordinarily tempts a man is that which would keep him from doing his duty, but in this case the temptation is itself the ethical . . . which would keep him from doing God's will. But what then is duty? Duty is precisely the expression for God's will.

Here is evident the necessity of a new category if one would understand Abraham. Such a relationship to the deity paganism did not know. The tragic hero does not enter into any private relationship with the deity, but for him the ethical is the divine, hence the paradox implied in his situation can be mediated in the universal.

Abraham cannot be mediated, and the same thing can be expressed also by saying that he cannot talk. So soon as I talk I express the universal, and if I do not do so, no one can understand me. Therefore if Abraham would express himself in terms of the universal, he must say that his situation is a temptation (*Anfechtung*), for he has no higher expression for that universal which stands above the universal which he transgresses.

Therefore, though Abraham arouses my admiration, he at the same time appalls me. He who denies himself and sacrifices himself for duty gives up the finite in order to grasp the infinite, and that man is secure enough. The tragic hero gives up the certain for the still more certain, and the eye of the beholder rests upon him confidently. But he who gives up the universal in order to grasp something still higher which is not the universal—what is he doing? Is it possible that this can be anything else but a temptation (*Anfechtung*)? And if it be possible . . . but the individual was mistaken—what can save him? He suffers all the pain of the tragic hero, he brings to naught his joy in the world, he renounces everything . . . and perhaps at the same instant debars himself from the sublime joy which to him was so precious that he would purchase it at any price. Him the beholder cannot understand nor let his eye rest confidently upon him. Perhaps it is not possible to do what the believer proposes, since it is indeed unthinkable. Or if it could be done, but if the individual had misunderstood the deity—what can save him? The tragic hero has need of tears and claims them, and where is the envious eye which would be so barren that it could not weep with Agamemnon; but where is the man with a soul so bewildered that he would have the presumption to weep for Abraham? The tragic hero accomplishes his act at a definite instant in time, but in the course of time he does something not less significant, he visits the man whose soul is beset with sorrow, whose breast for stifled sobs cannot draw breath, whose thoughts pregnant with tears weigh heavily upon him, to him he makes his appearance, dissolves the sorcery of sorrow, loosens his corslet, coaxes forth his tears by the fact that in his sufferings the sufferer forgets his own. One cannot weep over Abraham. One approaches him with a *horror religiosus*, as Israel approached Mount Sinai.—If then the solitary man who ascends Mount Moriah, which with its peak rises heaven-high above the plain of Aulis, if he be not a somnambulist who walks securely above the abyss while he who is stationed at the foot of the mountain and is looking on trembles with fear and out of reverence and dread dare not even call to him—if this man is disordered in his mind, if he had made a mistake! Thanks and thanks again to him who proffers to the man whom the sorrows of life have assaulted and left naked—proffers to him the fig-leaf of the word with which he can cover his wretchedness. Thanks be to thee, great Shakespeare, who art able to express everything, absolutely everything, precisely as it is—and yet why didst thou never pronounce this pang? Didst thou perhaps reserve it to thyself—like the loved one whose name one cannot endure that the world should mention? For the poet purchases the power of words, the power of uttering all the dread secrets of others, at the price of a little secret he is unable to utter . . . and a poet is not an apostle, he casts out devils only by the power of the devil.

But now when the ethical is thus teleologically suspended, how does the individual exist in whom it is suspended? He exists as the particular in opposition to the universal. Does he then sin? For this is the form of sin, as seen in the idea. Just as the infant, though it does not sin, because it is not as such yet conscious of its existence, yet its existence is sin, as seen in the idea, and the ethical makes its demands upon it every instant. If one denies that this form can be repeated [in the adult] in such a way that it is not sin, then the sentence of condemnation is pronounced upon Abraham. How then did Abraham exist? He believed. This is the paradox which keeps him upon the sheer edge and which he cannot make clear to any other man, for the paradox is that he as the individual puts himself in an absolute relation to the absolute. Is he justified in doing this? His justification is once more the paradox; for if he is justified, it is not by virtue of anything universal, but by virtue of being the particular individual.

How then does the individual assure himself that he is justified? It is easy enough to level down the whole of existence to the idea of the state or the idea of society. If one does this, one can also mediate easily enough, for then one does not encounter at all the paradox that the individual as the individual is higher than the universal—which I can aptly express also by the thesis of Pythagoras, that the uneven numbers are more perfect than the even. If in our age one occasionally hears a rejoinder which is pertinent to the paradox, it is likely to be to the following effect: "It is to be judged by the result." A hero who has become a σκάνδαλον[48] to his contemporaries because they are conscious that he is a paradox who cannot make himself intelligible, will cry out defiantly to his generation, "The result will surely prove that I am justified." In our age we hear this cry rather seldom, for as our age, to its disadvantage, does not produce heroes, it has also the advantage of producing few caricatures. When in our age one hears this saying, "It is to be judged according to the result," a man is at once clear as to who it is he has the honor of talking with. Those who talk thus are a numerous tribe, whom I will denominate by the common name of *Docents.*[49] In their thoughts they live secure in existence, they have a *solid* position and *sure* prospects in a well-ordered state, they have centuries and even millenniums between them and the concussions of existence, they do not fear that such things could recur—for what would the police say to that! and the newspapers! Their lifework is to judge the great, and to judge them according to the result. Such behavior toward the great betrays a strange mixture of arrogance and misery: of arrogance because they think they are called to be judges; of misery because they do not feel that their lives are even in the remotest degree akin to the great. Surely a man who possesses even a little *erectioris ingenii* [of the higher way of thinking] has not become entirely a cold and clammy mollusk, and when he approaches what is great it can never escape his mind that from the creation of the world it has been customary for the result to come last, and that, if one would truly learn anything from great actions, one must pay attention precisely to the beginning. In case he who should act were to judge himself according to the result, he would never get to the point of beginning. Even though the result may give joy to the whole world, it cannot help the hero, for he would get to know the result only when the whole thing was over, and it was not by this he became a hero, but he was such for the fact that he began.

Moreover, the result (inasmuch as it is the answer of finiteness to the infinite query) is in its dialectic entirely heterogeneous with the existence of the hero. Or is it possible to prove that Abraham was justified in assuming the position of the individual with relation to the universal . . . for the fact that he got Isaac by *miracle?* If Abraham had actually sacrificed Isaac, would he then have been less justified?

But people are curious about the result, as they are about the result in a book—they want to know nothing about dread, distress, the paradox. They flirt aesthetically with the result, it comes just as unexpectedly but also just as easily as a prize in the lottery; and when they have heard the result they are edified. And yet no robber of temples condemned to hard labor behind iron bars, is so base a criminal as the man who pillages the holy, and even Judas who sold his Master for thirty pieces of silver is not more despicable than the man who sells greatness.

It is abhorrent to my soul to talk inhumanly about greatness, to let it loom darkly at a distance in an indefinite form, to make out that it is great without making the human character of it evident—wherewith it ceases to be great. For it is not what happens to me that makes me great, but it is what I do, and there is surely no one who thinks that a man became great because he won the great prize in the lottery. Even if a man were born in humble circumstances, I would require of him nevertheless that he should not be so inhuman toward himself as not to be able to think of the King's castle except at a remote distance, dreaming vaguely of its greatness and wanting at the same time to exalt it and also to abolish it by the fact that he exalted it meanly. I require of him that he should be man enough to step forward confidently and worthily even in that place. He should not be unmanly enough to desire impudently to offend everybody by rushing straight from the street into the King's hall. By that he loses more than the King. On the contrary, he should find joy in observing every rule of propriety with a glad and confident enthusiasm which will make him frank and fearless. This is only a symbol, for the difference here remarked upon is only a very imperfect expression for spiritual distance. I require of every man that he should not think so inhumanly of himself as not to dare to enter those palaces where not merely the memory of the elect abides but where the elect themselves abide. He should not press forward impudently and impute to them kinship with himself; on the contrary, he should be blissful every time he bows before them, but he should be frank and confident and always be something more than a charwoman, for if he will not be more, he will never gain entrance. And what will help him is precisely the dread and distress by which the great are tried, for otherwise, if he has a bit of pith in him, they will merely arouse his justified envy. And what distance alone makes great, what people would make great by empty and hollow phrases, that they themselves reduce to naught.

Who was ever so great as that blessed woman, the Mother of God, the Virgin Mary? And yet how do we speak of her? We say that she was highly favored among women. And if it did not happen strangely that those who hear are able to think as inhumanly as those who talk, every young girl might well ask, "Why was not I too the highly favored?" And if I had nothing else to say, I would not dismiss such a question as stupid, for when it is a matter of favor, abstractly considered, everyone is equally entitled to it. What they leave out is the distress, the dread, the paradox. My thought is as pure as that of anyone, and the thought of the man who is able to think such things will surely become pure—and if this be not so, he may expect the dreadful; for he who once has evoked these images cannot be rid of them again, and if he sins against them, they avenge themselves with quiet wrath, more terrible than the vociferousness of ten ferocious reviewers. To be sure, Mary bore the child miraculously, but it came to pass with her after the manner of women, and that season is one of dread, distress and paradox. To be sure, the angel was a ministering spirit, but it was not a servile spirit which obliged her by saying to the other young maidens of Israel, "Despise not Mary. What befalls her is the extraordinary." But the Angel came only to Mary, and no one could understand her. After all, what woman was so mortified as Mary? And is it not true in this instance also that one whom God blesses He curses in the same breath? This is the spirit's interpretation of Mary, and she is not (as it shocks me to say, but shocks me still more to think that they have thoughtlessly and coquettishly interpreted her thus)—she is not a fine lady who sits in state and plays with an infant god. Nevertheless, when she says, "Behold the handmaid of the Lord"—then she is great, and I think it will not be found difficult to explain why she became the Mother of God. She has no need of worldly admiration, any more than Abraham has need of tears, for she was not a heroine, and he was not a hero, but both of them became greater than such, not at all because they were exempted from distress and torment and paradox, but they became great through these.[50]

It is great when the poet, presenting his tragic hero before the admiration of men, dares to say, "Weep for him, for he deserves it." For it is great to deserve the tears of those who are worthy to shed tears. It is great that the poet dares to hold the crowd in check, dares to castigate men, requiring that every man examine himself whether he be worthy to weep for the hero. For the waste-water of blubberers is a degradation of the holy.—But greater than all this it is that the knight of faith dares to say even to the noble man who would weep for him, "Weep not for me, but weep for thyself."

One is deeply moved, one longs to be back in those beautiful times, a sweet yearning conducts one to the desired goal, to see Christ wandering in the promised land. One forgets the dread, the distress, the paradox. Was it so easy a matter not to be mistaken? Was it not dreadful that this man who walks among the others—was it not dreadful that He was God? Was it not dreadful to sit at table with Him? Was it so easy a matter to become an Apostle? But the result, eighteen hundred years—that is a help, it helps to the shabby deceit wherewith one deceives oneself and others. I do not feel the courage to wish to be contemporary with such events, but hence I do not judge severely those who were mistaken, nor think meanly of those who saw aright.

I return, however, to Abraham. Before the result, either

Abraham was every minute a murderer, or we are confronted by a paradox which is higher than all mediation.

The story of Abraham contains therefore a teleological suspension of the ethical. As the individual he became higher than the universal. This is the paradox which does not permit of mediation. It is just as inexplicable how he got into it as it is inexplicable how he remained in it. If such is not the position of Abraham, then he is not even a tragic hero but a murderer. To want to continue to call him the father of faith, to talk of this to people who do not concern themselves with anything but words, is thoughtless. A man can become a tragic hero by his own powers—but not a knight of faith. When a man enters upon the way, in a certain sense the hard way of the tragic hero, many will be able to give him counsel; to him who follows the narrow way of faith no one can give counsel, him no one can understand. Faith is a miracle, and yet no man is excluded from it; for that in which all human life is unified is passion,* and faith is a passion.

*Lessing has somewhere given expression to a similar thought from a purely aesthetic point of view. What he would show expressly in this passage is that sorrow too can find a witty expression. To this end he quotes a rejoinder of the unhappy English king, Edward II. In contrast to this he quotes from Diderot a story of a peasant woman and a rejoinder of hers. Then he continues: "That too was wit, and the wit of a peasant at that; but the situation made it inevitable. Consequently one must not seek to find the excuse for the witty expressions of pain and of sorrow in the fact that the person who uttered them was a superior person, well educated, intelligent, and witty withal, *for the passions make all men again equal*—but the explanation is to be found in the fact that in all probability everyone would have said the same thing in the same situation. The thought of a peasant woman a queen could have had and must have had, just as what the king said in that instance a peasant too would have been able to say and doubtless would have said." Cf. *Sämtliche Werke*, XXX. p. 223.[51]

Is there such a thing as an
absolute duty toward God?

The ethical is the universal, and as such it is again the divine. One has therefore a right to say that fundamentally every duty is a duty toward God; but if one cannot say more, then one affirms at the same time that properly I have no duty toward God. Duty becomes duty by being referred to God, but in duty itself I do not come into relation with God. Thus it is a duty to love one's neighbor, but in performing this duty I do not come into relation with God but with the neighbor whom I love. If I say then in this connection that it is my duty to love God, I am really uttering only a tautology, inasmuch as "God" is in this instance used in an entirely abstract sense as the divine, i.e. the universal, i.e. duty. So the whole existence of the human race is rounded off completely like a sphere, and the ethical is at once its limit and its content. God becomes an invisible vanishing point, a powerless thought, His power being only in the ethical which is the content of existence. If in any way it might occur to any man to want to love God in any other sense than that here indicated, he is romantic, he loves a phantom which, if it had merely the power of being able to speak, would say to him, "I do not require your love. Stay where you belong." If in any way it might occur to a man to want to love God otherwise, this love would be open to suspicion, like that of which Rousseau speaks, referring to people who love the Kaffirs instead of their neighbors.

So in case what has been expounded here is correct, in case there is no incommensurability in a human life, and what there is of the incommensurable is only such by an accident from which no consequences can be drawn, in so far as existence is regarded in terms of the idea, Hegel is right;

but he is not right in talking about faith or in allowing Abraham to be regarded as the father of it; for by the latter he has pronounced judgment both upon Abraham and upon faith. In the Hegelian philosophy[52] *das Äussere* (*die Entäusserung*) is higher than *das Innere*. This is frequently illustrated by an example. The child is *das Innere*, the man *das Äussere*. Hence it is that the child is defined by the outward, and conversely, the man, as *das Äussere*, is defined precisely by *das Innere*. Faith, on the contrary, is the paradox that inwardness is higher than outwardness—or, to recall an expression used above, the uneven number is higher than the even.

In the ethical way of regarding life it is therefore the task of the individual to divest himself of the inward determinants and express them in an outward way. Whenever he shrinks from this, whenever he is inclined to persist in or to slip back again into the inward determinants of feeling, mood, etc., he sins, he is in a temptation (*Anfechtung*). The paradox of faith is this, that there is an inwardness which is incommensurable for the outward, an inwardness, be it observed, which is not identical with the first but is a new inwardness. This must not be overlooked. Modern philosophy[53] has permitted itself without further ado to substitute in place of "faith" the immediate. When one does that it is ridiculous to deny that faith has existed in all ages. In that way faith comes into rather simple company along with feeling, mood, idiosyncrasy, vapors, etc. To this extent philosophy may be right in saying that one ought not to stop there. But there is nothing to justify philosophy in using this phrase with regard to faith. Before faith there goes a movement of infinity, and only then, *necopinate*,[54] by virtue of the absurd, faith enters upon the scene. This I can well understand without maintaining on that account that I have faith. If faith is nothing but what philosophy makes it out to be, then Socrates already went further, much further, whereas the contrary is true, that he never reached it. In an intellectual respect he made the movement of infinity. His ignorance is infinite resignation. This task in itself is a match for human powers, even though people in our time disdain it; but only after it is done, only when the individual has evacuated himself in the infinite, only then is the point attained where faith can break forth.

The paradox of faith is this, that the individual is higher than the universal, that the individual (to recall a dogmatic distinction now rather seldom heard) determines his relation to the universal by his relation to the absolute, not his relation to the absolute by his relation to the universal. The paradox can also be expressed by saying that there is an absolute duty toward God; for in this relationship of duty the individual as an individual stands related absolutely to the absolute. So when in this connection it is said that it is a duty to love God, something different is said from that in the foregoing; for if this duty is absolute, the ethical is reduced to a position of relativity. From this, however, it does not follow that the ethical is to be abolished, but it acquires an entirely different expression, the paradoxical expression—that, for example, love to God may cause the knight of faith to give his love to his neighbor the opposite expression to that which, ethically speaking, is required by duty.

If such is not the case, then faith has no proper place in existence, then faith is a temptation (*Anfechtung*), and Abraham is lost, since he gave in to it.

This paradox does not permit of mediation, for it is founded precisely upon the fact that the individual is only the individual. As soon as this individual [who is aware of a direct command from God] wishes to express his absolute duty in [terms of] the universal [i.e. the ethical, and] is sure of his duty in that [i.e. the universal or ethical precept], he recognizes that he is in temptation [i.e. a trial of faith], and, if in fact he resists [the direct indication of God's will], he ends by not fulfilling the absolute duty so called [i.e. what here has been called the absolute duty]; and, if he doesn't do this, [i.e. doesn't put up a resistance to the direct intimation of God's will], he sins, even though *realiter* his deed were that which it was his absolute duty to do.* So what should

*The translator has ventured to render this muddy sentence very liberally (though he has bracketed his explanatory additions), in order to bring out the meaning this sentence must have if it is to express the anguishing paradox of a "teleological suspension of the

Abraham do? If he would say to another person, "Isaac I love more dearly than everything in the world, and hence it is so hard for me to sacrifice him"; then surely the other would have shaken his head and said, "Why will you sacrifice him then?" —or if the other had been a sly fellow, he surely would have seen through Abraham and perceived that he was making a show of feelings which were in strident contradiction to his act.

In the story of Abraham we find such a paradox. His relation to Isaac, ethically expressed, is this, that the father should love the son. This ethical relation is reduced to a relative position in contrast with the absolute relation to God. To the question, "Why?" Abraham has no answer except that it is a trial, a temptation (*Fristelse*)—terms which, as was remarked above, express the unity of the two points of view: that it is for God's sake and for his own sake. In common usage these two ways of regarding the matter are mutually exclusive. Thus when we see a man do something which does not comport with the universal, we say that he scarcely can be doing it for God's sake, and by that we imply that he does it for his own sake. The paradox of faith has lost the intermediate term, i.e. the universal. On the one side it has the expression for the extremest egoism (doing the dreadful thing it does for one's own sake); on the other side the expression for the most absolute self-sacrifice (doing it for God's sake). Faith itself cannot be mediated into the universal, for it would thereby be destroyed. Faith is this paradox, and the individual absolutely cannot make himself intelligible to anybody. People imagine maybe that the individual can make himself intelligible to another individual in the same case. Such a notion would be unthinkable if in our time

ethical." This is the meaning Niels Thulstrup gets out of it, and he tells me that this is the translation of Emanuel Hirsch. As S.K.'s sentence stands, without explanatory additions, it reminds me of a rigmarole I have often recited to the mystification of my hearers: "If a man were to signify, which he were not, if he had the power, which being denied him, he were to endeavor anyhow—merely because he don't, would you?" Much as I love Kierkegaard, I sometimes hate him for keeping me awake at night. Only between sleeping and waking am I able to unravel some of his most complicated sentences.

people did not in so many ways seek to creep slyly into greatness. The one knight of faith can render no aid to the other.
Either the individual becomes a knight of faith by assuming the burden of the paradox, or he never becomes one.
In these regions partnership is unthinkable. Every more
precise explication of what is to be understood by Isaac the
individual can give only to himself. And even if one were
able, generally speaking,[55] to define ever so precisely what
should be intended by Isaac (which moreover would be the
most ludicrous self-contradiction, i.e. that the particular individual who definitely stands outside the universal is subsumed
under universal categories precisely when he has to act as the
individual who stands outside the universal), the individual
nevertheless will never be able to assure himself by the aid
of others that this application is appropriate, but he can do
so only by himself as the individual. Hence even if a man
were cowardly and paltry enough to wish to become a knight
of faith on the responsibility of an outsider, he will never
become one; for only the individual becomes a knight of
faith as the particular individual, and this is the greatness of
this knighthood, as I can well understand without entering
the order, since I lack courage; but this is also its terror, as
I can comprehend even better.

In Luke 14:26, as everybody knows, there is a striking doctrine taught about the absolute duty toward God: "If any
man cometh unto me and hateth not his own father and
mother and wife and children and brethren and sisters, yea,
and his own life also, he cannot be my disciple." This is a
hard saying, who can bear to hear it? For this reason it is
heard very seldom. This silence, however, is only an evasion
which is of no avail. Nevertheless, the student of theology
learns to know that these words occur in the New Testament,
and in one or another exegetical aid[56] he finds the explanation
that μισεῖν in this passage and a few others is used in the sense
of μείσειν, signifying *minus diligo, posthabeo, non colo, nihili
facio.* However, the context in which these words occur does
not seem to strengthen this tasteful explanation. In the verse
immediately following there is a story about a man who desired to build a tower but first sat down to calculate whether

he was capable of doing it, lest people might laugh at him afterwards. The close connection of this story with the verse here cited seems precisely to indicate that the words are to be taken in as terrible a sense as possible, to the end that everyone may examine himself as to whether he is able to erect the building.

In case this pious and kindly exegete, who by abating the price thought he could smuggle Christianity into the world, were fortunate enough to convince a man that grammatically, linguistically and κατ' ἀναλογίαν [analogically] this was the meaning of that passage, it is to be hoped that the same moment he will be fortunate enough to convince the same man that Christianity is one of the most pitiable things in the world. For the doctrine which in one of its most lyrical outbursts, where the consciousness of its eternal validity swells in it most strongly, has nothing else to say but a noisy word which means nothing but only signifies that one is to be less kindly, less attentive, more indifferent; the doctrine which at the moment when it makes as if it would give utterance to the terrible ends by driveling instead of terrifying—that doctrine is not worth taking off my hat to.

The words are terrible, yet I fully believe that one can understand them without implying that he who understands them has courage to do them. One must at all events be honest enough to acknowledge what stands written and to admit that it is great, even though one has not the courage for it. He who behaves thus will not find himself excluded from having part in that beautiful story which follows, for after all it contains consolation of a sort for the man who had not courage to begin the tower. But we must be honest, and not interpret this lack of courage as humility, since it is really pride, whereas the courage of faith is the only humble courage.

One can easily perceive that if there is to be any sense in this passage, it must be understood literally. God it is who requires absolute love. But he who in demanding a person's love thinks that this love should be proved also by becoming lukewarm to everything which hitherto was dear—that man is not only an egoist but stupid as well, and he who would demand such love signs at the same moment his own death-warrant, supposing that his life was bound up with this coveted love. Thus a husband demands that his wife shall leave father and mother, but if he were to regard it as a proof of her extraordinary love for him that she for his sake became an indolent, lukewarm daughter etc., then he is the stupidest of the stupid. If he had any notion of what love is, he would wish to discover that as daughter and sister she was perfect in love, and would see therein the proof that she would love him more than anyone else in the realm. What therefore in the case of a man one would regard as a sign of egoism and stupidity, that one is to regard by the help of an exegete as a worthy conception of the Deity.

But how hate them? I will not recall here the human distinction between loving and hating—not because I have much to object to in it (for after all it is passionate), but because it is egoistic and is not in place here. However, if I regard the problem as a paradox, then I understand it, that is, I understand it in such a way as one can understand a paradox. The absolute duty may cause one to do what ethics would forbid, but by no means can it cause the knight of faith to cease to love. This is shown by Abraham. The instant he is ready to sacrifice Isaac the ethical expression for what he does is this: he hates Isaac. But if he really hates Isaac, he can be sure that God does not require this, for Cain and Abraham are not identical. Isaac he must love with his whole soul; when God requires Isaac he must love him if possible even more dearly, and only on this condition can he sacrifice him; for in fact it is this love for Isaac which, by its paradoxical opposition to his love for God, makes his act a sacrifice. But the distress and dread in this paradox is that, humanly speaking, he is entirely unable to make himself intelligible. Only at the moment when his act is in absolute contradiction to his feeling is his act a sacrifice, but the reality of his act is the factor by which he belongs to the universal, and in that aspect he is and remains a murderer.

Moreover, the passage in Luke must be understood in such a way as to make it clearly evident that the knight of faith has no higher expression of the universal (i.e. the ethical) by which he can save himself. Thus, for example, if we suppose that the Church requires such a sacrifice of one of its mem-

bers, we have in this case only a tragic hero. For the idea of
the Church is not qualitatively different from that of the State,
in so far as the individual comes into it by a simple mediation,
and in so far as the individual comes into the paradox he does
not reach the idea of the Church; he does not come out of
the paradox, but in it he must find either his blessedness or his
perdition. Such an ecclesiastical hero expresses in his act the
universal, and there will be no one in the Church—not even
his father and mother etc.—who fails to understand him. On
the other hand, he is not a knight of faith, and he has also a
different answer from that of Abraham: he does not say that it
is a trial or a temptation in which he is tested.

People commonly refrain from quoting such a text as this in
Luke. They are afraid of giving men a free rein, are afraid that
the worst will happen as soon as the individual takes it into
his head to comport himself as the individual. Moreover, they
think that to exist as the individual is the easiest thing of all,
and that therefore people have to be compelled to become the
universal. I cannot share either this fear or this opinion, and
both for the same reason. He who has learned that to exist as
the individual is the most terrible thing of all will not be fearful of saying that it is great, but then too he will say this in
such a way that his words will scarcely be a snare for the bewildered man, but rather will help him into the universal, even
though his words do to some extent make room for the great.
The man who does not dare to mention such texts will not
dare to mention Abraham either, and his notion that it is easy
enough to exist as the individual implies a very suspicious admission with regard to himself; for he who has a real respect
for himself and concern for his soul is convinced that the man
who lives under his own supervision, alone in the whole world,
lives more strictly and more secluded than a maiden in her
lady's bower. That there may be some who need compulsion,
some who, if they were free-footed, would riot in selfish
pleasures like unruly beasts, is doubtless true; but a man must
prove precisely that he is not of this number by the fact that he
knows how to speak with dread and trembling; and out of
reverence for the great one is bound to speak, lest it be forgotten for fear of the ill effect, which surely will fail to eventuate

when a man talks in such a way that one knows it for the great, knows its terror—and apart from the terror one does not know the great at all.

Let us consider a little more closely the distress and dread in the paradox of faith. The tragic hero renounces himself in order to express the universal, the knight of faith renounces the universal in order to become the individual. As has been said, everything depends upon how one is placed. He who believes that it is easy enough to be the individual can always be sure that he is not a knight of faith, for vagabonds and roving geniuses are not men of faith. The knight of faith knows, on the other hand, that it is glorious to belong to the universal. He knows that it is beautiful and salutary to be the individual who translates himself into the universal, who edits as it were a pure and elegant edition of himself, as free from errors as possible and which everyone can read. He knows that it is refreshing to become intelligible to oneself in the universal so that he understands it and so that every individual who understands him understands through him in turn the universal, and both rejoice in the security of the universal. He knows that it is beautiful to be born as the individual who has the universal as his home, his friendly abiding-place, which at once welcomes him with open arms when he would tarry in it. But he knows also that higher than this there winds a solitary path, narrow and steep; he knows that it is terrible to be born outside the universal, to walk without meeting a single traveller. He knows very well where he is and how he is related to men. Humanly speaking, he is crazy and cannot make himself intelligible to anyone. And yet it is the mildest expression, to say that he is crazy. If he is not supposed to be that, then he is a hypocrite, and the higher he climbs on this path, the more dreadful a hypocrite he is.

The knight of faith knows that to give up oneself for the universal inspires enthusiasm, and that it requires courage, but he also knows that security is to be found in this, precisely because it is for the universal. He knows that it is glorious to be understood by every noble mind, so glorious that the beholder is ennobled by it, and he feels as if he were bound; he could wish it were this task that had been allotted to him.

Thus Abraham could surely have wished now and then that the task were to love Isaac as becomes a father, in a way intelligible to all, memorable throughout all ages; he could wish that the task were to sacrifice Isaac for the universal, that he might incite the fathers to illustrious deeds— and he is almost terrified by the thought that for him such wishes are only temptations and must be dealt with as such, for he knows that it is a solitary path he treads and that he accomplishes nothing for the universal but only himself is tried and examined. Or what did Abraham accomplish for the universal? Let me speak humanly about it, quite humanly. He spent seventy years in getting a son of his old age. What other men get quickly enough and enjoy for a long time he spent seventy years in accomplishing. And why? Because he was tried and put to the test. Is not that crazy? But Abraham believed, and Sarah wavered and got him to take Hagar as a concubine—but therefore he also had to drive her away. He gets Isaac, then he has to be tried again. He knew that it is glorious to express the universal, glorious to live with Isaac. But this is not the task. He knew that it is a kingly thing to sacrifice such a son for the universal, he himself would have found repose in that, and all would have reposed in the commendation of his deed, as a vowel reposes in its consonant,[57] but that is not the task—he is tried. That Roman general who is celebrated by his name of Cunctator[58] checked the foe by procrastination—but what a procrastinator Abraham is in comparison with him! . . . yet he did not save the state. This is the content of one hundred and thirty years. Who can bear it? Would not his contemporary age, if we can speak of such a thing, have said of him, "Abraham is eternally procrastinating. Finally he gets a son. That took long enough. Now he wants to sacrifice him. So is he not mad? And if at least he could explain why he wants to do it—but he always says that it is a trial." Nor could Abraham explain more, for his life is like a book placed under a divine attachment and which never becomes *publici juris*.[59]

This is the terrible thing. He who does not see it can always be sure that he is no knight of faith, but he who sees it will not deny that even the most tried of tragic heroes walks with a dancing step compared with the knight of faith, who comes

slowly creeping forward. And if he has perceived this and assured himself that he has not courage to understand it, he will
at least have a presentiment of the marvellous glory this knight
attains in the fact that he becomes God's intimate acquaintance, the Lord's friend, and (to speak quite humanly) that
he says "Thou" to God in heaven, whereas even the tragic hero
only addresses Him in the third person.

The tragic hero is soon ready and has soon finished the
fight, he makes the infinite movement and then is secure in
the universal. The knight of faith, on the other hand, is kept
sleepless, for he is constantly tried, and every instant there is
the possibility of being able to return repentantly to the universal, and this possibility can just as well be a temptation as
the truth. He can derive evidence from no man which it is,
for with that query he is outside the paradox.

So the knight of faith has first and foremost the requisite
passion to concentrate upon a single factor the whole of the
ethical which he transgresses, so that he can give himself the
assurance that he really loves Isaac with his whole soul.* If he
cannot do that, he is in temptation (*Anfechtung*). In the next
place, he has enough passion to make this assurance available
in the twinkling of an eye and in such a way that it is as com-

---

*I would elucidate yet once more the difference between the col-
lisions which are encountered by the tragic hero and by the knight
of faith. The tragic hero assures himself that the ethical obligation
[i.e., the lower ethical obligation, which he puts aside for the higher;
in the present case, accordingly, it is the obligation to spare his
daughter's life] is totally present in him by the fact that he transforms
it into a wish. Thus Agamemnon can say, "The proof that I do not
offend against my parental duty is that my duty is my only wish." So
here we have wish and duty face to face with one another. The fortunate chance in life is that the two correspond, that my wish is my
duty and vice versa, and the task of most men in life is precisely to
remain within their duty and by their enthusiasm to transform it into
their wish. The tragic hero gives up his wish in order to accomplish
his duty. For the knight of faith wish and duty are also identical, but
he is required to give up both. Therefore when he would resign himself to giving up his wish he does not find repose, for that is after all
his duty. If he would remain within his duty and his wish, he is not
a knight of faith, for the absolute duty requires precisely that he
should give them up. The tragic hero apprehended a higher expression of duty but not an absolute duty.

pletely valid as it was in the first instance. If he is unable to do this, he can never budge from the spot, for he constantly has to begin all over again. The tragic hero also concentrated in one factor the ethical which he teleologically surpassed, but in this respect he had support in the universal. The knight of faith has only himself alone, and this constitutes the dreadfulness of the situation. Most men live in such a way under an ethical obligation that they can let the sorrow be sufficient for the day, but they never reach this passionate concentration, this energetic consciousness. The universal may in a certain sense help the tragic hero to attain this, but the knight of faith is left all to himself. The hero does the deed and finds repose in the universal, the knight of faith is kept in constant tension. Agamemnon gives up Iphigenia and thereby has found repose in the universal, then he takes the step of sacrificing her. If Agamemnon does not make the infinite movement, if his soul at the decisive instant, instead of having passionate concentration, is absorbed by the common twaddle that he had several daughters and *vielleicht* [perhaps] the *Ausserordentliche* [extraordinary] might occur—then he is of course not a hero but a hospital-case. The hero's concentration Abraham also has, even though in his case it is far more difficult, since he has no support in the universal; but he makes one more movement by which he concentrates his soul upon the miracle. If Abraham did not do that, he is only an Agamemnon—if in any way it is possible to explain how he can be justified in sacrificing Isaac when thereby no profit accrues to the universal.

Whether the individual is in temptation (*Anfechtung*) or is a knight of faith only the individual can decide. Nevertheless it is possible to construct from the paradox several criteria which he too can understand who is not within the paradox. The true knight of faith is always absolute isolation, the false knight is sectarian. This sectarianism is an attempt to leap away from the narrow path of the paradox and become a tragic hero at a cheap price. The tragic hero expresses the universal and sacrifices himself for it. The sectarian punchinello, instead of that, has a private theatre, i.e. several good friends and comrades who represent the universal just about as well as the beadles in *The Golden Snuffbox*[60] represent justice. The knight of faith, on the contrary, is the paradox, is the individual, absolutely nothing but the individual, without connections or pretensions. This is the terrible thing which the sectarian manikin cannot endure. For instead of learning from this terror that he is not capable of performing the great deed and then plainly admitting it (an act which I cannot but approve, because it is what I do) the manikin thinks that by uniting with several other manikins he will be able to do it. But that is quite out of the question. In the world of spirit no swindling is tolerated. A dozen sectaries join arms with one another, they know nothing whatever of the lonely temptations which await the knight of faith and which he dares not shun precisely because it would be still more dreadful if he were to press forward presumptuously. The sectaries deafen one another by their noise and racket, hold the dread off by their shrieks, and such a hallooing company of sportsmen think they are storming heaven and think they are on the same path as the kight of faith who in the solitude of the universe never hears any human voice but walks alone with his dreadful responsibility.

The knight of faith is obliged to rely upon himself alone, he feels the pain of not being able to make himself intelligible to others, but he feels no vain desire to guide others. The pain is his assurance that he is in the right way, this vain desire he does not know, he is too serious for that. The false knight of faith readily betrays himself by this proficiency in guiding which he has acquired in an instant. He does not comprehend what it is all about, that if another individual is to take the same path, he must become entirely in the same way the individual and have no need of any man's guidance, least of all the guidance of a man who would obtrude himself. At this point men leap aside, they cannot bear the martyrdom of being uncomprehended, and instead of this they choose conveniently enough the worldly admiration of their proficiency. The true knight of faith is a witness, never a teacher, and therein lies his deep humanity, which is worth a good deal more than this silly participation in others' weal and woe which is honored by the name of sympathy, whereas in fact it is nothing but vanity.

He who would only be a witness thereby avows that no man, not even the lowliest, needs another man's sympathy or should be abased that another may be exalted. But since he did not win what he won at a cheap price, neither does he sell it out at a cheap price, he is not petty enough to take men's admiration and give them in return his silent contempt, he knows that what is truly great is equally accessible to all.

Either there is an absolute duty toward God, and if so it is the paradox here described, that the individual as the individual is higher than the universal and as the individual stands in an absolute relation to the absolute/or else faith never existed, because it has always existed, or, to put it differently, Abraham is lost, or one must explain the passage in the fourteenth chapter of Luke as did that tasteful exegete, and explain in the same way the corresponding passages and similar ones.[61]

PROBLEM III

Was Abraham ethically defensible in keeping silent about his purpose before Sarah, before Eleazar, before Isaac?

The ethical as such is the universal, again, as the universal it is the manifest, the revealed. The individual regarded as he is immediately, that is, as a physical and psychical being, is the hidden, the concealed. So his ethical task is to develop out of this concealment and to reveal himself in the universal. Hence whenever he wills to remain in concealment he sins and lies in temptation (*Anfechtung*), out of which he can come only by revealing himself.

With this we are back again at the same point. If there is not a concealment which has its ground in the fact that the individual as the individual is higher than the universal, then Abraham's conduct is indefensible, for he paid no heed to the intermediate ethical determinants. If on the other hand there is such a concealment, we are in the presence of the paradox which cannot be mediated inasmuch as it rests upon the consideration that the individual as the individual is higher than the universal, but it is the universal precisely which is mediation. The Hegelian philosophy holds that there is no justified concealment, no justified incommensurability. So it is self-consistent when it requires revelation, but it is not warranted in regarding Abraham as the father of faith and in talking about faith. For faith is not the first immediacy but a subsequent immediacy. The first immediacy is the aesthetical, and about this the Hegelian philosophy may be in the right. But faith is not the aesthetical—or else faith has never existed because it has always existed.

It will be best to regard the whole matter from a purely aesthetical point of view, and with that intent to embark upon an aesthetic deliberation, to which I beg the reader to abandon himself completely for the moment, while I, to contribute my share, will modify my presentation in conformity with the subject. The category I would consider a little more closely is *the interesting*, a category which especially in our age (precisely because our age lives *in discrimine rerum*) [at a turning point in history] has acquired great importance, for it is properly the category of the turning-point. Therefore we, after having loved this category *pro virili* [with all our power], should not scorn it as some do because we have outgrown it, but neither should we be too greedy to attain it, for certain it is that to be interesting or to have an interesting life is not a task for industrial art but a fateful privilege, which like every privilege in the world of spirit is bought only by deep pain. Thus, for example, Socrates was the most interesting man that ever lived, his life the most interesting that has been recorded, but this existence was alloted to him by the Deity, and in so far as he himself had to acquire it he was not unacquainted with trouble and pain. To take such a life in vain does not beseem a man who takes life seriously, and yet it is not rare to see in our age examples of such an endeavor. Moreover the interesting is a border-category, a boundary between aesthetics and ethics. For this reason our deliberation must constantly glance over into the field of ethics, while in order to be able to acquire significance it must grasp the problem with aesthetic intensity and concupiscence. With such matters ethics seldom deals in our age.

The reason is supposed to be that there is no appropriate place for it in the System. Then surely one might do it in a monograph, and moreover, if one would not do it prolixly, one might do it briefly and yet attain the same end—if, that is to say, a man has the predicate in his power, for one or two predicates can betray a whole world. Might there not be some place in the System for a little word like the predicate?

In his immortal *Poetics* (Chapter 11) Aristotle says,[62] δύο μὲν οὖν τοῦ μύθου μέρη περὶ ταῦτ' ἐστί, περιπέτεια καὶ ἀναγνώρισις. I am of course concerned here only with the second factor, ἀναγνώρισις, recognition. Where there can be question of a recognition there is implied *eo ipso* a previous concealment. So just as recognition is the relieving, the relaxing factor in the dramatic life, so is concealment the factor of tension. What Aristotle has to say in the same chapter about the merits of tragedy which are variously appraised in proportion as περιπέτεια and ἀναγνώρισις impinge[63] upon one another, and also what he says about the "individual" and the "double recognition," I cannot take into consideration here, although by its inwardness and quiet concentration what he says is peculiarly tempting to one who is weary of the superficial omniscience of encyclopedic scholars. A more general observation may be appropriate here. In Greek tragedy concealment (and consequently recognition) is an epic survival grounded upon a fate in which the dramatic action disappears from view and from which it derives its obscure and enigmatic origin. Hence it is that the effect produced by a Greek tragedy is like the impression of a marble statue which lacks the power of the eye. Greek tragedy is blind. Hence a certain abstraction is necessary in order to appreciate it properly. A son[64] murders his father, but only afterwards does he learn that it was his father. A sister[65] wants to sacrifice her brother, but at the decisive moment she learns who he is. This dramatic motive is not so apt to interest our reflective age. Modern drama has given up fate, has emancipated itself dramatically, sees with its eyes, scrutinizes itself, resolves fate in its dramatic consciousness. Concealment and revelation are in this case the hero's free act for which he is responsible.

Recognition and concealment are also present as an essential element in modern drama. To adduce examples of this would be too prolix. I am courteous enough to assume that everybody in our age, which is so aesthetically wanton, so potent and so enflamed that the act of conception comes as easy to it as to the partridge hen, which, according to Aristotle's affirmation,[66] needs only to hear the voice of the cock or the sound of its flight overhead—I assume that everyone, merely upon hearing the word "concealment" will be able to shake half a score of romances and comedies out of his sleeve. Wherefore I express myself briefly and so will throw out at once a general observation. In case one who plays hide and seek (and thereby introduces into the play the dramatic ferment) hides something nonsensical, we get a comedy; if on the other hand he stands in relation to the idea, he may come near being a tragic hero. I give here merely an example of the comic. A man rouges his face and wears a periwig. The same man is eager to try his fortune with the fair sex, he is perfectly sure of conquering by the aid of the rouge and the periwig which make him absolutely irresistible. He captures a girl and is at the acme of happiness. Now comes the gist of the matter: if he is able to admit this embellishment, he does not lose all of his infatuating power; when he reveals himself as a plain ordinary man, and bald at that, he does not thereby lose the loved one. —Concealment is his free act, for which aesthetics also holds him responsible. This science is no friend of bald hypocrites, it abandons him to the mercy of laughter. This must suffice as a mere hint of what I mean—the comical cannot be a subject of interest for this investigation.

It is incumbent upon me to examine dialectically the part played by concealment in aesthetics and ethics, for the point is to show the absolute difference between the aesthetic concealment and the paradox.

A couple of examples. A girl is secretly in love with a man, although they have not definitely avowed their love to one another. Her parents compel her to marry another (there may be moreover a consideration of filial piety which determines her), she obeys her parents, she conceals her love, "so as not to make the other unhappy, and no one will ever know what she suffers."—A young man is able by a single word to get possession of the object of his longings and his restless dreams. This little word, however, will compromise, yea, perhaps (who knows?) bring to ruin a whole family, he resolves magnanimously to remain in his concealment, "the girl shall never get to know it, so that she may perhaps become happy by giving her hand to another." What a pity that these two persons, both of whom were concealed from their respective beloveds, were also concealed from one another, otherwise a remarkable higher unity might have been brought about.—Their concealment is a free act, for which they are responsible also to aesthetics. Aesthetics, however, is a courteous and sentimental science which knows of more expedients than a pawnbroker. So what does it do? It makes everything possible for the lovers. By the help of a chance the partners to the projected marriage get a hint of the magnanimous resolution of the other part, it comes to an explanation, they get one another and at the same time attain rank with real heroes. For in spite of the fact that they did not even get time to sleep over their resolution, aesthetics treats them nevertheless as if they had courageously fought for their resolution during many years. For aesthetics does not trouble itself greatly about time, whether in jest or seriousness time flies equally fast for it.

But ethics knows nothing about that chance or about that sentimentality, nor has it so speedy a concept of time. Thereby the matter receives a different aspect. It is no good arguing with ethics for it has pure categories. It does not appeal to experience, which of all ludicrous things is the most ludicrous, and which so far from making a man wise rather makes him mad if he knows nothing higher than this. Ethics has in its possession no chance, and so matters do not come to an explanation, it does not jest with dignities, it lays a prodigious responsibility upon the shoulders of the puny hero, it denounces as presumption his wanting to play providence by his actions, but it also denounces him for wanting to do it by his suffering. It bids a man believe in reality and have courage to fight against all the afflictions of reality, and still more against the bloodless sufferings he has assumed on his own responsibility. It warns against believing the calculations of the understanding, which are more perfidious than the oracles of ancient times. It warns against every untimely magnanimity. Let reality decide—then is the time to show courage, but then ethics itself offers all possible assistance. If, however, there was something deeper which moved in these two, if there was seriousness to see the task, seriousness to commence it, then something will come of them; but ethics cannot help, it is offended, for they keep a secret from it, a secret they hold at their own peril.

So aesthetics required concealment and rewarded it, ethics required revelation and punished concealment.

At times, however, even aesthetics requires revelation. When the hero ensnared in the aesthetic illusion thinks by his silence to save another man, then it requires silence and rewards it. On the other hand, when the hero by his action intervenes disturbingly in another man's life, then it requires revelation. I am now on the subject of the tragic hero. I would consider for a moment Euripides' *Iphigenia in Aulis*. Agamemnon must sacrifice Iphigenia. Now aesthetics requires silence of Agamemnon inasmuch as it would be unworthy of the hero to seek comfort from any other man, and out of solicitude for the women too he ought to conceal this from them as long as possible. On the other hand, the hero, precisely in order to be a hero, must be tried by dreadful temptations which the tears of Clytemnestra and Iphigenia provide for him. What does aesthetics do? It has an expedient, it has in readiness an old servant who reveals everything to Clytemnestra. Then all is as it should be.

Ethics, however, has at hand no chance and no old servant. The aesthetical idea contradicts itself as soon as it must be carried out in reality. Hence ethics requires revelation. The tragic hero displays his ethical courage precisely by the fact that it is he who, without being ensnared in any aesthetic illusion, himself announces to Iphigenia her fate. If the tragic hero does this, then he is the beloved son of ethics in whom it is well pleased. If he keeps silent, it may be because he thinks thereby to make it easier for others, but it may also be because thereby he makes it easier for himself. However, he knows that he is not influenced by this latter motive. If he keeps silent, he assumes as the individual a serious responsibility inasmuch as he ignores an argument which may come from without. As a tragic hero he cannot do this, for ethics loves him precisely because he constantly expresses the universal. His heroic action demands courage, but it belongs to this courage that he shall shun no argumentation. Now it is certain that tears are a dreadful *argumentum ad hominem*, and doubtless there are those who are moved by nothing yet are touched by tears. In the play Iphigenia had leave to weep, really she ought to have been allowed like Jephthah's daughter two months for weeping, not in solitude but at her father's feet, allowed to employ all her art "which is but tears," and to twine about his knees instead of presenting the olive branch of the suppliant.

Aesthetics required revelation but helped itself out by a chance; ethics required revelation and found in the tragic hero its satisfaction.

In spite of the severity with which ethics requires revelation, it cannot be denied that secrecy and silence really make a man great precisely because they are characteristics of inwardness. When Amor leaves Psyche he says to her, "Thou shalt give birth to a child which will be a divine infant if thou dost keep silence, but a human being if thou dost reveal the secret." The tragic hero who is the favorite of ethics is the purely human, and him I can understand, and all he does is in the light of the revealed. If I go further, then I stumble upon the paradox, either the divine or the demoniac, for silence is both. Silence is the snare of the demon, and the more one keeps silent, the more terrifying the demon becomes; but silence is also the mutual understanding between the Deity and the individual.

Before going on to the story of Abraham, however, I would call before the curtain several poetic personages. By the power of dialectic I keep them upon tiptoe, and by wielding over them the scourge of despair I shall surely keep them from standing still, in order that in their dread they may reveal one thing and another.*

*These movements and attitudes might well be a subject for further aesthetic treatment. However, I leave it undecided to what extent faith and the whole life of faith might be a fit subject for such treatment. Only, because it is always a joy to me to thank him to

In his *Poetics*[67] Aristotle relates a story of a political disturbance at Delphi which was provoked by a question of marriage. *The bridegroom, when the augurs*[68] *foretell to him that a misfortune would follow his marriage, suddenly changes his plan at the decisive moment when he comes to fetch the bride —he will not celebrate the wedding. I have no need of more.** In Delphi this event hardly passed without tears; if a poet were to have adopted it as his theme, he might have dared to count very surely upon sympathy. Is it not dreadful that love, which in human life often enough was cast into exile, is now deprived of the support of heaven? Is not the old proverb that "marriages are made in heaven" here put to shame? Usually it is all the afflictions and difficulties of the finite which like evil spirits separate the lovers, but love has heaven on its side, and therefore this holy alliance overcomes all enemies. In this case

---

whom I am indebted, I would thank Lessing for some hints of a Christian drama which is found in his *Hamburgische Dramaturgie.*[69] He, however, fixed his glance upon the purely divine side of the Christian life (the consummated victory) and hence he had misgivings; perhaps he would have expressed a different judgment if he had paid more attention to the purely human side (*theologia viatorum*).[70] Doubtless what he says is very brief, in part evasive, but since I am always glad to have the company of Lessing, I seize it at once. Lessing was not merely one of the most comprehensive minds Germany has had, he not only was possessed of rare exactitude in his learning (for which reason one can securely rely upon him and upon his autopsy without fear of being duped by inaccurate quotations which can be traced nowhere, by half-understood phrases which are drawn from untrustworthy compendiums, or to be disoriented by a foolish trumpeting of novelties which the ancients have expounded far better) but he possessed at the same time an exceedingly uncommon gift of explaining what he himself had understood. There he stopped. In our age people go further and explain more than they have understood.

*According to Aristotle the historic catastrophe was as follows. To avenge themselves the family of the bride introduced a temple-vessel among his household goods, and he is sentenced as a temple-robber. This, however, is of no consequence, for the question is not whether the family is shrewd or stupid in taking revenge. The family has an ideal significance only in so far as it is drawn into the dialectic of the hero. Besides it is fateful enough that he, when he would shun danger by not marrying, plunges into it, and also that his life comes into contact with the divine in a double way: first by the saying of the augurs, and then by being condemned for sacrilege.

it is heaven itself which separates what heaven itself has joined together. And who would have guessed such a thing? The young bride least of all. Only a moment before she was sitting in her chamber in all her beauty, and the lovely maidens had conscientiously adorned her so that they could justify before all the world what they had done, so that they not merely derived joy from it but envy, yea, joy for the fact that it was not possible for them to become more envious, because it was not possible for her to become more beautiful. She sat alone in her chamber and was transformed from beauty unto beauty, for every means was employed that feminine art was capable of to adorn worthily the worthy. But there still was lacking something which the young maidens had not dreamed of: a veil finer, lighter and yet more impenetrable than that in which the young maidens had enveloped her, a bridal dress which no young maiden knew of or could help her to obtain, yea, even the bride herself did not know how to obtain it. It was an invisible, a friendly power, taking pleasure in adorning a bride, which enveloped her in it without her knowledge; for she saw only how the bridegroom passed by and went up to the temple. She saw the door shut behind him, and she became even more calm and blissful, for she only knew that he now belonged to her more than ever. The door of the temple opened, he stepped out, but maidenly she cast down her eyes and therefore did not see that his countenance was troubled, but he saw that heaven was jealous of the bride's loveliness and of his good fortune. The door of the temple opened, and the young maidens saw the bridegroom step out, but they did not see that his countenance was troubled, they were busy fetching the bride. Then forth she stepped in all her maidenly modesty and yet like a queen surrounded by her maids of honor, who bowed before her as the young maiden always bows before a bride. Thus she stood at the head of her lovely band and waited—it was only an instant, for the temple was near at hand—and the bridegroom came . . . but he passed by her door.

But here I break off—I am not a poet, I go about things only dialectically. It must be remembered first of all that it is at the decisive instant the hero gets this elucidation, so he is pure and blameless, has not light-mindedly tied himself to the fiancée. In the next place, he has a divine utterance for him, or rather against him,[71] he is therefore not guided like those puny lovers by his own conceit. Moreover, it goes without saying that this utterance makes him just as unhappy as the bride, yea, a little more so, since he after all is the occasion of her unhappiness. It is true enough that the augurs only foretold a misfortune to *him*, but the question is whether this misfortune is not of such a sort that in injuring him it would also affect injuriously their conjugal happiness. What then is he to do? (1) Shall he preserve silence and celebrate the wedding?—with the thought that "perhaps the misfortune will not come at once, at any rate I have upheld love and have not feared to make myself unhappy. But keep silent I must, for otherwise even the short moment is wasted." This seems plausible, but it is not so by any means, for in doing this he has insulted the girl. He has in a way made the girl guilty by his silence, for in case she had known the truth she never would have consented to such a union. So in the hour of need he would not only have to bear the misfortune but also the responsibility for having kept silent and her justified indignation that he had kept silent. Or (2) shall he keep silent and give up celebrating the wedding? In this case he must embroil himself in a mystification by which he reduces himself to naught in relation to her. Aesthetics would perhaps approve of this. The catastrophe might then be fashioned like that of the real story, except that at the last instant an explanation would be forthcoming—however, that would be after it was all over, since aesthetically viewed it is a necessity to let him die . . . unless this science should see its way to annul the fateful prophecy. Still, this behavior, magnanimous as it is, implies an offense against the girl and against the reality of her love. Or (3) shall he speak? One of course must not forget that our hero is a little too poetical for us to suppose that to sign away his love might not have for him a significance very different from the result of an unsuccessful business speculation. If he speaks, the whole thing becomes a story of unhappy love in the style of Axel and Valborg.* This is a pair which heaven it-

*Moreover, from this point one might conduct the dialectical movements in another direction. Heaven foretells a misfortune con-

self separates.[72] However, in the present case the separation is to be conceived somewhat differently since it results at the same time from the free act of the individuals. What is so very difficult in the dialectic of this case is that the misfortune is to fall only upon him. So the two lovers do not find like Axel and Valborg a common expression for their suffering, inasmuch as heaven levels its decree equally against Axel and Valborg because they are equally near of kin to one another. If this were the case here, a way out would be thinkable. For since heaven does not employ any visible power to separate them but leaves this to them, it is thinkable that they might resolve between them to defy heaven and its misfortune too.

Ethics, however, will require him to speak. His heroism then is essentially to be found in the fact that he gives up aesthetic magnanimity, which in this case, however, could not easily be thought to have any admixture of the vanity which consists in being hidden, for it must indeed be clear to him that he makes

---

sequent upon his marriage, so in fact he might give up the wedding but not for this reason give up the girl, rather live with her in a romantic union which for the lovers would be more than satisfactory. This implies, however, an offense against the girl because in his love for her he does not express the universal. However, this would be a theme both for a poet and for an ethicist who would defend marriage. On the whole, if poetry were to pay attention to the religious and to the inwardness of personalities, it would find themes of far greater importance than those with which it now busies itself. In poetry one hears again and again this story: a man is bound to a girl whom he once loved—or perhaps never sincerely loved, for now he has seen another girl who is the ideal. A man makes a mistake in life, it was in the right street but it was in the wrong house, for opposite, on the second floor, dwells the ideal—this people think a theme for poetry. A lover has made a mistake, he saw his fiancée by lamplight and thought she had dark hair, but, lo, on closer inspection she is blonde —but her sister, she is the ideal! This they think is a theme for poetry! My opinion is that every such man is a lout who may be intolerable enough in real life but ought instantly to be hissed off the stage when he would give himself airs in poetry. Only passion against passion provides a poetic collision, not the rumpus of these particulars within the same passion. If, for example, a girl in the Middle Ages, after having fallen in love, convinces herself that all earthly love is a sin and prefers a heavenly, here is a poetic collision, and the girl is poetic, for her life is in the idea.

the girl unhappy. The reality of this heroism depends, however, upon the fact that he had had his opportunity [for a genuine love] and annulled it; for if such heroism could be acquired without this, we should have plenty of heroes in our age, in our age which has attained an unparalleled proficiency in forgery and does the highest things by leaping over the intermediate steps.

But then why this sketch, since I get no further after all than the tragic hero? Well, because it is at least possible that it might throw light upon the paradox. Everything depends upon how this man stands related to the utterance of the augurs which is in one way or another decisive for his life. Is this utterance *publici juris*, or is it a *privatissimum?* The scene is laid in Greece, the utterance of the augur is intelligible to all. I do not mean merely that the ordinary man is able to understand its content lexically, but that the ordinary man can understand that an augur announces to the individual the decision of heaven. So the utterance of the augur is not intelligible only to the hero but to all, and no private relationship to the deity results from it. Do what he will, that which is foretold will come to pass, and neither by doing nor by leaving undone does he come into closer relationship with the deity, or become either the object of its grace or of its wrath. The result foretold is a thing which any ordinary man will be just as well able as the hero to understand, and there is no secret writing which is legible to the hero only. Inasmuch as he would speak, he can do so perfectly well, for he is able to make himself intelligible; inasmuch as he would keep silent, it is because by virtue of being the individual he would be higher than the universal, would delude himself with all sorts of fantastic notions about how she will soon forget the sorrow, etc. On the other hand, in case the will of heaven had not been announced to him by an augur, in case it had come to his knowledge in an entirely private way, in case it had put itself into an entirely private relationship with him, then we encounter the paradox (supposing there is such a thing—for my reflection takes the form of a dilemma), then he could not speak, however much he might wish to.[73] He did not then enjoy himself in the silence but suffered pain—but this precisely was to him the assurance that he was justified. So the reason for his silence is not that he as the individual would place himself in an absolute relation to the *universal*, but that he as the individual was placed in an absolute relation to the *absolute*. In this then he would also be able to find repose (as well as I am able to figure it to myself), whereas his magnanimous silence would constantly have been disquieted by the requirements of the ethical. It is very much to be desired that aesthetics would for once essay to begin at the point where for so many years it has ended, with the illusory magnanimity. Once it were to do this it would work directly in the interest of the religious, for religion is the only power which can deliver the aesthetical out of its conflict with the ethical. Queen Elizabeth[74] sacrificed to the State her love for Essex by signing his death-warrant. This was a heroic act, even if there was involved a little personal grievance for the fact that he had not sent her the ring. He had in fact sent it, as we know, but it was kept back by the malice of a lady of the court. Elizabeth received intelligence of this (so it is related, *ni fallor*), thereupon she sat for ten days with one finger in her mouth and bit it without saying a word, and thereupon she died. This would be a theme for a poet who knew how to wrench the mouth open—without this condition it is at the most serviceable to a conductor of the ballet, with whom in our time the poet too often confuses himself.

I will follow this with a sketch which involves the demoniacal. The legend of *Agnes and the Merman* will serve my purpose. The merman is a seducer who shoots up from his hiding-place in the abyss, with wild lust grasps and breaks the innocent flower which stood in all its grace on the seashore and pensively inclined its head to listen to the howling of the ocean. This is what the poets hitherto have meant by it. Let us make an alteration. The merman was a seducer. He had called to Agnes, had by his smooth speech enticed from her the hidden sentiments, she has found in the merman what she sought, what she was gazing after down at the bottom of the sea.

Agnes would like to follow him. The merman has lifted her up in his arms, Agnes twines about his neck, with her whole soul she trustingly abandons herself to the stronger one; he already stands upon the brink, he leans over the sea, about to plunge into it with his prey—then Agnes looks at him once more, not timidly, not doubtingly, not proud of her good fortune, not intoxicated by pleasure, but with absolute faith in him, with absolute humility, like the lowly flower she conceived herself to be; by this look she entrusts to him with absolute confidence her whole fate.[75] And, behold, the sea roars no more, its voice is mute, nature's passion which is the merman's strength leaves him in the lurch, a dead calm ensues—and still Agnes continues to look at him thus. Then the merman collapses, he is not able to resist the power of innocence, his native element is unfaithful to him, he cannot seduce Agnes. He leads her back again, he explains to her that he only wanted to show her how beautiful the sea is when it is calm, and Agnes believes him.—Then he turns back alone and the sea rages, but despair in the merman rages more wildly. He is able to seduce Agnes, he is able to seduce a hundred Agneses, he is able to infatuate every girl—but Agnes has conquered, and the merman has lost her. Only as a prey can she become his, he cannot belong faithfully to any girl, for in fact he is only a merman. Here I have taken the liberty of making a little alteration* in the merman;

*One might also treat this legend in another way. The merman does not want to seduce Agnes, although previously he had seduced many. He is no longer a merman, or, if one so will, he is a miserable merman who already has long been sitting on the floor of the sea and sorrowing. However, he knows (as the legend in fact teaches),[76] that he can be delivered by the love of an innocent girl. But he has a bad conscience with respect to girls and does not dare to approach them. Then he sees Agnes. Already many a time when he was hidden in the reeds he had seen her walking on the shore.[77] Her beauty, her quiet occupation with herself, fixes his attention upon her; but only sadness prevails in his soul, no wild desire stirs in it. And so when the merman mingles his sighs with the soughing of the reeds she turns her ear thither, and then stands still and falls to dreaming, more charming than any woman and yet beautiful as a liberating angel which inspires the merman with confidence. The merman plucks up courage, he approaches Agnes, he wins her love, he hopes for his deliverance. But Agnes was no quiet maiden, she was fond of the roar of the sea, and the sad sighing beside the inland lake pleased her only

substantially I have also altered Agnes a little, for in the legend Agnes is not entirely without fault—and generally speaking it is nonsense and coquetry and an insult to the feminine sex to imagine a case of seduction where the girl is not the least bit to blame. In the legend Agnes is (to modernize my expression a little) a woman who craves "the interesting," and every such woman can always be sure that there is a merman in the offing, for with half an eye mermen discover the like of that and steer for it like a shark after its prey. It is therefore very stupid to suppose (or is it a rumor which a merman has spread abroad?) that the so-called culture protects a girl against seduction. No, existence is more righteous and fair: there is only one protection, and that is innocence.

We will now bestow upon the merman a human consciousness and suppose that the fact of his being a merman indicates a human pre-existence in the consequences of which his life is entangled. There is nothing to prevent him from becoming a hero, for the step he now takes is one of reconciliation. He is saved by Agnes, the seducer is crushed, he has bowed to the power of innocence, he can never seduce again. But at the same instant two powers are striving for possession of him: repentance; and Agnes and repentance. If repentance alone takes possession of him, then he is hidden; if Agnes and repentance take possession of him, then he is revealed.

Now in case repentance grips the merman and he remains concealed, he has clearly made Agnes unhappy, for Agnes loved him in all her innocence, she believed that at the instant when even to her he seemed changed, however well he hid it, he was telling the truth in saying that he only wanted to show her the beautiful calmness of the sea. However, with respect to

---

because then she seethed more strongly within. She would be off and away, she would rush wildly out into the infinite with the merman whom she loved—so she incites the merman. She disdained his humility, now pride awakens. And the sea roars and the waves foam and the merman embraces Agnes and plunges with her into the deep. Never had he been so wild, never so full of desire, for he had hoped by this girl to find deliverance. He soon became tired of Agnes, yet no one ever found her corpse, for she became a mermaid who tempted men by her songs.

passion the merman himself becomes still more unhappy, for he loved Agnes with a multiplicity of passions and had besides a new guilt to bear. The demoniacal element in repentance will now explain to him that this is precisely his punishment [for the faults of his pre-existent state], and that the more it tortures him the better.

If he abandons himself to this demoniacal influence, he then perhaps makes still another attempt to save Agnes, in such a way as one can, in a certain sense, save a person by means of the evil. He knows that Agnes loves him. If he could wrest from Agnes this love, then in a way she is saved. But how? The merman has too much sense to depend upon the notion that an open-hearted confession would awaken her disgust. He will therefore try perhaps to incite in her all dark passions, will scorn her, mock her, hold up her love to ridicule, if possible he will stir up her pride. He will not spare himself any torment; for this is the profound contradiction in the demoniacal, and in a certain sense there dwells infinitely more good in a demoniac than in a trivial person. The more selfish Agnes is, the easier the deceit will prove for him (for it is only very inexperienced people who suppose that it is easy to deceive innocence; existence is very profound, and it is in fact the easiest thing for the shrewd to fool the shrewd)—but all the more terrible will be the merman's sufferings. The more cunningly his deceit is planned, the less will Agnes bashfully hide from him her suffering; she will resort to every means, nor will they be without effect—not to shake his resolution, I mean, but to torture him.

So by help of the demoniacal the merman desires to be the individual who as the individual is higher than the universal. The demoniacal has the same characteristic as the divine inasmuch as the individual can enter into an absolute relation to it. This is the analogy, the counterpart, to that paradox of which we are talking. It has therefore a certain resemblance which may deceive one. Thus the merman has apparently the proof that his silence is justified for the fact that by it he suffers all his pain. However, there is no doubt that he can talk. He can thus become a tragic hero, to my mind a grandiose tragic hero, if he talks. Some, perhaps, will only understand wherein this is grandiose.* He will then be able to wrest from his mind every self-deceit about his being able to make Agnes happy by his trick, he will have courage, humanly speaking, to crush Agnes. Here I would make in conclusion only one psychological observation. The more selfishly Agnes has been developed, the more dazzling will the self-deception be, indeed it is not inconceivable that in reality it might come to pass that a merman by his demoniac shrewdness has, humanly speaking, not only saved an Agnes but brought something extraordinary out of her; for a demon knows how to torture powers out of even the weakest person, and in his way he may have the best intentions toward a human being.

The merman stands at the dialectical turning-point. If he is delivered out of the demoniacal into repentance there are two paths open to him. He may hold back, remain in his concealment, but not rely upon his shrewdness. He does not come as the individual into an absolute relationship with the demoniacal but finds repose in the counter-paradox that the deity will save Agnes. (So it is the Middle Ages would perform the movement, for according to its conception the merman is absolutely dedicated to the cloister.) Or else he may be saved along with Agnes. Now this is not to be understood to mean that by the love of Agnes for him he might be saved from being henceforth a deceiver (this is the aesthetic way of performing a rescue, which always goes around the main point, which is the continuity of the merman's life); for so far as that goes

*Aesthetics sometimes treats a similar subject with its customary coquetry. The merman is saved by Agnes, and the whole thing ends in a happy marriage. A happy marriage! That's easy enough. On the other hand, if ethics were to deliver the address at the wedding service, it would be quite another thing, I imagine. Aesthetics throws the cloak of love over the merman, and so everything is forgotten. It is also careless enough to suppose that at a wedding things go as they do at an auction where everything is sold in the state it is in when the hammer falls. All it cares for is that the lovers get one another, it doesn't trouble about the rest. If only it could see what happens afterwards—but for that it has no time, it is at once in full swing with the business of clapping together a new pair of lovers. Aesthetics is the most faithless of all sciences. Everyone who has deeply loved it becomes in a certain sense unhappy, but he who has never loved it is and remains a pecus.

he is already saved, he is saved inasmuch as he becomes revealed. Then he marries Agnes. But still he must have recourse
to the paradox. For when the individual by his guilt has gone
outside the universal he can return to it only by virtue of having come as the individual into an absolute relationship with
the absolute. Here I will make an observation by which I say
more than was said at any point in the foregoing discussion.*
Sin is not the first immediacy, sin is a later immediacy. By sin
the individual is already higher (in the direction of the demoniacal paradox) than the universal, because it is a contradiction on the part of the universal to impose itself upon a man
who lacks the *conditio sine qua non.* If philosophy among
other vagaries were also to have the notion that it could occur
to a man to act in accordance with its teaching, one might
make out of that a queer comedy. An ethics which disregards
sin is a perfectly idle science; but if it asserts sin, it is *eo ipso*
well beyond itself. Philosophy teaches that the immediate
must be annulled (*aufgehoben*). That is true enough; but what
is not true in this is that sin is as a matter of course the immediate, for that is no more true than that faith as a matter of
course is the immediate.

As long as I move in these spheres everything goes smoothly,
but what is said here does not by any means explain Abraham;
for it was not by sin Abraham became the individual, on the
contrary, he was a righteous man, he is God's elect. So the
analogy to Abraham will not appear until after the individual
has been brought to the point of being able to accomplish the
universal, and then the paradox repeats itself.

The movements of the merman I can understand, whereas I
cannot understand Abraham; for it is precisely through the
paradox that the merman comes to the point of realizing the
universal. For if he remains hidden and initiates himself into
all the torments of repentance, then he becomes a demon and

---

*In the foregoing discussion I have intentionally refrained from
any consideration of sin and its reality. The whole discussion points
to Abraham, and him I can still approach by immediate categories—
in so far, that is to say, as I am able to understand him. As soon as
sin makes its appearance ethics comes to grief precisely upon repentance; for repentance is the highest ethical expression, but precisely as such it is the deepest ethical self-contradiction.

as such is brought to naught. If he remains concealed but does not think cunningly that being himself tormented in the bondage of repentence he could work Agnes loose, then he finds peace indeed but is lost for this world. If he becomes revealed and allows himself to be saved by Agnes, then he is the greatest man I can picture to myself; for it is only the aesthetic writer who thinks lightmindedly that he extols the power of love by letting the lost man be loved by an innocent girl and thereby saved, it is only the aesthetic writer who sees amiss and believes that the girl is the heroine, instead of the man being the hero. So the merman cannot belong to Agnes unless, after having made the infinite movement, the movement of repentance, he makes still one more movement by virtue of the absurd. By his own strength he can make the movement of repentance, but for that he uses up absolutely all his strength and hence he cannot by his own strength return and grasp reality. If a man has not enough passion to make either the one movement or the other, if he loiters through life, repenting a little, and thinks that the rest will take care of itself, he has once for all renounced the effort to live in the idea—and then he can very easily reach and help others to reach the highest attainments, i.e. delude himself and others with the notion that in the world of spirit everything goes as in a well-known game of cards where everything depends on haphazard. One can therefore divert oneself by reflecting how strange it is that precisely in our age when everyone is able to accomplish the highest things doubt about the immortality of the soul could be so widespread, for the man who has really made even so much as the movement of infinity is hardly a doubter. The conclusions of passion are the only reliable ones, that is, the only convincing conclusions. Fortunately existence is in this instance more kindly and more faithful than the wise maintain, for it excludes no man, not even the lowliest, it fools no one, for in the world of spirit only he is fooled who fools himself.

It is the opinion of all, and so far as I dare permit myself to pass judgment it is also my opinion, that it is not the highest thing to enter the monastery; but for all that it is by no means my opinion that in our age when nobody enters the monastery everybody is greater than the deep and earnest souls who found repose in a monastery. How many are there in our age who have passion enough to think this thought and then to judge themselves honestly? This mere thought of taking time upon one's conscience, of giving it time to explore with its sleepless vigilance every secret thought, with such effect that, if every instant one does not make the movement by virtue of the highest and holiest there is in a man, one is able with dread and horror to discover* and by dread itself, if in no other way, to lure forth the obscure libido[78] which is concealed after all in every human life, whereas on the contrary when one lives in society with others one so easily forgets, is let off so easily, is sustained in so many ways, gets opportunity to start afresh—this mere thought, conceived with proper respect, I would suppose, must chasten many an individual in our age which imagines it has already reached the highest attainment. But about this people concern themselves very little in our age which has reached the highest attainment, whereas in truth no age has so fallen victim to the comic as this has, and it is incomprehensible that this age has not already by a *generatio aequivoca* [breeding without mating] given birth to its hero, the demon who would remorselessly produce the dreadful spectacle of making the whole age laugh and making it forget that it was laughing at itself. Or what is existence for but to be laughed at if men in their twenties have already attained the utmost? And for all that, what loftier emotion has the age found since men gave up entering the monastery? Is it not a pitiable prudence, shrewdness, faintheartedness, it has found, which sits in high places and cravenly makes men believe they have accomplished the greatest things and insidiously withholds them from attempting to do even the lesser things? The man who has performed the cloister-movement has only one movement more to make, that is, the movement of the absurd. How many in our age understand what the ab-

---

*People do not believe this in our serious age, and yet it is remarkable that even in paganism, more easy-going and less given to reflection, the two outstanding representatives of the Greek γνῶθι σαυτόν [know thyself] as a conception of existence intimated each in his way that by delving deep into oneself one would first of all discover the disposition to evil. I surely do not need to say that I am thinking of Pythagoras and Socrates.

surd is? How many of our contemporaries so live that they have renounced all or have gained all? How many are even so honest with themselves that they know what they can do and what they cannot? And is it not true that in so far as one finds such people one finds them rather among the less cultured and in part among women? The age in a kind of clairvoyance reveals its weak point, as a demoniac always reveals himself without understanding himself, for over and over again it is demanding the comic. If it really were this the age needed, the theater might perhaps need a new play in which it was made a subject of laughter that a person died of love—or would it not rather be salutary for this age if such a thing were to happen among us, if the age were to witness such an occurrence, in order that for once it might acquire courage to believe in the power of spirit, courage to stop quenching cravenly the better impulses in oneself and quenching enviously the better impulses in others . . . by laughter? Does the age really need a ridiculous exhibition by a religious enthusiast in order to get something to laugh at, or does it not need rather that such an enthusiastic figure should remind it of that which has been forgotten?

If one would like to have a story written on a similar theme but more touching for the fact that the passion of repentance was not awakened, one might use to this effect a tale which is narrated in the book of Tobit. The young Tobias wanted to marry Sarah the daughter of Raguel and Edna. But a sad fatality hung over this young girl. She had been given to seven husbands, all of whom had perished in the bride-chamber. With a view to my plan this feature is a blemish in the narrative, for almost irresistibly a comic effect is produced by the thought of seven fruitless attempts to get married notwithstanding she was very near to it—just as near as a student who seven times failed to get his diploma. In the book of Tobit the accent falls on a different spot, therefore the high figure is significant and in a certain sense is contributary to the tragic effect, for it enhances the courage of Tobias, which was the more notable because he was the only son of his parents (6:14) and because the deterrent was so striking. So this feature must be left out. Sarah is a maiden who has never been in love, who treasures still a young maiden's bliss, her enormous first mortgage upon life, her *Vollmachtbrief zum Glücke*,[79] the privilege of loving a man with her whole heart. And yet she is the most unhappy maiden, for she knows that the evil demon who loves her will kill the bridegroom the night of the wedding. I have read of many a sorrow, but I doubt if there is anywhere to be found so deep a sorrow as that which we discover in the life of this girl. However, if the misfortune comes from without, there is some consolation to be found after all. Although existence did not bring one that which might have made one happy, there is still consolation in the thought that one would have been able to receive it. But the unfathomable sorrow which time can never divert, which time can never heal: To be aware that it was of no avail though existence were to do everything! A Greek writer conceals so infinitely much by his simple naïveté when he says: πάντως γὰρ οὐδεὶς ἔρωτα ἔφυγεν ἤ φεύξεται, μέχρις ἂν κάλλος ἦ καὶ ὀφθαλμοὶ βλέπωσιν (cf. Longi *Pastoralia*).[80] There has been many a girl who became unhappy in love, but after all she *became* so, Sarah *was* so before she became so. It is hard not to find the man to whom one can surrender oneself devotedly, but it is unspeakably hard not to be able to surrender oneself. A young girl surrenders herself, and then they say, "Now she is no longer free"; but Sarah was never free, and yet she had never surrendered herself. It is hard if a girl surrendered herself and then was cheated,[81] but Sarah was cheated before she surrendered herself. What a world of sorrow is implied in what follows, when finally Tobias wishes to marry Sarah! What wedding ceremonies! What preparations! No maiden has ever been so cheated as Sarah, for she was cheated out of the most sacred thing of all, the absolute wealth which even the poorest girl possesses, cheated out of the secure, boundless, unrestrained, unbridled devotion of surrender—for first there had to be a fumigation by laying the heart of the fish and its liver upon glowing coals. And think of how the mother had to take leave of her daughter, who having herself been cheated out of all, in continuity with this must cheat the mother out of her most beautiful possession. Just read the narrative. "Edna prepared the chamber and brought Sarah thither and wept and received the tears of her daughter. And she said unto her, Be of good comfort, my child, the Lord of heaven and earth give thee joy for this thy sorrow! Be of good courage, my daughter." And then the moment of the nuptials! Let one read it if one can for tears. "But after they were both shut in together Tobias rose up from the bed and said, Sister, arise, and let us pray that the Lord may have mercy upon us" (8:4).

In case a poet were to read this narrative, in case he were to make use of it, I wager a hundred to one that he would lay all the emphasis upon the young Tobias. His heroic courage in being willing to risk his life in such evident danger—which the narrative recalls once again, for the morning after the nuptials Raguel says to Edna, "Send one of the maidservants and let her see whether he be alive; but if not, that we may bury him and no man know of it" (8:12)—this heroic courage would be the poet's theme. I take the liberty of proposing another. Tobias acted bravely, stoutheartedly and chivalrously, but any man who has not the courage for this is a molly-coddle who does not know what love is, or what it is to be a man, or what is worth living for; he had not even comprehended the little mystery, that it is better to give than to receive, and has no inkling of the great one, that it is far more difficult to receive than to give—that is, if one has had courage to do without and in the hour of need did not become cowardly. No, it is Sarah that is the heroine. I desire to draw near to her as I never have drawn near to any girl or felt tempted in thought to draw near to any girl I have read about. For what love to God it requires to be willing to let oneself be healed when from the beginning one has been thus bungled without one's fault, from the beginning has been an abortive specimen of humanity![82] What ethical maturity was required for assuming the responsibility of allowing the loved one to do such a daring deed! What humility before the face of another person! What faith in God to believe that the next instant she would not hate the husband to whom she owed everything!

Let Sarah be a man, and with that the demoniacal is close at hand. The proud and noble nature can endure everything, but one thing it cannot endure, it cannot endure pity. In that there is implied an indignity which can only be inflicted upon one by a higher power, for by oneself one can never become an object of pity. If a man has sinned, he can bear the punishment for it without despairing; but without blame to be singled out from his mother's womb as a sacrifice to pity, as a sweet-smelling savor in its nostrils, that he cannot put up with. Pity has a strange dialectic, at one moment it requires guilt, the next moment it will not have it, and so it is that to be predestinated to pity is more and more dreadful the more the individual's misfortune is in the direction of the spiritual. But Sarah had no blame attaching to her, she is cast forth as a prey to every suffering and in addition to this has to endure the torture of pity—for even I who admire her more than Tobias loved her, even I cannot mention her name without saying, "Poor girl." Put a man in Sarah's place, let him know that in case he were to love a girl a spirit of hell would come and murder his loved one—it might well be possible that he would choose the demoniacal part, that he would shut himself up within himself and say in the way a demoniacal nature talks in secret, "Many thanks, I am no friend of courteous and prolix phrases, I do not absolutely need the pleasure of love, I can become a Blue Beard, finding my delight in seeing maidens perish during the night of their nuptials." Commonly one hears little about the demoniacal, notwithstanding that this field, particularly in our time, has a valid claim to be explored, and notwithstanding that the observer, in case he knows how to get a little in *rapport* with the demon, can, at least occasionally, make use of almost every man for this purpose. As such an explorer Shakespeare is and constantly remains a hero. That horrible demon, the most demoniacal figure Shakespeare has depicted and depicted incomparably, the Duke of Gloucester (afterwards to become Richard III)—what made him a demon? Evidently the fact that he could not bear the pity he had been subjected to since childhood. His monologue in the first act of Richard III is worth more than all the moral systems which have no inkling of the terrors of existence or of the explanation of them.

I, that am rudely stamped, and want love's majesty
To strut before a wanton ambling nymph;
I, that am curtail'd of this fair proportion,
Cheated of feature by dissembling nature,
Deformed, unfinished, sent before my time
Into this breathing world, scarse half made up,
And that so lamely and unfashionable
That dogs bark at me as I halt by them.

Such natures as that of Gloucester one cannot save by
mediating them into an idea of society. Ethics in fact only
makes game of them, just as it would be a mockery of Sarah if
ethics were to say to her, "Why dost thou not express the universal and get married?" Essentially such natures are in the
paradox and are no more imperfect than other men, but are
either lost in the demoniacal paradox or saved in the divine.
Now from time out of mind people have been pleased to think
that witches, hobgoblins, gnomes etc. were deformed, and un-
deniably every man on seeing a deformed person has at once
an inclination to associate this with the notion of moral de-
pravity. What a monstrous injustice! For the situation must
rather be inverted, in the sense that existence itself has cor-
rupted them, in the same way that a stepmother makes the
children wicked. The fact of being originally set outside of the
universal, by nature or by a historical circumstance, is the beginning of the demoniacal, for which the individual himself
however is not to blame. Thus Cumberland's Jew[83] is also a
demon notwithstanding he does what is good. Thus too the
demoniacal may express itself as contempt for men—a contempt, be it observed, which does not cause a man to behave
contemptibly, since on the contrary he counts it his forte that
he is better than all who condemn him.—In view of such cases
the poets ought to lose no time in sounding the alarm. God
knows what books are read now by the younger generation of
verse makers! Their study likely consists in learning rhymes by
rote. God knows what significance in existence these men
have! At this moment I do not know what use they are except
to furnish an edifying proof of the immortality of the soul, for
the fact that one can say of them as Baggesen says[84] of the

poet of our town, Kildevalle, "If he is immortal, then we all are."—What has here been said about Sarah, almost as a sort of poetic production and therefore with a fantastic presupposition, acquires its full significance if one with psychological interest will delve deep into the meaning of the old saying: *Nullum unquam exstitit magnum ingenium sine aliqua dementia.*[85] For this *dementia* is the suffering allotted to genius in existence, it is the expression, if I may say so, of the divine jealousy, whereas the gift of genius is the expression of the divine favor. So from the start the genius is disoriented in relation to the universal and is brought into relation with the paradox—whether it be that in despair at his limitation (which in his eyes transforms his omnipotence into impotence) he seeks a demoniacal reassurance and therefore will not admit such limitation either before God or men, or whether he reassures himself religiously by love to the Deity. Here are implied psychological topics to which, it seems to me, one might gladly sacrifice a whole life—and yet one so seldom hears a word about them.[86] What relation has madness to genius? Can we construct the one out of the other? In what sense and how far is the genius master of his madness? For it goes without saying that to a certain degree he is master of it, since otherwise he would be actually a madman. For such observations, however, ingenuity in a high degree is requisite, and love; for to make observation upon a superior mind is very difficult. If with due attention to this difficulty one were to read through the works of particular authors most celebrated for their genius, it might in barely a single instance perhaps be possible, though with much pains, to discover a little.

I would consider still another case, that of an individual who by being hidden and by his silence would save the universal. To this end I make use of the legend of Faust.[87] Faust is a doubter,* an apostate against the spirit, who takes the path

---

*If one would prefer not to make use of a doubter, one might choose a similar figure, an ironist, for example, whose sharp sight has discovered fundamentally the ludicrousness of existence, who by a secret understanding with the forces of life ascertains what the patient wishes. He knows that he possesses the power of laughter if he

of the flesh. This is what the poets mean by it, and whereas again and again it is repeated that every age has its Faust, yet one poet after another follows indefatigably the same beaten track. Let us make a little alteration. Faust is the doubter *par excellence*, but he is a sympathetic nature. Even in Goethe's interpretation of Faust I sense the lack of a deeper psychological insight into the secret conversations of doubt with itself. In our age, when indeed all have experienced doubt, no poet has yet made a step in this direction. So I think I might well offer them Royal Securities[88] to write on, so that

---

would use it, he is sure of his victory, yea, also of his good fortune. He knows that an individual voice will be raised in resistance, but he knows that he is stronger, he knows that for an instant one still can cause men to seem serious, but he knows also that privately they long to laugh with him; he knows that for an instant one can still cause a woman to hold a fan before her eyes when he talks, but he knows that she is laughing behind the fan, that the fan is not absolutely impervious to vision, he knows that one can write on it an invisible inscription, he knows that when a woman strikes at him with her fan it is because she has understood him, he knows without the least danger of deception how laughter sneaks in, and how when once it has taken up its lodging it lies in ambush and waits. Let us imagine such an Aristophanes, such a Voltaire, a little altered, for he is at the same time a sympathetic nature, he loves existence, he loves men, and he knows that even though the reproof of laughter will perhaps educate a saved young race, yet in the contemporary generation a multitude of men will be ruined. So he keeps silent and as far as possible forgets how to laugh. But dare he keep silent? Perhaps there are sundry persons who do not in the least understand the difficulty I have in mind. They are likely of the opinion that it is an admirable act of magnanimity to keep silent. That is not at all my opinion, for I think that every such character, if he has not had the magnanimity to keep silent, is a traitor against existence. So I require of him this magnanimity; but when he possesses it, dare he then keep silent? Ethics is a dangerous science, and it might be possible that Aristophanes was determined by purely ethical considerations in resolving to reprove by laughter his misguided age. Aesthetical magnanimity does not help [to solve the question whether one ought to keep silent], for on the credit of that one does not take such a risk. If he is to keep silent, then into the paradox he must go.—I will suggest still another plan for a story. Suppose e.g. that a man possessed a explanation of a heroic life which explained it in a sorry way, and yet a whole generation reposes securely in an absolute belief in this hero, without suspecting anything of the sort.

they could write down all they have experienced in this respect—they would hardly write more than there is room for on the left hand margin.

Only when one thus deflects Faust back into himself, only then can doubt appear poetic, only then too does he himself discover in reality all its sufferings. He knows that it is spirit which sustains existence, but he knows then too that the security and joy in which men live is not founded upon the power of spirit but is easily explicable as an unreflected happiness. As a doubter, as the doubter, he is higher than all this, and if anyone would deceive him by making him believe that he has passed through a course of training in doubt, he readily sees through the deception; for the man who has made a movement in the world of spirit, hence an infinite movement, can at once hear through the spoken word whether it is a tried and experienced man who is speaking or a Münchhausen. What a Tamberlane is able to accomplish by means of his Huns, that Faust is able to accomplish by means of his doubt: to frighten men up in dismay, to cause existence to quake beneath their feet, to disperse men abroad, to cause the shriek of dread to be heard on all sides. And if he does it, he is nevertheless no Tamberlane, he is in a certain sense warranted and has the warranty of thought. But Faust is a sympathetic nature, he loves existence, his soul is acquainted with no envy, he perceives that he is unable to check the raging he is well able to arouse, he desires no Herostratic honor[89]—he keeps silent, he hides the doubt in his soul more carefully than the girl who hides under her heart the fruit of a sinful love, he endeavors as well as he can to walk in step with other men, but what goes on within him he consumes within himself, and thus he offers himself a sacrifice for the universal.

When an eccentric pate raises a whirlwind of doubt one may sometimes hear people say, "Would that he had kept silent." Faust realizes this idea. He who has a conception of what it means to live upon spirit knows also what the hunger of doubt is, and that the doubter hungers just as much for the daily bread of life as for the nutriment of the spirit. Although all the pain Faust suffers may be a fairly good argument that is was not pride possessed him, yet to test this further I will employ a little precautionary expedient which I invent with great ease. For as Gregory of Rimini was called *tortor infantium*[90] because he espoused the view of the damnation of infants, so I might be tempted to call myself *tortor heroum;* for I am very inventive when it is a question of putting heroes to the torture. Faust sees Marguerite—not after he had made the choice of pleasure, for my Faust does not choose pleasure—he sees Marguerite, not in the concave mirror of Mephistopheles but in all her lovable innocence, and as his soul has preserved love for mankind he can perfectly well fall in love with her. But he is a doubter, his doubt has annihilated reality for him; for so ideal is my Faust that he does not belong to these scientific doubters who doubt one hour every semester in the professorial chair, but at other times are able to do everything else, as indeed they do this, without the support of spirit or by virtue of spirit. He is a doubter, and the doubter hungers just as much for the daily bread of joy as for the food of the spirit. He remains, however, true to his resolution and keeps silent, and he talks to no man of his doubt, nor to Marguerite of his love.

It goes without saying that Faust is too ideal a figure to be content with the tattle that if he were to talk he would give occasion to an ordinary discussion and the whole thing would pass off without any consequences—or perhaps, and perhaps. . . . (Here, as every poet will easily see, the comic is latent in the plan, threatening to bring Faust into an ironical relation to these fools of low comedy who in our age run after doubt, produce an external argument, e.g. a doctor's diploma, to prove that they really have doubted, or take their oath that they have doubted everything, or prove it by the fact that on a journey they met a doubter—these express-messengers and foot-racers in the world of spirit, who in the greatest haste get from one man a little hint of doubt, from another a little hint of faith, and then turn it to account as best they can, according as the congregation wants to have fine sand or coarse sand.)[91] Faust is too ideal a figure to go about in carpet-slippers. He who has not an infinite passion is not the ideal, and he who has an infinite passion has long ago saved his soul out of such nonsense. He keeps silent and sacrifices himself/or he talks with the consciousness that he will confound everything.

If he keeps silent, ethics condemns him, for it says, "Thou shalt acknowledge the universal, and it is precisely by speaking thou dost acknowledge it, and thou must not have compassion upon the universal." One ought not to forget this consideration when sometimes one judges a doubter severely for talking. I am not inclined to judge such conduct leniently, but in this case as everywhere all depends upon whether the movements occur normally. If worse comes to worst, a doubter, even though by talking he were to bring down all possible misfortune upon the world, is much to be preferred to these miserable sweet-tooths who taste a little of everything, and who would heal doubt without being acquainted with it, and who are therefore usually the proximate cause of it when doubt breaks out wildly and with ungovernable rage.—If he speaks, then he confounds everything—for though this does not actually occur, he does not get to know it till afterwards, and the upshot cannot help a man either at the moment of action or with regard to his responsibility.

If he keeps silent on his own responsibility, he may indeed be acting magnanimously, but to his other pains he adds a little temptation (*Anfechtung*), for the universal will constantly torture him and say, "You ought to have talked. Where will you find the certainty that it was not after all a hidden pride which governed your resolution?"

If on the other hand the doubter is able to become the particular individual who as the individual stands in an absolute relation to the absolute, then he can get a warrant for his silence. In this case he must transform his doubt into guilt. In this case he is within the paradox, but in this case his doubt is cured, even though he may get another doubt.

Even the New Testament would approve of such a silence. There are even passages in the New Testament which commend irony—if only it is used to conceal something good. This movement, however, is as properly a movement of irony as is any other which has its ground in the fact that subjectivity is higher than reality. In our age people want to hear nothing about this, generally they want to know no more about irony than Hegel has said about it[92]—who strangely enough had not much understanding of it, and bore a grudge against it, which our age has good reason not to give up, for it had better beware of irony. In the Sermon on the Mount it is said, "When thou fastest, anoint thy head and wash thy face, that thou be not seen of men to fast." This passage bears witness directly to the truth that subjectivity is incommensurable with reality, yea, that it has leave to deceive. If only the people who in our age go gadding about with vague talk about the congregational idea[93] were to read the New Testament, they would perhaps get other ideas into their heads.

But now as for Abraham—how did he act? For I have not forgotten, and the reader will perhaps be kind enough to remember, that it was with the aim of reaching this point I entered into the whole foregoing discussion—not as though Abraham would thereby become more intelligible, but in order that the unintelligibility might become more desultory.[94] For, as I have said, Abraham I cannot understand, I can only admire him. It was also observed that the stages I have described do none of them contain an analogy to Abraham. The examples were simply educed in order that while they were shown in their own proper sphere they might at the moment of variation [from Abraham's case] indicate as it were the boundary of the unknown land. If there might be any analogy, this must be found in the paradox of sin, but this again lies in another sphere and cannot explain Abraham and is itself far easier to explain than Abraham.

So then, Abraham did not speak, he did not speak to Sarah, nor to Eleazar, nor to Isaac, he passed over three ethical authorities; for the ethical had for Abraham no higher expression than the family life.

Aesthetics permitted, yea, required of the individual silence, when he knew that by keeping silent he could save another. This is already sufficient proof that Abraham does not lie within the circumference of aesthetics. His silence has by no means the intention of saving Isaac, and in general his whole task of sacrificing Isaac for his own sake and for God's sake is an offense to aesthetics, for aesthetics can well understand that I sacrifice myself, but not that I sacrifice another for my own sake. The aesthetic hero was silent. Ethics condemned him, however, because he was silent by virtue of his accidental particularity. His human foreknowledge was what determined him to keep silent. This ethics cannot forgive, every such human knowledge is only an illusion, ethics requires an infinite movement, it requires revelation. So the aesthetic hero can speak but will not.

The genuine tragic hero sacrifices himself and all that is his for the universal, his deed and every emotion with him belong to the universal, he is revealed, and in this self-revelation he is the beloved son of ethics. This does not fit the case of Abraham: he does nothing for the universal, and he is concealed.

Now we reach the paradox. Either the individual as the individual is able to stand in an absolute relation to the absolute (and then the ethical is not the highest) /or Abraham is lost—he is neither a tragic hero, nor an aesthetic hero.

Here again it may seem as if the paradox were the easiest and most convenient thing of all. However, I must repeat that he who counts himself convinced of this is not a knight of faith, for distress and anguish are the only legitimations that can be thought of, and they cannot be thought in general terms, for with that the paradox is annulled.

Abraham keeps silent—but he *cannot* speak. Therein lies the distress and anguish. For if I when I speak am unable to make myself intelligible, then I am not speaking—even though I were to talk uninterruptedly day and night. Such is the case with Abraham. He is able to utter everything, but one thing he cannot say, i.e. say it in such a way that another understands it, and so he is not speaking. The relief of speech is that it translates me into the universal. Now Abraham is able to say the most beautiful things any language can express about how he loves Isaac. But it is not this he has at heart to say, it is the profounder thought that he would sacrifice him because it is a trial. This latter thought no one can understand, and hence everyone can only misunderstand the former. This distress the tragic hero does not know. He has first of all the comfort that every counter-argument has received due consideration, that he has been able to give to Clytemnestra, to Iphigenia, to Achilles, to the chorus, to every living being, to every voice from the heart of humanity, to every cunning, every alarming, every accusing, every compassionate thought, opportunity to stand up against him. He can be sure that everything that can be said against him has been said, unsparingly, mercilessly—and to strive against the whole world is a comfort, to strive with oneself is dreadful. He has no reason to fear that he has overlooked anything, so that afterwards he must cry out as did King Edward the Fourth at the news of the death of Clarence:[95]

> Who su'd to me for him? who, in my wrath,
> Kneel'd at my feet and bade me be advised?
> Who spoke of brotherhood? who spoke of love?

The tragic hero does not know the terrible responsibility of solitude. In the next place he has the comfort that he can weep and lament with Clytemnestra and Iphigenia—and tears and cries are assuaging, but unutterable sighs are torture. Agamemnon can quickly collect his soul into the certainty that he will act, and then he still has time to comfort and exhort. This Abraham is unable to do. When his heart is moved, when his words would contain a blessed comfort for the whole world, he does not dare to offer comfort, for would not Sarah, would not Eleazar, would not Isaac say, "Why wilt thou do it? Thou canst refrain"? And if in his distress he would give vent to his feelings and would embrace all his dear ones before taking the final step, this might perhaps bring about the dreadful consequence that Sarah, that Eleazar, that Isaac would be offended in him and would believe he was a hypocrite. He is unable to speak, he speaks no human language. Though he himself understood all the tongues of the world, though his loved ones also understood them, he nevertheless cannot speak—he speaks a divine language . . . he "speaks with tongues."

This distress I can well understand, I can admire Abraham,

I am not afraid that anyone might be tempted by this narrative light-heartedly to want to be the individual, but I admit also that I have not the courage for it, and that I renounce gladly any prospect of getting further—if only it were possible that in any way, however late, I might get so far. Every instant Abraham is able to break off, he can repent the whole thing as a temptation (*Anfechtung*), then he can speak, then all could understand him—but then he is no longer Abraham.

Abraham cannot speak, for he cannot utter the word which explains all (that is, not so that it is intelligible), he cannot say that it is a test, and a test of such a sort, be it noted, that the ethical is the temptation (*Versuchung*). He who is so situated is an emigrant from the sphere of the universal. But the next word he is still less able to utter. For, as was sufficiently set forth earlier, Abraham makes two movements: he makes the infinite movement of resignation and gives up Isaac (this no one can understand because it is a private venture); but in the next place, he makes the movement of faith every instant. This is his comfort, for he says: "But yet this will not come to pass, or, if it does come to pass, then the Lord will give me a new Isaac, by virtue viz. of the absurd." The tragic hero does at last get to the end of the story. Iphigenia bows to her father's resolution, she herself makes the infinite movement of resignation, and now they are on good terms with one another. She can understand Agamemnon because his undertaking expresses the universal. If on the other hand Agamemnon were to say to her, "In spite of the fact that the deity demands thee as a sacrifice, it might yet be possible that he did not demand it—by virtue viz. of the absurd," he would that very instant become unintelligible to Iphigenia. If he could say this by virtue of human calculation, Iphigenia would surely understand him, but from that it would follow that Agamemnon had not made the infinite movement of resignation, and so he is not a hero, and so the utterance of the seer is a sea-captain's tale and the whole occurrence a vaudeville.

Abraham did not speak. Only one word of his has been preserved, the only reply to Isaac, which also is sufficient proof that he had not spoken previously. Isaac asks Abraham where the lamb is for the burnt offering. "And Abraham said, God will provide Himself the lamb for the burnt offering, my son."

This last word of Abraham I shall consider a little more closely. If there were not this word, the whole event would have lacked something; if it were to another effect, everything perhaps would be resolved into confusion.

I have often reflected upon the question whether a tragic hero, be the culmination of his tragedy a suffering or an action, ought to have a last rejoinder. In my opinion it depends upon the life-sphere to which he belongs, whether his life has intellectual significance, whether his suffering or his action stands in relation to spirit.

It goes without saying that the tragic hero, like every other man who is not deprived of the power of speech, can at the instant of his culmination utter a few words, perhaps a few appropriate words, but the question is whether it is appropriate for him to utter them. If the significance of his life consists in an outward act, then he has nothing to say, since all he says is essentially chatter whereby he only weakens the impression he makes, whereas the ceremonial of tragedy requires that he perform his task in silence, whether this consists in action or in suffering. Not to go too far afield, I will take an example which lies nearest to our discussion. If Agamemnon himself and not Calchas had had to draw the knife against Iphigenia, then he would have only demeaned himself by wanting at the last moment to say a few words, for the significance of his act was notorious, the juridical procedure of piety, of compassion, of emotion, of tears was completed, and moreover his life had no relation to spirit, he was not a teacher or a witness to the spirit. On the other hand, if the significance of a hero's life is in the direction of spirit, then the lack of a rejoinder would weaken the impression he makes. What he has to say is not a few appropriate words, a little piece of declamation, but the significance of his rejoinder is that in the decisive moment he carries himself through. Such an intellectual tragic hero ought to have what in other circumstances is too often striven for in ludicrous ways, he ought to have and he ought to keep the last word. One requires of him the same exalted bearing which is seemly in every tragic hero, but in addition to this there is required of him one word. So when such an intellectual tragic hero has his culmination in suffering (in death), then by his last word he becomes immortal before he dies, whereas the ordinary tragic hero on the other hand does not become immortal till after his death.

One may take Socrates as an example. He was an intellectual tragic hero. His death sentence was announced to him. That instant he dies—for one who does not understand that the whole power of the spirit is required for dying, and that the hero always dies before he dies, that man will not get so very far with his conception of life. So as a hero it is required of Socrates that he repose tranquilly in himself, but as an intellectual tragic hero it is required of him that he at the last moment have spiritual strength sufficient to carry himself through. So he cannot like the ordinary tragic hero concentrate upon keeping himself face to face with death, but he must make this movement so quickly that at the same instant he is consciously well over and beyond this strife and asserts himself. If Socrates had been silent in the crisis of death, he would have weakened the effect of his life and aroused the suspicion that in him the elasticity of irony was not an elemental power but a game, the flexibility of which he had to employ at the decisive moment to sustain him emotionally.*

What is briefly suggested here has to be sure no application to Abraham in case one might think it possible to find out by analogy an appropriate word for Abraham to end with, but it does apply to this extent, that one thereby perceives how necessary it is that Abraham at the last moment must

---

*Opinions may be divided as to which rejoinder of Socrates is to be regarded as the decisive one, inasmuch as Socrates has been in so many ways volatilized by Plato. I propose the following. The sentence of death is announced to him, the same instant he dies, the same instant he overcomes death and carries himself through in the famous reply which expresses surprise that he had been condemned by a majority of three votes.⁹⁶ With no vague and idle talk in the marketplace, with no foolish remark of an idiot, could he have jested more ironically than with the sentence which condemned him to death.

carry himself through, must not silently draw the knife, but must have a word to say, since as the father of faith he has absolute significance in a spiritual sense. As to what he must say, I can form no conception beforehand; after he has said it I can maybe understand it, maybe in a certain sense can understand Abraham in what he says, though without getting any closer to him than I have been in the foregoing discussion. In case no last rejoinder of Socrates had existed, I should have been able to think myself into him and formulate such a word; if I were unable to do it, a poet could, but no poet can catch up with Abraham.

Before I go on to consider Abraham's last word more closely I would call attention to the difficulty Abraham had in saying anything at all. The distress and anguish in the paradox consisted (as was set forth above) in silence—Abraham cannot speak.* So in view of this fact it is a contradiction to require him to speak, unless one would have him out of the paradox again, in such a sense 'that at the last moment he suspends it, whereby he ceases to be Abraham and annuls all that went before. So then if Abraham at the last moment were to say to Isaac, "To thee it applies," this would only have been a weakness. For if he could speak at all, he ought to have spoken long before, and the weakness in this case would consist in the fact that he did not possess the maturity of spirit and the concentration to think in advance the whole pain but had thrust something away from him, so that the actual pain contained a plus over and above the thought pain. Moreover, by such a speech he would fall out of the rôle of the paradox, and if he really wanted to speak to Isaac, he must transform his situation into a temptation (*Anfechtung*), for otherwise he could say nothing, and if he were to do that, then he is not even so much as a tragic hero.

However, a last word of Abraham has been preserved, and in so far as I can understand the paradox I can also appre-

---

*If there can be any question of an analogy, the circumstance of the death of Pythagoras furnishes it, for the silence which he had always maintained he had to carry through in his last moment, and therefore [being compelled to speak] he *said*, "It is better to be put to death than to speak" (cf. Diogenes Laertius, viii. 39).

hend the total presence of Abraham in this word. First and foremost, he does not say anything, and it is in this form he says what he has to say. His reply to Isaac has the form of irony, for it always is irony when I say something and do not say anything. Isaac interrogates Abraham on the supposition that Abraham knows. So then if Abraham were to have replied, "I know nothing," he would have uttered an untruth. He cannot say anything, for what he knows he cannot say. So he replies, "God will provide Himself the lamb for the burnt offering, my son." Here the double movement in Abraham's soul is evident, as it was described in the foregoing discussion. If Abraham had merely renounced his claim to Isaac and had done no more, he would in this last word be saying an untruth, for he knows that God demands Isaac as a sacrifice, and he knows that he himself at that instant precisely is ready to sacrifice him. We see then that after making this movement he made every instant the next movement, the movement of faith by virtue of the absurd. Because of this he utters no falsehood, for in virtue of the absurd it is of course possible that God could do something entirely different. Hence he is speaking no untruth, but neither is he saying anything, for he speaks a foreign language. This becomes still more evident when we consider that it was Abraham himself who must perform the sacrifice of Isaac. Had the task been a different one, had the Lord commanded Abraham to bring Isaac out to Mount Moriah and then would Himself have Isaac struck by lightning and in this way receive him as a sacrifice, then, taking his words in a plain sense, Abraham might have been right in speaking enigmatically as he did, for he could not himself know what would occur. But in the way the task was prescribed to Abraham he himself had to act, and at the decisive moment he must know what he himself would do, he must know that Isaac will be sacrificed. In case he did not know this definitely, then he has not made the infinite movement of resignation, then, though his word is not indeed an untruth, he is very far from being Abraham, he has less significance than the tragic hero, yea, he is an irresolute man who is unable to resolve either on one thing or another, and for this reason will always be uttering riddles. But such a hesitator is a sheer parody of a knight of faith.

Here again it appears that one may have an understanding of Abraham, but can understand him only in the same way as one understands the paradox. For my part I can in a way understand Abraham, but at the same time I apprehend that I have not the courage to speak, and still less to act as he did —but by this I do not by any means intend to say that what he did was insignificant, for on the contrary it is the one only marvel.

And what did the contemporary age think of the tragic hero? They thought that he was great, and they admired him. And that honorable assembly of nobles, the jury which every generation impanels to pass judgment upon the foregoing generation, passed the same judgment upon him. But as for Abraham there was no one who could understand him. And yet think what he attained! He remained true to his love. But he who loves God has no need of tears, no need of admiration, in his love he forgets his suffering, yea, so completely has he forgotten it that afterwards there would not even be the least inkling of his pain if God Himself did not recall it, for God sees in secret and knows the distress and counts the tears and forgets nothing.

So either there is a paradox, that the individual as the individual stands in an absolute relation to the absolute/or Abraham is lost.

EPILOGUE

One time in Holland when the market was rather dull for spices the merchants had several cargoes dumped into the sea to peg up prices. This was a pardonable, perhaps a necessary device for deluding people. Is it something like that we need now in the world of spirit? Are we so thoroughly convinced that we have attained the highest point that there is nothing left for us but to make ourselves believe piously that we have not got so far—just for the sake of having something left to occupy our time? Is it such a self-deception the present generation has need of, does it need to be trained to virtuosity in self-deception, or is it not rather sufficiently perfected already in the art of deceiving itself? Or rather is not the thing most needed an honest seriousness which dauntlessly and incorruptibly points to the tasks, an honest seriousness which lovingly watches over the tasks, which does not frighten men into being over hasty in getting the highest tasks accomplished, but keeps the tasks young and beautiful and charming to look upon and yet difficult withal and appealing to noble minds. For the enthusiasm of noble natures is aroused only by difficulties. Whatever the one generation may learn from the other, that which is genuinely human no generation learns from the foregoing. In this respect every generation begins primitively, has no different task from that of every previous generation, nor does it get further, except in so far as the preceding generation shirked its task and deluded itself. This authentically human factor is passion, in which also the one generation perfectly understands the other and understands itself. Thus no generation has learned from another to love, no generation begins at any other point than at the beginning, no generation has a shorter task assigned to it than had the preceding generation, and if here one is not willing like the previous generations to stop with love but would go further, this is but idle and foolish talk.

But the highest passion in a man is faith, and here no generation begins at any other point than did the preceding generation, every generation begins all over again, the subsequent generation gets no further than the foregoing—in so far as this remained faithful to its task and did not leave it in the lurch. That this should be wearisome is of course something the generation cannot say, for the generation has in fact the task to perform and has nothing to do with the consideration that the foregoing generation had the same task— unless the particular generation or the particular individuals within it were presumptuous enough to assume the place which belongs by right only to the Spirit which governs the world and has patience enough not to grow weary. If the generation begins that sort of thing, it is upside down, and what wonder then that the whole of existence seems to it upside down, for there surely is no one who has found the world so upside down as did the tailor in the fairy tale[97] who went up in his lifetime to heaven and from that standpoint contemplated the world. If the generation would only concern itself about its task, which is the highest thing it can do, it cannot grow weary, for the task is always sufficient for a human life. When the children on a holiday have already got through playing all their games before the clock strikes twelve and say impatiently, "Is there nobody can think of a new game?" does this prove that these children are more developed and more advanced than the children of the same generation or of a previous one who could stretch out the familiar games, to last the whole day long? Or does it not prove rather that these children lack what I would call the lovable seriousness which belongs essentially to play?

Faith is the highest passion in a man. There are perhaps many in every generation who do not even reach it, but no one gets further. Whether there be many in our age who do not discover it, I will not decide, I dare only appeal to myself as a witness who makes no secret that the prospects for him are not the best, without for all that wanting to delude himself and to betray the great thing which is faith by reducing it to an insignificance, to an ailment of childhood which one must wish to get over as soon as possible. But for the man also who does not so much as reach faith life has tasks enough, and if one loves them sincerely, life will by no means be wasted, even though it never is comparable to the life of those who sensed and grasped the highest. But he who reached faith (it makes no difference whether he be a man of distinguished talents or a simple man) does not remain standing at faith, yea, he would be offended if anyone were to say this of him, just as the lover would be indignant if one said that he remained standing at love, for he would reply, "I do not remain standing by any means, my whole life is in this." Nevertheless he does not get further, does not reach anything different, for if he discovers this, he has a different explanation for it.

"One must go further, one must go further." This impulse to go further is an ancient thing in the world. Heraclitus the obscure, who deposited his thoughts in his writings and his writings in the Temple of Diana (for his thoughts had been his armor during his life, and therefore he hung them up in the temple of the goddess),[98] Heraclitus the obscure said, "One cannot pass twice through the same stream."* Heraclitus the obscure had a disciple who did not stop with that, he went further and added, "One cannot do it even once."† Poor Heraclitus, to have such a disciple! By this amendment the thesis of Heraclitus was so improved that it became an Eleatic thesis which denies movement, and yet that disciple desired only to be a disciple of Heraclitus . . . and to go further—not back to the position Heraclitus had abandoned.

*Plato's Cratyllus, §402.
†Cf. Tennemann, Geschichte der Philosophie, I, p. 220.

THE SICKNESS UNTO DEATH

THE SICKNESS UNTO DEATH

TRANSLATOR'S INTRODUCTION*

The Sickness unto Death is a "repetition" in maturer years of *Fear and Trembling*, one of S.K.'s earliest works (1843), in which the completely non-religious pseudonym Johannes de silentio investigated the problems of repentance and faith.

A part of this work, as S.K. says, "was written before the catastrophe" (i.e. the war with Germany and the Danish constitutional revolution, both of which were compressed within a period of a month in the spring of 1848), and hence before his Easter experience which altered radically the character of his writing. The polemical tone of the later chapters attests the effect of it.

Hirsch speaks of this work and the *Training in Christianity* as "the two masterpieces of Kierkegaard as a Christian writer," and he affirms that along with *The Point of View* "no other Christian-religious or Christian-theological works of the nineteenth century stand so good a chance of being introduced into the rank of the imperishable works of the Christian Church."

S.K.'s purpose in this work was essentially religious. He proposed to preface the book with a prayer, as he did all of his Edifying Discourses; but he discarded this thought when he reflected that "a prayer would give the book almost too much the semblance of the edifying" (VIII B 143). Yet the prayer may well be cited here:

"Father in heaven, to Thee the congregation often makes its petition for all who are sick and sorrowful, and when someone amongst us lies ill, alas, of mortal sickness the con-

*My book on *Kierkegaard* (pp. 408–449) furnishes a more ample introduction to the works of this period of S.K.'s life, and to this work in particular, than can be given here, and the following chapter (pp. 450–483) gives an account of the difficulty he encountered in deciding to publish them. A more searching analysis of the whole situation may be found in the *Kierkegaard-Studien* of Professor Emanuel Hirsch, pp. 357–389.

gregation sometimes desires a special petition; Grant that we may each one of us become in good time aware what sickness it is which is the sickness unto death, and aware that we are all of us suffering from this sickness. O Lord Jesus Christ, who didst come to earth to heal them that suffer from this sickness, from which, alas, we all suffer, but from which Thou art able to heal only those who are conscious that they are sick in this way; help Thou us in this sickness to hold fast to Thee, to the end that we may be healed of it. O God the Holy Ghost, who comest to help us in this sickness if we honestly desire to be healed; remain with us so that for no single instant we may to our own destruction shun the Physician, but may remain with Him—delivered from sickness. For to be with Him is to be delivered from our sickness, and when we are with Him we are saved from all sickness."

The word "psychological" was substituted in the title of this book for "edifying." Making a subtle distinction, S.K. declared, "for edification is not my category." He meant, I suppose, that this expression implied authority, whereas when he called his Discourses "edifying" he was asserting merely that they were of a sort that might have this effect. It is significant therefore that this word ultimately found its way back into the title in the form which hitherto he had not ventured to use—except in the last section of the *Christian Discourses*, "Thoughts which Wound from Behind—for edification."

In all his works S.K. gives evidence of a profound knowledge of human psychology, but only this work and *The Concept of Dread* are described in the title as "psychological." No one can deny the appropriateness of this characterization—but how different all this is from what today passes for psychology!

In the preliminary notes for this book S.K. remarks (VIII B 151), "In Section III of Part First I will now describe psychologically the forms of despair as they display themselves in reality, in actual men, whereas in Section I despair was treated as abstractly as possible, and in Section II it was shown that consciousness is the decisive characteristic of despair."

On the date of May 13, 1848, when the book was finished, S.K. made an entry in his *Journal* (VIII A 651ff.) which he entitled "A Report about *The Sickness unto Death*." He says, "There is one difficulty about this book: it is too dialectical and strict to permit of the employment of rhetoric, of revival, of moving effect. The title itself seems to indicate discourses, the title is lyrical. Perhaps the title cannot be used; but at any rate the book has enriched me with a capital *schema* which can always be used in discourses, but without being apparent. The fact is that before I can begin to employ the rhetorical I always must have the dialectical at my finger tips, must go through it many times. This was not the case with this subject." He proceeds to suggest eight themes for discourses.

Before this work had assumed a definite form S.K. proposed (VIII A 558, February 1848) to publish it along with others he then had in hand under the common title:

THOUGHTS WHICH HEAL FUNDAMENTALLY,
CHRISTIAN THERAPEUTIC

"Here the doctrine of the atonement shall be treated. First it is to be shown where the sickness is: sin. So it will be in two parts—or better in three.

(1). Thoughts which Wound from Behind—for Edification.
(2). About the Consciousness of Sin.
   The Sickness unto Death
   Christian Discourses.
(3). Fundamental Healing
   The Christian Therapeutic.
   The Atonement."

In November of 1848 he proposed to include all the works produced in that year, except *The Point of View*, under a single title: "The Collected Works of Completion."

About the beginning of 1850, looking back upon the year 1848, S.K. said of it in his *Journal* (X⁶ B 249), "for me it was incomparably the richest and most fruitful year I have experienced as an author. The productions of the year 1848 I have not yet published, with exception of the little work by the new pseudonym Anti-Climacus, *The Sickness unto Death*, a part of which antedates the catastrophe of '48. The remaining productions are lying completely finished and ready for publication so soon as I understand that the moment has come." In another place (X^4 A 560, June 19, 1852) he says, "Then came '48. I was raised to such a height as I never had known, and I understood myself completely in what was past and already accomplished." This was in fact the zenith of his productivity as an author. He pursued with singleness of aim "the task of making clear what Christianity is," and he performed it with a degree of success which could be attained only by the rare combination of dialectical acumen and poetical genuis which he possessed. But naturally this prodigious labor, carried on throughout a year which for him was marked by more emotional experiences than any other, almost exhausted the strength of this frail man, or, as he said (X^2 A 66), "to put it in my language, God has run me to a standstill."

And not for physical weariness only was S.K. at a standstill in 1849. Having produced this great literature, he did not know what to do with it. From the thought of publishing such trenchant works he recoiled in dismay. Difficulty after difficulty presented itself to his mind. These were of many sorts. The difficulty about publishing *The Point of View* was simple but very singular: it was the doubt "whether a man has a right to let people know how good he is." That proved an insurmountable obstacle. Hence he resolved to leave this work to be published after his death, "as a report to history," and even the "abbreviation" which he wrote in place of it he could not bring himself to publish until August 1851. There were more practical obstacles in the way of publishing the other works, which might well be regarded, even if they had not been so described, as "a condemnation of Christendom," as "an attempt to introduce Christianity into Christendom"; and as such they were sure to be resented, even though they were introduced by the statement that they were written "poetically, without authority," and merely " to call attention." If he were to publish these books, or, as he put it, "to step forth in character," he expected to encounter the most serious sort of persecution, at least that he would find it impossible to obtain a post in the Established Church, either as a country parson (as he had thought at an earlier time), or in a seminary (which now seemed to him more appropriate). At that moment such a post seemed essential to his physical welfare, for he was then faced by the gravest economic difficulties. But he also entertained the hope that after suffering so much by reason of his "heterogeneity" he might find happiness in working like normal men, working "more extensively," as he put it, instead of "intensively" as hitherto he had worked. And we find to our surprise that there was another reason, the hope that if he became "homogeneous" he might look for a *rapprochement* with Regina, who was now Madame Schlegel. For all of these reasons combined the publication of such works seemed to him a very bold "venture," which would deprive him of all the conditions which had made his life tolerable, or indeed which made it possible.

His debate with himself was excruciating and long drawn out. It was not until the middle of the year 1849 that, by a combination of circumstances, his resolution was formed to publish at least *The Sickness unto Death*, that being the work which seemed likely to give the least offense. When the book was published he was agreeably surprised that Bishop Mynster made no great fuss about it. For this he was so grateful that he proposed to dedicate to the old Bishop one of the smaller and least offensive of the works he had ready—perhaps it was the *Cyclus of Ethico-Religious Treatises*. Among his published papers there are six pages (X⁶ B 162–170) devoted to various drafts of an elaborate dedication to the Bishop, which were never used because in the meanwhile the breach between the two men became wider.

But it would be unjust to S.K. were we to stop here, without seeking a nobler and more generous reason for his desperate solicitude. In fact the principal obstacle which he discovered was not unlike that which prevented him from publishing *The Point of View*; for it seemed to him inhuman, even "demoniacal," to confront Christendom with such an "assault of thoughts," unless one had the authority of an Apostle or the attestation which only martyrdom could give to a "witness for the truth." He felt that while he was a very imperfect Christian he might seem to be exacting perfection of others, whereas in fact he regarded these works as his own education in Christianity (cf. especially X⁴ A 560, 666).

That this was the principal obstacle is shown by his almost childish delight in the discovery of the new pseudonym Anti-Climacus (X² A 147, 177; cf. my *Kierkegaard*, pp. 456f.), who figured first as the author of *The Sickness unto Death*, and again as the author of *Training in Christianity*. It must be understood that this manifest fiction could not in the least degree protect S.K. from the external dangers he apprehended, for no one could be in doubt who was the author, even if S.K.'s name had not appeared on the title page as editor. This pseudonym was adopted merely to relieve his own fine feeling of propriety. It must be understood also that this form of pseudonymity was totally different from that which hitherto he had used. In the case of the other pseudonymous works S.K. was scrupulous to make the text agree with the character he ascribed to the pseudonym. Hence he was justified in affirming that not a word uttered by his pseudonyms could properly be referred to him as an expression of his personal view. There is nothing of the sort here, for these later works were the sincerest expression of his own belief, and he had expected to publish them under his own name. The pseudonym was an afterthought. Here therefore every word can be regarded as his own, when now for the first time, with complete frank-heartedness, without resort to the device of "indirect communication," as in the earlier pseudonymous works, and without the "economy" (to use a word which is not his) he employed in the Edifying Discourses, he essays to tell directly and as plainly as possible what Christianity is and all that it is, even if no man can live up to the obligations which it imposes.

The Sickness unto Death is (to recall the title of Robert Burton's famous book) an "Anatomy of Melancholy." But so also was *The Concept of Dread*, and some of the other pseudonymous works are hardly less deserving of this title—

Either/Or most of all, and in some measure *Repetition*, *Fear and Trembling*, and the *Stages*. But S.K. was not content with a diagnosis, he also prescribed the remedy. In his earlier works (inasmuch as he himself had not yet been healed) he could only indicate in a general way that the remedy was to be sought in religion. Here (in the last word of the book, which repeats one of the first words) he gives, if not the prescription for medication of this sickness in the self, at least the precise formula for health, that is, for the condition of the self when this sickness is completely eradicated: that the self "by relating itself to its own self and by willing to be itself is grounded transparently in the Power which constituted it." And "this," he says emphatically, "is the definition of faith."

W. L.

THE SICKNESS UNTO DEATH

A CHRISTIAN PSYCHOLOGICAL EXPOSITION
FOR EDIFICATION AND AWAKENING

By *Anti-Climacus*

EDITED BY S. KIERKEGAARD

COPENHAGEN 1849
[July 30]

Herr! gieb uns blöde Augen für Dinge, die nichts taugen, und Augen voller Klarheit in alle deine Wahrheit. [Lord! Give us weak eyes for things which are of no account, and clear eyes for all your truth.]

In the manuscript S.K. indicated the source of this motto as follows: A sermon by Bishop Albertini, cf. *Handbuch deutscher Beredsamkeit* v. Dr. D. L. B. Wolff, Leipzig, 1845, 1ste D. p. 293.

To many the form of this "exposition" will perhaps seem strange; it will seem to them too strict to be edifying, and too edifying to be strictly scientific. As to this latter point I have no opinion. As to the first, however, this does not express my opinion of the matter; and if it were true that the form is too strict to be edifying, that, according to my conception, would be a fault. It is one question whether it cannot be edifying to everyone, seeing that not everyone possesses the capacity for following it; it is another question whether it possesses the specific character of the edifying. From the Christian point of view everything, absolutely everything should serve for edification. The sort of learning which is not in the last resort edifying is precisely for that reason unchristian. Everything that is Christian must bear some resemblance to the address which a physician makes beside the sick-bed: although it can be fully understood only by one who is versed in medicine, yet it must never be forgotten that it is pronounced beside the sick-bed. This relation of the Christian teaching to life (in contrast with a scientific aloofness from life), or this ethical side of Christianity, is essentially the edifying, and the form in which it is presented, however strict it may be, is altogether different, qualitatively different, from that sort of learning which is "indifferent," the lofty heroism of which is from a Christian point of view so far from being heroism that from a Christian point of view it is an inhuman sort of curiosity. The Christian heroism (and perhaps it is rarely to be seen) is to venture wholly to be oneself, as an individual man, this definite individual man, alone before the face of God, alone in this tremendous exertion and this tremendous responsibility; but it is not Christian heroism to be humbugged by the pure idea of humanity or to play the game of marvelling at world-history. All Christian knowledge, however strict its form, ought to be anxiously concerned; but this concern is precisely the note of the edifying. Concern implies relationship to life, to the reality of personal existence, and thus in a Christian sense it is seriousness; the high aloofness of indifferent learning, is, from the Christian point of view, far from being seriousness, it is, from the Christian point of view, jest and vanity. But seriousness again is the edifying.

This little book therefore is in one sense composed in a way that a seminary student could write it; in another sense, however, in a way that perhaps not every professor could write it.

But the fact that the form in which this treatise is clothed is what it is, is at least the result of due reflection, and at all events it is certainly correct from a psychological point of view. There is a more solemn style which is so solemn that it does not signify much, and since one is too well accustomed to it, it easily becomes entirely meaningless.

Only one remark more, doubtless a superfluity, but for that I am willing to assume the blame: I would call attention once for all to the fact that in this whole book, as the title indeed says, despair is conceived as the sickness, not as the cure. So dialectical is despair. So also in the Christian terminology death is the expression for the greatest spiritual wretchedness, and yet the cure is simply to die, to "die from."

1848.

"This sickness is not unto death" (John 11:4), and yet Lazarus died; for when the disciples misunderstood the words which Christ adjoined later, "Lazarus our friend is asleep, but I go to wake him out of his sleep" (11:11), He said plainly, "Lazarus is dead" (11:14). So then Lazarus is dead, and yet this sickness was not unto death; he was dead, and yet this sickness is not unto death. Now we know that Christ was thinking of the miracle which would permit the bystanders, "if they believed, to see the glory of God" (11:40), the miracle by which He awoke Lazarus from the dead, so that this sickness was not only not unto death, but, as Christ had foretold, "for the glory of God, that the Son of God might be glorified thereby" (11:4). Oh, but even if Christ had not awakened Lazarus from the dead, is it not true that this sickness, that death itself, was not a sickness unto death? When Christ comes to the grave and cries with a loud voice, "Lazarus, come forth" (11:43), it is evident enough that "this" sickness is not unto death. But even if Christ had not said these words— merely the fact that He, who is "the resurrection and the life" (11:25), comes to the grave, is not this a sufficient sign that *this* sickness is not unto death, does not the fact that Christ exists mean that *this* sickness is not unto death? And what help would it have been to Lazarus to be awakened from the dead, if the thing must end after all with his dying—how would that have helped Lazarus, if He did not live who is the resurrection and the life for everyone who believes in Him? No, it is not because Lazarus was awakened from the dead, not for this can one say that *this* sickness is not unto death; but because He lives, therefore this sickness is not unto death. For, humanly speaking, death is the last thing of all; and, humanly speaking, there is hope only so long as there is life. But Christianly understood death is by no means the last thing of all, hence it is only a little event within that which is all, an eternal life; and Christianly understood there is in death infinitely much more hope than merely humanly speaking there is when there not only is life but this life exhibits the fullest health and vigor.

So then in the Christian understanding of it not even death is the sickness unto death, still less everything which is called earthly and temporal suffering: want, sickness, wretchedness, affliction, adversities, torments, mental sufferings, sorrow, grief. And even if such things are so painful and hard to bear that we men say, or at all events the sufferer says, "This is worse than death"—everything of the sort, which, if it is not a sickness, is comparable to a sickness, is nevertheless, in the Christian understanding of it, not the sickness unto death.

So it is that Christianity has taught the Christian to think dauntlessly of everything earthly and worldly, including death. It is almost as though the Christian must be puffed up because of this proud elevation above everything men commonly call misfortune, above that which men commonly call the greatest evil. But then in turn Christianity has discovered an evil which man as such does not know of; this misery is the sickness unto death. What the natural man considers horrible—when he has in this wise enumerated everything and knows nothing more he can mention, this for the Christian is like a jest. Such is the relation between the natural man and the Christian; it is like the relation between a child and a man: what the child shudders at, the man regards as nothing. The child does not know what the dreadful is; this the man knows, and he shudders at it. The child's imperfection consists, first of all, in not knowing what the dreadful is; and then again, as an implication of this, in shuddering at that which is not dreadful. And so it is also with the natural man, he is ignorant of what the dreadful truly is, yet he is not thereby exempted from shuddering; no, he shudders at that which is not the dreadful: he does not know the true God, but this is not the whole of it, he worships an idol as God.

Only the Christian knows what is meant by the sickness unto death. He acquires as a Christian a courage which the natural man does not know—this courage he acquires by learning fear for the still more dreadful. Such is the way a man always acquires courage; when one fears a greater danger, it is as though the other did not exist. But the dreadful thing the Christian learned to know is "the sickness unto death."

I. THAT DESPAIR IS THE SICKNESS
UNTO DEATH

A. Despair is a Sickness in the Spirit, in the Self, and So It May Assume a Triple Form: in Despair at Not Being Conscious of Having a Self (Despair Improperly So Called); in Despair at Not Willing to Be Oneself; in Despair at Willing to Be Oneself.[1]

Man is spirit. But what is spirit? Spirit is the self. But what is the self? The self is a relation which relates itself to its own self, or it is that in the relation [which accounts for it] that the relation relates itself to its own self; the self is not the relation but [consists in the fact] that the relation relates itself to its own self. Man is a synthesis of the infinite and the finite, of the temporal and the eternal, of freedom and necessity, in short it is a synthesis. A synthesis is a relation between two factors. So regarded, man is not yet a self.

In the relation between two, the relation is the third term as a negative unity, and the two relate themselves to the relation, and in the relation to the relation; such a relation is that between soul and body, when man is regarded as soul. If on the contrary the relation relates itself to its own self, the relation is then the positive third term, and this is the self.

Such a relation which relates itself to its own self (that is to say, a self) must either have constituted itself or have been constituted by another.

If this relation which relates itself to its own self is constituted by another, the relation doubtless is the third term, but this relation (the third term) is in turn a relation relating itself to that which constituted the whole relation.

Such a derived, constituted, relation is the human self, a relation which relates itself to its own self, and in relating itself to its own self relates itself to another. Hence it is that there can be two forms of despair properly so called. If the human self had constituted itself, there could be a question only of one form, that of not willing to be one's own self, of willing to get rid of oneself, but there would be no question of despairingly willing to be oneself. This formula [i.e. that the self is constituted by another] is the expression for the total dependence of the relation (the self namely), the expression for the fact that the self cannot of itself attain and remain in equilibrium and rest by itself, but only by relating itself to that Power which constituted the whole relation. Indeed, so far is it from being true that this second form of despair (despair at willing to be one's own self) denotes only a particular kind of despair, that on the contrary all despair can in the last analysis be reduced to this. If a man in despair is as he thinks conscious of his despair, does not talk about it meaninglessly as of something which befell him (pretty much as when a man who suffers from vertigo talks with nervous self-deception about a weight upon his head or about its being like something falling upon him, etc., this weight and this pressure being in fact not something external but an inverse reflection from an inward experience), and if by himself and by himself only he would abolish the despair, then by all the labor he expends he is only laboring himself deeper into a deeper despair. The disrelationship of despair is not a simple disrelationship but a disrelationship in a relation which relates itself to its own self and is constituted by another, so that the disrelationship in that self-relation reflects itself infinitely in the relation to the Power which constituted it.

This then is the formula which describes the condition of the self when despair is completely eradicated: by relating itself to its own self and by willing to be itself the self is grounded transparently in the Power which posited it.

B. Possibility and Actuality of Despair

Is despair an advantage or a drawback? Regarded in a purely dialectical way it is both. If one were to stick to the abstract notion of despair, without thinking of any concrete despairer, one might say that it is an immense advantage. The possibility of this sickness is man's advantage over the beast, and this advantage distinguishes him far more essentially than the erect posture, for it implies the infinite erectness or loftiness of being spirit. The possibility of this sickness is man's advantage over the beast; to be sharply observant of this sickness constitutes the Christian's advantage over the natural man; to be healed of this sickness is the Christian's bliss.

So then it is an infinite advantage to be able to despair; and yet it is not only the greatest misfortune and misery to be in despair; no, it is perdition. Ordinarily there is no such relation between possibility and actuality; if it is an advantage to be able to be this or that, it is a still greater advantage to be such a thing. That is to say, being is related to the ability to be as an ascent. In the case of despair, on the contrary, being is related to the ability to be as a fall. Infinite as is the advantage of the possibility, just so great is the measure of the fall. So in the case of despair the ascent consists in not being in despair. Yet this statement is open to misunderstanding. The thing of not being in despair is not like not being lame, blind, etc. In case the not being in despair means neither more nor less than not being this, then it is precisely to be it. The thing of not being in despair must mean the annihilation of the possibility of being this; if it is to be true that a man is not in despair, one must annihilate the possibility every instant. Such is not ordinarily the relation between possibility and actuality. Although thinkers say[2] that actuality is the annihilated possibility, yet this is not entirely true; it is the fulfilled, the effective possibility. Here, on the contrary, the actuality (not being in despair), which in its very form is a negation, is the impotent, annihilated possibility; ordinarily, actuality in comparison with possibility is a confirmation, here it is a negation.

Despair is the disrelationship in a relation which relates itself to itself. But the synthesis is not the disrelationship, it is merely the possibility, or, in the synthesis is latent the possibility of the disrelationship. If the synthesis were the disrelationship, there would be no such thing as despair, for despair would then be something inherent in human nature as such, that is, it would not be despair, it would be something that befell a man, something he suffered passively, like an illness into which a man falls, or like death which is the lot of all. No, this thing of despairing is inherent in man himself; but if he were not a synthesis, he could not despair, neither could he despair if the synthesis were not originally from God's hand in the right relationship.

Whence then comes despair? From the relation wherein the synthesis relates itself to itself, in that God who made man a relationship lets this go as it were out of His hand, that is, in the fact that the relation relates itself to itself. And herein, in the fact that the relation is spirit, is the self, consists the responsibility under which all despair lies, and so lies every instant it exists, however much and however ingeniously the despairer, deceiving himself and others, may talk of his despair as a misfortune which has befallen him, with a confusion of things different, as in the case of vertigo aforementioned, with which, though it is qualitatively different, despair has much in common, since vertigo is under the rubric soul what despair is under the rubric spirit, and is pregnant with analogies to despair.

So when the disrelationship—that is, despair—has set in, does it follow as a matter of course that it continues? No, it does not follow as a matter of course; if the disrelationship continues, it does not follow as a consequence of the disrelation but as a consequence of the relation which relates itself to itself. That is to say, every time the disrelation expresses itself, and every instant it exists, it is to the relation one must revert. Observe that we speak of a man contracting a disease, maybe through carelessness. Then the illness sets in, and from that instant it affirms itself and is now an *actuality*, the origin of which recedes more and more into the *past*. It would be cruel and inhuman if one were to continue to say incessantly, "This instant thou, the sick man, art contracting this disease"; that is, if every instant one were to resolve the actuality of the disease into its possibility. It is true that he did contract the disease, but this he did only once; the continuance of the disease is a simple consequence of the fact that he once contracted it, its progress is not to be referred every instant to him as the cause; he contracted it, but one cannot say that he *is* contracting it. Not so with despair: every actual instant of despair is to be referred back to possibility, every instant the man in despair is *contracting* it, it is constantly in the present tense, nothing comes to pass here as a consequence of a bygone actuality superseded; at every actual instant of despair the despairer bears as his responsibility all the foregoing experience in possibility as a present. This comes from the fact that despair is a qualification of spirit, that it is related to the eternal in man. But the eternal he cannot get rid of, no, not to all eternity; he cannot cast it from him once for all, nothing is more impossible; every instant he does not possess it he must have cast it or be casting it from him—but it comes back, every instant he is in despair he contracts despair. For despair is not a result of the disrelationship but of the relation which relates itself to itself. And the relation to himself a man cannot get rid of, any more than he can get rid of himself, which moreover is one and the same thing, since the self is the relationship to onself.

C. Despair is "The Sickness unto Death."

The concept of the sickness unto death must be understood, however, in a peculiar sense. Literally it means a sickness the end and outcome of which is death. Thus one speaks of a mortal sickness as synonymous with a sickness unto death. In this sense despair cannot be called the sickness unto death. But in the Christian understanding of it death itself is a transition unto life. In view of this, there is from the Christian standpoint no earthly, bodily sickness unto death. For death is doubtless the last phase of the sickness, but death is not the last thing. If in the strictest sense we are to speak of a sickness unto death, it must be one in which the last thing is death, and death the last thing. And this precisely is despair.

Yet in another and still more definite sense despair is the sickness unto death. It is indeed very far from being true that, literally understood, one dies of this sickness, or that this sickness ends with bodily death. On the contrary, the torment of despair is precisely this, not to be able to die. So it has much in common with the situation of the moribund when he lies and struggles with death, and cannot die. So to be sick unto death is, not to be able to die—yet not as though there were hope of life; no, the hopelessness in this case is that even the last hope, death, is not available. When death is the greatest danger, one hopes for life; but when one becomes acquainted with an even more dreadful danger, one hopes for death. So when the danger is so great that death has become one's hope, despair is the disconsolateness of not being able to die.

It is in this last sense that despair is the sickness unto death, this agonizing contradiction, this sickness in the self, everlastingly to die, to die and yet not to die, to die the death. For dying means that it is all over, but dying the death means to live to experience death; and if for a single instant this experience is possible, it is tantamount to experiencing it forever. If one might die of despair as one dies of a sickness, then the eternal in him, the self, must be capable of dying in the same sense that the body dies of sickness. But this is an impossibility; the dying of despair transforms itself constantly into a living. The despairing man cannot die; no more than "the dagger can slay thoughts" can despair consume the eternal thing, the self, which is the ground of despair, whose worm dieth not, and whose fire is not quenched. Yet despair is precisely *self*-consuming, but it is an impotent self-consumption which is not able to do what it wills; and this impotence is a new form of self-consumption, in which again, however, the despairer is not able to do what he wills, namely, to consume himself. This is despair raised to a higher potency, or it is the law for the potentiation. This is the hot incitement, or the cold fire in despair, the gnawing canker whose movement is constantly inward, deeper and deeper, in impotent self-consumption. The fact that despair does not consume him is so far from being any comfort to the despairing man that it is precisely the opposite, this comfort is precisely the torment, it is precisely this that keeps the gnawing pain alive and keeps life in the pain. This precisely is the reason why he despairs—not to say despaired—because he cannot consume himself, cannot get rid of himself, cannot become nothing. This is the potentiated formula for despair, the rising of the fever in the sickness of the self.

A despairing man is in despair over *something*. So it seems for an instant, but only for an instant; that same instant the true despair manifests itself, or despair manifests itself in its true character. For in the fact that he despaired of *something,* he really despaired of himself, and now would be rid of himself. Thus when the ambitious man whose watchword was "Either Caesar or nothing"[3] does not become Caesar, he is in despair thereat. But this signifies something else, namely, that precisely because he did not become Caesar he now cannot endure to be himself. So properly he is not in despair over the fact that he did not become Caesar, but he is in despair over himself for the fact that he did not become Caesar. This self which, had he become Caesar, would have been to him a sheer delight (though in another sense equally in despair), this self is now absolutely intolerable to him. In a profounder sense it is not the fact that he did not become Caesar which is intolerable to him, but the self which did not become Caesar is the thing that is intolerable; or, more correctly, what is intolerable to him is that he cannot get rid of himself. If he had become Caesar he would have been rid of himself in desperation, but now that he did not become Caesar he cannot in desperation get rid of himself. Essentially he is equally in despair in either case, for he does not possess himself, he is not himself. By becoming Caesar he would not after all have become himself but have got rid of himself, and by not becoming Caesar he falls into despair over the fact that he cannot get rid of himself. Hence it is a superficial view (which presumably has never seen a person in despair, not even one's own self) when it is said of a man in despair, "He is consuming himself." For precisely this it is he despairs of, and to his torment it is precisely this he cannot do, since by despair fire has entered into something that cannot burn, or cannot burn up, that is, into the self.

So to despair over something is not yet properly despair. It is the beginning, or it is as when the physician says of a sickness that it has not yet declared itself. The next step is the declared despair, despair over oneself. A young girl is in despair over love, and so she despairs over her lover, because he died, or because he was unfaithful to her. This is not a declared despair; no, she is in despair over herself. This self of hers, which, if it had become "his" beloved, she would have been rid of in the most blissful way, or would have lost, this self is now a torment to her when it has to be a self without "him"; this self which would have been to her her riches (though in another sense equally in despair) has now become to her a loathsome void, since "he" is dead, or it has become to her an abhorrence, since it reminds her of the fact that she was betrayed. Try it now, say to such a girl, "Thou art consuming thyself," and thou shalt hear her reply, "Oh, no, the torment is precisely this, that I cannot do it."

To despair over oneself, in despair to will to be rid of oneself, is the formula for all despair, and hence the second form of despair (in despair at willing to be oneself) can be followed back to the first (in despair at not willing to be oneself), just as in the foregoing we resolved the first into the second (cf. I). A despairing man wants despairingly to be himself. But if he despairingly wants to be himself, he will not want to get rid of himself. Yes, so it seems; but if one inspects more closely, one perceives that after all the contradiction is the same. That self which he despairingly wills to be is a self which he is not (for to will to be that self which one truly is, is indeed the opposite of despair); what he really wills is to tear his self away from the Power which constituted it. But notwithstanding all his despair, this he is unable to do, notwithstanding all the efforts of despair, that Power is the stronger, and it compels him to be the self he does not will to be. But for all that he wills to be rid of himself, to be rid of the self which he is, in order to be the self he himself has chanced to chose. To be *self* as he wills to be would be his delight (though in another sense it would be equally in despair), but to be compelled to be *self* as he does not will to be is his torment, namely, that he cannot get rid of himself.

Socrates proved the immortality of the soul from the fact that the sickness of the soul (sin) does not consume it as sickness of the body consumes the body. So also we can demonstrate the eternal in man from the fact that despair cannot consume his self, that this precisely is the torment of contradiction in despair. If there were nothing eternal in a man, he could not despair; but if despair could consume his self, there would still be no despair.

Thus it is that despair, this sickness in the self, is the sickness unto death. The despairing man is mortally ill. In an entirely different sense than can appropriately be said of any disease, we may say that the sickness has attacked the noblest part; and yet the man cannot die. Death is not the last phase of the sickness, but death is continually the last. To be delivered from this sickness by death is an impossibility, for the sickness and its torment . . . and death consist in not being able to die.

This is the situation in despair. And however thoroughly it eludes the attention of the despairer, and however thoroughly the despairer may succeed (as in the case of that kind of despair which is characterized by unawareness of being in despair) in losing himself entirely, and losing himself in such a way that it is not noticed in the least—eternity nevertheless will make it manifest that his situation was despair, and it will so nail him to himself that the torment nevertheless remains that he cannot get rid of himself, and it becomes manifest that he was deluded in thinking that he succeeded. And thus it is eternity must act, because to have a self, to be a self, is the greatest concession made to man, but at the same time it is eternity's demand upon him.

Just as the physician might say that there lives perhaps not one single man who is in perfect health, so one might say perhaps that there lives not one single man who after all is not to some extent in despair, in whose inmost parts there does not dwell a disquietude, a perturbation, a discord, an anxious dread of an unknown something, or of a something he does not even dare to make acquaintance with, dread of a possibility of life, or dread of himself, so that, after all, as physicians speak of a man going about with a disease in him, this man is going about and carrying a sickness of the spirit, which only rarely and in glimpses, by and with a dread which to him is inexplicable, gives evidence of its presence within. At any rate there has lived no one and there lives no one outside of Christendom who is not in despair, and no one in Christendom, unless he be a true Christian, and if he is not quite that, he is somewhat in despair after all.

This view will doubtless seem to many a paradox, an exaggeration, and a gloomy and depressing view at that. Yet it is nothing of the sort. It is not gloomy; on the contrary, it seeks to throw light upon a subject which ordinarily is left in obscurity. It is not depressing; on the contrary it is uplifting, since it views every man in the aspect of the highest demand made upon him, that he be spirit. Nor is it a paradox; on the contrary, it is a fundamental apprehension consistently carried through, and hence it is no exaggeration.

On the other hand, the ordinary view of despair remains content with appearances, and so it is a superficial view, that is, no view at all. It assumes that every man must know by himself better than anyone else whether he is in despair or not. So whoever says that he is in despair is regarded as being in despair, but whoever thinks he is not in despair is not so regarded. Consequently despair becomes a rather rare phenomenon, whereas in fact it is quite universal. It is not a rare exception that one is in despair; no, the rare, the very rare exception is that one is not in despair.

But the vulgar view has a very poor understanding of despair. Among other things (to mention only one which, if rightly understood, would bring thousands, yea, millions under this category), it completely overlooks the fact that one form of despair is precisely this of not being in despair, that is, not being aware of it. The vulgar view is exposed, though in a much deeper sense, to the same fallacy it sometimes falls into when it would determine whether a man is sick or not. In a much deeper sense, I say, for the vulgar view has a far more inadequate notion of spirit than of sickness and health—and without understanding spirit it is impossible to understand despair. It is ordinarily assumed that a man is well when he does not himself say that he is sick, and still more confidently when he says that he is well. The physician on the other hand regards sickness differently. And why? Because he has a definite and well thought out conception of what it is to be in sound health, and by this he tests the man's condition. The physician knows that just as there is sickness which is only imaginary, so also there is such a thing as fictitious health. In the latter case, therefore, the physician first employs medicines to cause the disease to become manifest. Generally the physician, just because he is a physician, i.e. the competent man, has no unconditional faith in a person's own assertion about the state of his health. If it were true that what every man says about the state of his health (as to whether he is sick or well, where he suffers, etc.) were absolutely to be relied upon, it would be an illusion to be a physician. For a physician does not merely have to prescribe medicines, but first and foremost he has to be acquainted with sickness, and so first and foremost to know whether a supposedly sick man really is sick, or whether a supposedly well man is not really sick. So it is also with the physician of souls when dealing with despair. He knows what despair is, he is acquainted with it, and hence he is not satisfied with a man's assertion that he is in despair or that he is not. For it must be observed that in a certain sense not even all who say they are in despair always are so. One may affect despair, and one may make a mistake and confuse despair with all sorts of transitory dejection or grief which pass away without coming to the point of despair. However, the physician of souls does, it is true, regard these states also as forms of despair. He perceives very well that this is affectation—but precisely this affectation is despair. He perceives very well that this dejection etc. does not mean much—but precisely this fact, that it does not mean much, is despair.

Furthermore, the vulgar view overlooks the fact that, as compared with sickness, despair is much more dialectical than what is commonly called sickness, because it is a sickness of the spirit. And this dialectical quality, rightly understood, again brings thousands under the category of despair. For in case at a given moment a physician is convinced that this or that person is in good health and at a later moment becomes sick—the physician may be right in affirming that the person *was* well then, and at a later moment became sick. With despair it is different. As soon as despair manifests itself in a person, it is manifest that the person *was* in despair. For this reason one cannot at a given moment decide anything about a person who is not saved by the fact that he has been in despair. For in case the condition comes about which brings him to despair, it is at that same moment manifest that he has been in despair throughout the whole of his previous life. On the other hand, one is by no means justified in saying, when a man has a fever, that he has had a fever throughout his whole life. But despair is a phenomenon of the spirit, is related to the eternal, and therefore has something of the eternal in its dialectic.

Not only is despair far more dialectical than an illness, but all its symptoms are dialectical, and for this reason the superficial view is so readily deceived in determining whether despair is present or not. For not to be in despair may mean to be in despair, and it may also mean to be delivered from being in despair. A sense of security and tranquillity may mean that one is in despair, precisely this security, this tranquillity, may be despair; and it may mean that one has overcome despair and gained peace. In this respect despair is unlike bodily sickness; for not to be sick cannot possibly mean to be sick; but not to be despairing may mean precisely to be despairing. It is not true of despair, as it is of bodily sickness, that the feeling of indisposition is the sickness. By no means. The feeling of indisposition is again dialectical. Never to have been sensible of this indisposition is precisely to be in despair.

This points to the fact, and has its ground therein, that man, regarded as spirit, is always in a critical condition—and if one is to talk of despair, one must conceive of man as spirit. In relation to sickness we talk of a crisis, but not in relation to health. And why not? Because bodily health is an "immediate" qualification, and only becomes dialectical in sickness, when one can speak of the crisis. But spiritually, or when man is regarded as spirit, both health and sickness are critical. There is no such thing as "immediate" health of the spirit.

So long as one does not regard man as spirit (in which case we cannot talk about despair) but only as a synthesis of soul and body, health is an "immediate" determinant, and only the sickness of soul or body is a dialectical determinant. But despair is expressed precisely by the fact that a person is unaware of being characterized as spirit. Even that which, humanly speaking, is the most beautiful and lovable thing of all, a feminine youthfulness which is sheer peace and harmony and joy—even that is despair. For this indeed is happiness, but happiness is not a characteristic of spirit, and in the remote depths, in the most inward parts, in the hidden recesses of happiness, there dwells also the anxious dread which is despair; it would be only too glad to be allowed to remain therein, for the dearest and most attractive dwelling-place of despair is in the very heart of immediate happiness. All immediacy, in spite of its illusory peace and tranquillity, is dread, and hence, quite consistently, it is dread of nothing; one cannot make immediacy so anxious by the most horrifying description of the most dreadful something, as by a crafty, apparently casual half word about an unknown peril which is thrown out with the surely calculated aim of reflection; yea, one can put immediacy most in dread by slyly imputing to it knowledge of the matter referred to. For immediacy doubtless does not know; but never does reflection catch its prey so surely as when it makes its snare out of nothing, and never is reflection so thoroughly itself as when it is . . . nothing. There is need of an eminent reflection, or rather of a great faith, to support a reflection based upon nothing, i.e. an infinite reflection. So even the most beautiful and lovable thing of all, a feminine youthfulness which is sheer peace and harmony and joy, is nevertheless despair, is happiness. Hardly will one have the good hap to get through life on the strength of this immediacy. And if this happiness has the hap to get through, it would be of little help for it is despair. Despair, just because it is wholly dialectical, is in fact the sickness of which it holds that it is the greatest misfortune not to have had it—the true good hap to get it, although it is the most dangerous sickness of all, if one does not wish to be healed of it. In other cases one can only speak of the good fortune of being healed of a sickness, sickness itself being misfortune.

Therefore it is as far as possible from being true that the vulgar view is right in assuming that despair is a rarity; on the contrary, it is quite universal. It is as far as possible from being true that the vulgar view is right in assuming that everyone who does not think or feel that he is in despair is not so at all, and that only he is in despair who says that he is. On the contrary, one who without affectation says that he is in despair is after all a little bit nearer, a dialectical step nearer to being cured than all those who are not regarded and do not regard themselves as being in despair. But precisely this is the common situation (as the physician of souls will doubtless concede), that the majority of men live without being thoroughly conscious that they are spiritual beings—and to this is referable all the security, contentment with life, etc., etc., which precisely is despair. Those, on the other hand, who say that they are in despair are generally such as have a nature so much more profound that they must become conscious of themselves as spirit, or such as by the hard vicissitudes of life and its dreadful decisions have been helped to become conscious of themselves as spirit—either one or the other, for rare is the man who truly is free from despair.

Ah, so much is said about human want and misery—I seek to understand it, I have also had some acquaintance with it at close range; so much is said about wasted lives—but only that man's life is wasted who lived on, so deceived by the joys of life or by its sorrows that he never became eternally and decisively conscious of himself as spirit, as self, or (what is the same thing) never became aware and in the deepest sense received an impression of the fact that there is a God, and that he, he himself, his self, exists before this God, which gain of infinity is never attained except through despair. And, oh, this misery, that so many live on and are defrauded of this most blessed of all thoughts; this misery, that people employ themselves about everything else, or, as for the masses of men, that people employ them about everything else, utilize them to generate the power for the theater of life, but never remind them of their blessedness; that they heap them in a mass and defraud them, instead of splitting them apart so that they might gain the highest thing, the only thing worth living for, and enough to live in for an eternity—it seems to me that I could weep for an eternity over the fact that such misery exists! And, oh, to my thinking this is one expression the more of the dreadfulness of this most dreadful sickness and misery, namely, its hiddenness—not only that he who suffers from it may wish to hide it and may be able to do so, to the effect that it can so dwell in a man that no one, no one whatever discovers it; no, rather that it can be so hidden in a man that he himself does not know it! And, oh, when the hour-glass has run out, the hour-glass of time, when the noise of worldliness is silenced, and the restless or the ineffectual busyness comes to an end, when everything is still about thee as it is in eternity—whether thou wast man or woman, rich or poor, dependent or independent, fortunate or unfortunate, whether thou didst bear the splendor of the crown in a lofty station, or didst bear only the labor and heat of the day in an inconspicuous lot; whether thy name shall be remembered as long as the world stands (and so was remembered as long as the world stood), or without a name thou didst cohere as nameless with the countless multitude; whether the glory which surrounded thee surpassed all human description, or the judgment passed upon thee was the most severe and dishonoring human judgement can pass—eternity asks of thee and of every individual among these million millions only one question, whether thou hast lived in despair or not, whether thou wast in despair in such a way that thou didst not know thou wast in despair, or in such a way that thou didst hiddenly carry this sickness in thine inward parts as thy gnawing secret, carry it under thy heart as the fruit of a sinful love, or in such a way that thou, a horror to others, didst rave in despair. And if so, if thou hast lived in despair (whether for the rest thou didst win or lose), then for thee all is lost, eternity knows thee not, it never knew thee, or (even more dreadful) it knows thee as thou art known, it puts thee under arrest by thyself in despair.

The forms of despair must be discoverable abstractly by reflecting upon the factors which compose the self as a synthesis.
The self is composed of infinity and finiteness. But the synthesis is a relationship, and it is a relationship which, though
it is derived, relates itself to itself, which means freedom. The
self is freedom. But freedom is the dialectical element in the
terms possibility and necessity.

Principally, however, despair must be viewed under the
category of consciousness: the question whether despair is conscious or not, determines the qualitative difference between
despair and despair. In its concept all despair is doubtless conscious; but from this it does not follow that he in whom it
exists, he to whom it can rightly be attributed in conformity
with the concept, is himself conscious of it. It is in this sense
that consciousness is decisive. Generally speaking, consciousness, i.e. consciousness of self, is the decisive criterion of the
self. The more consciousness, the more self; the more consciousness, the more will, and the more will the more self. A
man who has no will at all is no self; the more will he has, the
more consciousness of self he has also.

A. Despair Regarded in Such a Way That One Does Not Reflect Whether It Is Conscious or Not, So That One Reflects
Only upon the Factors of the Synthesis.

(a). *Despair viewed under the aspects of Finitude/Infinitude.*

The self is the conscious synthesis of infinitude and finitude
which relates itself to itself, whose task is to become itself, a
task which can be performed only by means of a relationship
to God. But to become oneself is to become concrete. But to
become concrete means neither to become finite nor infinite,
for that which is to become concrete is a synthesis. Accordingly, the development consists in moving away from oneself

infinitely by the process of infinitizing oneself, and in returning to oneself infinitely by the process of finitizing. If on the
contrary the self does not become itself, it is in despair,
whether it knows it or not. However, a self, every instant it
exists, is in process of becoming, for the self κατὰ δύναμιν [po-
tentially] does not actually exist, it is only that which it is to
become. In so far as the self does not become itself, it is not
its own self; but not to be one's own self is despair.

(1). THE DESPAIR OF INFINITUDE IS DUE TO THE LACK OF FINITUDE.

The truth of this is inherent in the dialectical fact that the
self is a synthesis [of two factors], the one of which is constantly the opposite of the other. No kind of despair can be
defined directly (i.e. undialectically), but only by reflecting
upon the opposite factor. The despairing person's condition of
despair can be directly described, as the poet does in fact by
attributing to him the appropriate lines. But to describe despair
is possible only by its opposite; and if the lines are to have
poetic value, they must contain in their coloring a reflection of
the dialectical opposite. So then every human existence which
supposedly has become or merely wills to become infinite is
despair. For the self is a synthesis in which the finite is the
limiting factor, and the infinite is the expanding factor. Infinitude's despair is therefore the fantastical, the limitless. The
self is in sound health and free from despair only when, precisely by having been in despair, it is grounded transparently
in God.

The fantastical is doubtless most closely related to fantasy,
imagination, but imagination in turn is related to feeling,
knowledge, and will, so that a person may have a fantastic feeling, or knowledge, or will. Generally speaking, imagination is
the medium of the process of infinitizing; it is not one faculty
on a par with others, but, if one would so speak, it is the faculty
instar omnium [for all faculties]. What feeling, knowledge,
or will a man has, depends in the last resort upon what imagination he has, that is to say, upon how these things are reflected, i.e. it depends upon imagination. Imagination is the

reflection of the process of infinitizing, and hence the elder Fichte quite rightly assumed, even in relation to knowledge, that imagination is the origin of the categories.[4] The self is reflection, and imagination is reflection, it is the counterfeit presentment of the self, which is the possibility of the self. Imagination is the possibility of all reflection, and the intensity of this medium is the possibility of the intensity of the self.

Generally the fantastical is that which so carries a man out into the infinite that it merely carries him away from himself and therewith prevents him from returning to himself.

So when feeling becomes fantastic, the self is simply volatilized more and more, at last becoming a sort of abstract sentimentality which is so inhuman that it does not apply to any person, but inhumanly participates feelingly, so to speak, in the fate of one or another abstraction, e.g. that of mankind *in abstracto.* As the sufferer from rheumatism is unable to master his physical feelings which are under the sway of wind and weather, with the result that he is involuntarily aware of a change in the air etc., so it is with him whose feeling has become fantastic; he becomes in a way infinitized, but not in such a way that he becomes more and more himself, for he loses himself more and more.

So it is with knowledge when it becomes fantastic. The law for the development of the self with respect to knowledge, in so far as it is true that the self becomes itself, is this, that the increasing degree of knowledge corresponds with the degree of self-knowledge, that the more the self knows, the more it knows itself. If this does not occur, then the more knowledge increases, the more it becomes a kind of inhuman knowing for the production of which man's self is squandered, pretty much as men were squandered for the building of the Pyramids, or as men were squandered in the Russian horn-bands to produce one note, neither more nor less.[5]

When the will becomes fantastic, the self likewise is volatilized more and more. In this case the will does not constantly become concrete in the same degree that it is abstract, in such a way that the more it is infinitized in purpose and resolution, the more present and contemporaneous with itself does it become in the small part of the task which can be realized at once, so that in being infinitized it returns in the strictest sense to its self, so that what is *farthest* from itself (when it is most infinitized in purpose and resolution) is in the same instant *nearest* to itself in accomplishing the infinitely small part of the task which can be done even today, even at this hour, even at this instant.

And when feeling, or knowledge, or will have thus become fantastic, the entire self may at last become so, whether in a more active form, as when a man runs headlong into the fantastic, or in a more passive form, when he is carried away, but in either case with moral responsibility. The self thus leads a fantastic existence in abstract endeavor after infinity, or in abstract isolation, constantly lacking itself, from which it merely gets further and further away. So, for example, in the religious sphere. The God-relationship infinitizes; but this may so carry a man away that it becomes an inebriation, it may seem to a man as though it were unendurable to exist before God—for the reason that a man cannot return to himself, cannot become himself. Such a fantastic religious individual would say (to characterize him by putting into his mouth these lines), "That a sparrow can live is comprehensible; it does not know anything about existing before God. But to know that one exists before God—and then not to go crazy or be brought to naught!"[6]

But in spite of the fact that a man has become fantastic in this fashion, he may nevertheless (although most commonly it becomes manifest) be perfectly well able to live on, to be a man, as it seems, to occupy himself with temporal things, get married, beget children, win honor and esteem—and perhaps no one notices that in a deeper sense he lacks a self. About such a thing as that not much fuss is made in the world; for a self is the thing the world is least apt to inquire about, and the thing of all things the most dangerous for a man to let people notice that he has it. The greatest danger, that of losing one's own self, may pass off as quietly as if it were nothing; every other loss, that of an arm, a leg, five dollars, a wife, etc., is sure to be noticed.

(2). THE DESPAIR OF FINITUDE IS DUE TO
THE LACK OF INFINITUDE.

The truth of this (as was shown under 1) is inherent in the dialectical fact that the self is a synthesis [of two factors], one of which is the opposite of the other.

The lack of infinitude means to be desperately narrow-minded and mean-spirited. Here of course it is only a question of ethical meanness and narrowness. The world really never talks of any narrowness but intellectual or aesthetic narrowness —or about the indifferent, which is always the principal subject of the world's talk; for worldliness means precisely attributing infinite value to the indifferent. The worldly view always clings fast to the difference between man and man, and naturally it has no understanding of the one thing needful (for to have that is spirituality), and therefore no understanding of the narrowness and meanness of mind which is exemplified in having lost one's self—not by evaporation in the infinite, but by being entirely finitized, by having become, instead of a self, a number, just one man more, one more repetition of this everlasting *Einerlei*.

Despairing narrowness consists in the lack of primitiveness, or of the fact one has deprived oneself of one's primitiveness; it consists in having emasculated oneself, in a spiritual sense. For every man is primitively planned to be a self, appointed to become oneself; and while it is true that every self as such is angular, the logical consequence of this merely is that it has to be polished, not that it has to be ground smooth, not that for fear of men it has to give up entirely being itself, nor even that for fear of men it dare not be itself in its essential accidentality (which precisely is what should not be ground away), by which in fine it is itself. But while one sort of despair plunges wildly into the infinite and loses itself, a second sort permits itself as it were to be defrauded by "the others." By seeing the multitude of men about it, by getting engaged in all sorts of worldly affairs, by becoming wise about how things go in this world, such a man forgets himself, forgets what his name is (in the divine understanding of it), does not dare to believe in himself, finds it too venturesome a thing to be himself, far easier and safer to be like the others, to become an imitation, a number, a cipher in the crowd.

This form of despair is hardly ever noticed in the world. Such a man, precisely by losing his self in this way, has gained perfectibility in adjusting himself to business, yea, in making a success in the world. Here there is no hindrance, no difficulty, occasioned by his self and his infinitization, he is ground smooth as a pebble, *courant* as a well-used coin. So far from being considered in despair, he is just what a man ought to be. In general the world has of course no understanding of what is truly dreadful. The despair which not only occasions no embarrassment but makes one's life easy and comfortable is naturally not regarded as despair. That this is the view of the world can also be seen in almost all the proverbs, which are merely rules for shrewd behavior. It is said, for example, that a man ten times regrets having spoken, for the once he regrets his silence. And why? Because the fact of having spoken is an external fact, which may involve one in annoyances, since it is an actuality. But the fact of having kept silent! Yet this is the most dangerous thing of all. For by keeping silent one is relegated solely to oneself, no actuality comes to a man's aid by punishing him, by bringing down upon him the consequences of his speech. No, in this respect, to be silent is the easy way. But he who knows what the dreadful is, must for this very reason be most fearful of every fault, of every sin, which takes an inward direction and leaves no outward trace. So it is too that in the eyes of the world it is dangerous to venture. And why? Because one may lose. But not to venture is shrewd. And yet, by not venturing, it is so dreadfully easy to lose that which it would be difficult to lose in even the most venturesome venture, and in any case never so easily, so completely as if it were nothing . . . one's self. For if I have ventured amiss—very well, then life helps me by its punishment. But if I have not ventured at all—who then helps me? And, moreover, if by not venturing at all in the highest sense (and to venture in the highest sense is precisely to become conscious of oneself) I have gained all earthly advantages . . . and lose my self! What of that?

And thus it is precisely with the despair of finitude. In spite of the fact that a man is in despair he can perfectly well live on in the temporal, in fact all the better for it; he may be praised by men, be honored and esteemed, and pursue all the aims of temporal life. What is called worldliness is made up of just such men, who (if one may use the expression) pawn themselves to the world. They use their talents, accumulate money, carry on worldly affairs, calculate shrewdly, etc., etc., are perhaps mentioned in history, but themselves they are not; spiritually understood, they have no self, no self for whose sake they could venture everything, no self before God—however selfish they may be for all that.

(b). *Despair viewed under the aspects of Possibility/Necessity.*

For the purpose of becoming (and it is the task of the self freely to become itself) possibility and necessity are equally essential. Just as infinitude and finitude ($\H{\alpha}\pi\epsilon\iota\rho\rho\nu$ $\pi\epsilon\rho\alpha s$)* both belong to the self, so also do possibility and necessity. A self which has no possibility is in despair, and so in turn is the self which has no necessity.

(1). THE DESPAIR OF POSSIBILITY IS DUE TO THE LACK OF NECESSITY.

The truth of this proposition, as was shown, is inherent in the dialectical situation.

Just as finitude is the limiting factor in relation to infinitude, so in relation to possibility it is necessity which serves as a check. When the self as a synthesis of finitude and infinitude is once constituted, when already it is $\kappa\alpha\tau\grave{\alpha}$ $\delta\acute{\upsilon}\nu\alpha\mu\iota\nu$, then in order to become it reflects itself in the medium of imagination, and with that the infinite possibility comes into view. The self $\kappa\alpha\tau\grave{\alpha}$ $\delta\acute{\upsilon}\nu\alpha\mu\iota\nu$ is just as possible as it is necessary; for though it is itself, it has to become itself. Inasmuch as it is itself, it is the necessary, and inasmuch as it has to become itself, it is a possibility.

*[The limitless/the finite—important terms in Plato's philosophy, especially in his Philebus, 30.]

Now if possibility outruns necessity, the self runs away from itself, so that it has no necessity whereto it is bound to return —then this is the despair of possibility. The self becomes an abstract possibility which tries itself out with floundering in the possible, but does not budge from the spot, nor get to any spot, for precisely the necessary is the spot; to become oneself is precisely a movement at the spot. To become is a movement from the spot, but to become oneself is a movement at the spot.

Possibility then appears to the self ever greater and greater, more and more things become possible, because nothing becomes actual. At last it is as if everything were possible—but this is precisely when the abyss has swallowed up the self. Every little possibility even would require some time to become actuality. But finally the time which should be available for actuality becomes shorter and shorter, everything becomes more and more instantaneous. Possibility becomes more and more intense—but only in the sense of possibility, not in the sense of actuality; for in the sense of actuality the meaning of intensity is that at least something of that which is possible becomes actual. At the instant something appears possible, and then a new possibility makes its appearance, at last this phantasmagoria moves so rapidly that it is as if everything were possible—and this is precisely the last moment, when the individual becomes for himself a mirage.

What the self now lacks is surely reality—so one would commonly say, as one says of a man that he has become unreal. But upon closer inspection it is really necessity the man lacks. For it is not true, as the philosophers explain, that necessity is a unity of possibility and actuality; no, actuality is a unity of possibility and necessity. Nor is it merely due to lack of strength when the soul goes astray in possibility—at least this is not to be understood as people commonly understand it. What really is lacking is the power to obey, to submit to the necessary in oneself, to what may be called one's limit. Therefore the misfortune does not consist in the fact that such a self did not amount to anything in the world; no, the misfortune is that the man did not become aware of himself, aware that the self he is, is a perfectly definite something, and so is the necessary. On the contrary, he lost himself, owing to the fact that this self was seen fantastically reflected in the possible. Even in looking at one's self in a mirror it is requisite to know oneself; for, if not, one does not behold one's self but merely a man. But the mirror of possibility is not an ordinary mirror, it must be used with the utmost precaution. For of this mirror it is true in the highest sense that it is a false mirror. That the self looks so and so in the possibility of itself is only half truth; for in the possibility of itself the self is still far from itself, or only half itself. So the question is how the necessity of the self determines it more precisely. A case analogous to possibility is when a child is invited to participate in some pleasure or another: the child is at once willing, but now it is a question whether the parents will permit it—and as with the parents, so it is with necessity.

In possibility, however, everything is possible. Hence in possibility one can go astray in all possible ways, but essentially in two. One form is the wishful, yearning form, the other is the melancholy fantastic—on the one hand hope; on the other, fear or anguished dread. Fairy-tales and legends so often relate that a knight suddenly perceived a rare bird, which he continues to run after, since at the beginning it seemed as if it were so very near—but then it flies off again, until at last night falls, and he has become separated from his companions, being unable to find his way in the wilderness where he now is. So it is with the possibility of the wish. Instead of summoning back possibility into necessity, the man pursues the possibility—and at last he cannot find his way back to himself.—In the melancholy form the opposite result is reached in the same way. The individual pursues with melancholy love a possibility of agonizing dread, which at last leads him away from himself, so that he perishes in the dread, or perishes in that in which he was in dread of perishing.

(2). THE DESPAIR OF NECESSITY IS DUE TO THE LACK OF POSSIBILITY.

If one will compare the tendency to run wild in possibility with the efforts of a child to enunciate words, the lack of possibility is like being dumb. Necessity is like a sequence of consonants only, but in order to utter them there must in addition be possibility. When this is lacking, when a human existence is brought to the pass that it lacks possibility, it is in despair, and every instant it lacks possibility it is in despair.[7]

One commonly thinks that there is a certain age which is especially rich in hope, or one talks about being or having been at a certain period or a particular moment of one's life so rich in hope and possibility. All this is merely human talk, which never reaches the truth. All this hoping and all this despairing is not yet the true hope and the true despair.

The decisive thing is, that for God all things are possible. This is eternally true, and true therefore every instant. This is commonly enough recognized in a way, and in a way it is commonly affirmed; but the decisive affirmation comes only when a man is brought to the utmost extremity, so that humanly speaking no possibility exists. Then the question is whether he will believe that for God all things are possible—that is to say, whether he will *believe*. But this is completely the formula for losing one's mind or understanding; to believe is precisely to lose one's understanding in order to win God. Suppose it occurs as follows. Picture a man who with all the shuddering revolt of a terrified imagination has represented to himself some horror as a thing absolutely not to be endured. Now it befalls him, precisely this horror befalls him. Humanly speaking his destruction is the most certain of all things—and the despair in his soul fights desperately to get leave to despair, to get, if you will, repose for despair, the consent of his whole personality to despair, so that he would curse nothing and nobody more fiercely than him who attempted (or it may be the attempt) to prevent him from despairing, as the poet's poet so capitally, so incomparably expresses it in *Richard II*, Act 3, Scene 2:

Beshrew thee, cousin, which didst lead me forth
Of that sweet way I was in to despair.

So then, salvation is humanly speaking the most impossible thing of all; but for God all things are possible! This is the fight of *faith*, which fights madly (if one would so express it) for possibility. For possibility is the only power to save. When one swoons people shout for water, *Eau-de-Cologne*, Hoffman's Drops; but when one is about to despair the cry is, Procure me possibility, procure possibility! Possibility is the only saving remedy; given a possibility, and with that the desperate man breathes once more, he revives again; for without possibility a man cannot, as if were, draw breath. Sometimes the inventiveness of a human imagination suffices to procure possibility, but in the last resort, that is, when the point is to *believe*, the only help is this, that for God all things are possible.

Thus is the fight carried on. Whether he who is engaged in this fight will be defeated, depends solely and alone upon whether he has the will to procure for himself possibility, that is to say, whether he will believe. And yet he understands that humanly speaking his destruction is the most certain thing of all. This is the dialectical character of faith. For the most part a man knows no more than that this or that, as he has reason to hope, as seems probable, etc., will not befall him. If it befalls him, then he succumbs. The foolhardy man plunges into a danger involving this or that possibility; if it befalls him, he despairs and succumbs. The *believer* perceives and understands, humanly speaking, his destruction (in what has befallen him and in what he has ventured), but he believes. Therefore he does not succumb. He leaves it wholly to God how he is to be helped, but he believes that for God all things are possible. To *believe* in his own destruction is impossible. To understand that, humanly, it is his own destruction, and then nevertheless to believe in the possibility, is what is meant by faith. So then God helps him—perhaps by letting him escape the terror, perhaps by means of the terror—in the fact that here, unexpectedly, miraculously, divinely, help appears. Miraculously—for it is a strange pedantry to assume that only eighteen hundred years ago it could occur that a man was helped miraculously. Whether a man has been helped by a miracle depends essentially upon the degree of intellectual passion he has employed to understand that help was impossible, and next upon how honest he is toward the Power which helped him nevertheless. But usually it is neither the one thing nor the other: men cry that there is no help, without having strained the understanding to find help, and afterwards they lie ungratefully.

The believer possesses the eternally certain antidote to despair, viz. possibility; for with God all things are possible every instant. This is the sound health of faith which resolves contradictions. The contradiction in this case is that, humanly speaking, destruction is certain, and that nevertheless there is possibility. Health consists essentially in being able to resolve contradictions. So it is bodily or physically: a draft is indifferently cold and warm, disparate qualities undialectically combined; but a healthy body resolves this contradiction and does not notice the draft. So it is also with faith.

The loss of possibility signifies: either that everything has become necessary to a man/or that everything has become trivial.

The determinist or the fatalist is in despair, and in despair he has lost his self, because for him everything is necessary. He is like that king who died of hunger because all his food was transformed into gold. Personality is a synthesis of possibility and necessity. The condition of its survival is therefore analogous to breathing (respiration), which is an in- and an a-spiration. The self of the determinist cannot breathe, for it is impossible to breathe necessity alone, which taken pure and simple suffocates the human self.

The fatalist is in despair—he has lost God, and therefore himself as well; for if he has no God, neither has he a self. But the fatalist has no God—or, what is the same thing, his god is necessity. Inasmuch as for God all things are possible, it may be said that this is what God is, viz. one for whom all things are possible. The worship of the fatalist is therefore at its maximum an exclamation, and essentially it is dumbness, dumb submission, he is unable to pray. So to pray is to breathe, and possibility is for the self what oxygen is for breathing. But for possibility alone or for necessity alone to supply the conditions for the breathing of prayer is no more possible than it is for a man to breathe oxygen alone or nitrogen alone. For in order to pray there must be a God, there must be a self plus possibility, or a self and possibility in the pregnant sense; for God is that all things are possible, and that all things are possible is God; and only the man whose being has been so shaken that he became spirit by understanding that all things are possible, only he has had dealings with God. The fact that God's will is the possible makes it possible for me to pray; if God's will is only the necessary, man is essentially as speechless as the brutes.

In the case of philistinism or triviality, which also lacks possibility, the situation is somewhat different. Philistinism is spiritlessness, in the literal sense of the word; determinism and fatalism are spiritual despair; but such spiritlessness is also despair. Philistinism lacks every determinant of spirit and terminates in probability, within which the possible finds its insignificant place. Thus it lacks sufficient possibility to take notice of God. Devoid of imagination, as the Philistine always is, he lives in a certain trivial province of experience as to how things go, what is possible, what usually occurs. Thus the Philistine has lost his self and God. For in order to be aware of oneself and God imagination must enable a man to soar higher than the misty precinct of the probable, it must wrench one out of this and, by making possible that which transcends the *quantum satis* of every experience, it must teach him to hope and fear, or to fear and hope. But imagination the Philistine does not possess, he does not want to have it, he abhors it. So here there is no help. And if sometimes reality helps by terrors which transcend the parrot-wisdom of trivial experience, then philistinism despairs—that is, it becomes manifest that it was in despair. It lacks the possibility of faith in order by God's help to be able to deliver itself from certain destruction.

Fatalism and determinism, however, have enough imagination to despair of possibility, and have possibility enough to discover impossibility. Philistinism tranquilizes itself in the trivial, being equally in despair whether things go well or ill. Fatalism or determinism lacks the possibility of relaxing and soothing, of tempering necessity, and so it lacks possibility as assuagement. Philistinism lacks possibility as revival from spiritlessness. For philistinism thinks it is in control of possibility, it thinks that when it has decoyed this prodigious elasticity into the field of probability or into the mad-house it holds it a prisoner; it carries possibility around like a prisoner in the cage of the probable, shows it off, imagines itself to be the master, does not take note that precisely thereby it has taken itself captive to be the slave of spiritlessness and to be the most pitiful of all things. For with the audacity of despair that man soared aloft who ran wild in possibility; but crushed down by despair that man strains himself against existence to whom everything has become necessary. But philistinism spiritlessly celebrates its triumph.

B. Despair Viewed under the Aspect of Consciousness.

With every increase in the degree of consciousness, and in proportion to that increase, the intensity of despair increases: the more consciousness, the more intense the despair. This is everywhere to be seen, most clearly in the maximum and minimum of despair. The devil's despair is the most intense despair, for the devil is sheer spirit, and therefore absolute consciousness and transparency; in the devil there is no obscurity which might serve as a mitigating excuse, his despair is therefore absolute defiance. This is the maximum of despair. The minimum of despair is a state which (as one might humanly be tempted to express it) by reason of a sort of innocence does not even know that there is such a thing as despair. So when consciousness is at its minimum the despair is least; it is almost as if it were a dialectical problem whether one is justified in calling such a state despair.

(a). *The Despair which is Unconscious that it is Despair, or the Despairing Unconsciousness of having a Self and an Eternal Self.*

That this condition is nevertheless despair and is rightly so denominated may be taken as an expression for a trait which we may call, in a good sense, the opinionativeness of truth. *Veritas est index sui et falsi.*[8] But this opinionativeness of truth is, to be sure, held in scant honor, as also it is far from being the case that men in general regard relationship to the truth, the fact of standing in relationship to the truth, as the highest good, and it is very far from being the case that they,

Socratically, regard being under a delusion as the greatest misfortune;[9] their sensuous nature is generally predominant over their intellectuality. So when a man is supposed to be happy, he imagines that he is happy (whereas viewed in the light of the truth he is unhappy), and in this case he is generally very far from wishing to be torn away from that delusion. On the contrary, he becomes furious, he regards the man who does this as his most spiteful enemy, he considers it an insult, something near to murder, in the sense that one speaks of killing joy. What is the reason of this? The reason is that the sensuous nature and the psycho-sensuous completely dominate him; the reason is that he lives in the sensuous categories agreeable/disagreeable, and says goodbye to truth etc.; the reason is that he is too sensuous to have the courage to venture to be spirit or to endure it. However vain and conceited men may be, they have nevertheless for the most part a very lowly conception of themselves, that is to say, they have no conception of being spirit, the absolute of all that a man can be—but vain and conceited they are . . . by way of comparison. In case one were to think of a house, consisting of cellar, ground-floor and premier étage, so tenanted, or rather so arranged, that it was planned for a distinction of rank between the dwellers on the several floors; and in case one were to make a comparison between such a house and what it is to be a man—then unfortunately this is the sorry and ludicrous condition of the majority of men, that in their own house they prefer to live in the cellar. The soulish-bodily synthesis in every man is planned with a view to being spirit, such is the building; but the man prefers to dwell in the cellar, that is, in the determinants of sensuousness. And not only does he prefer to dwell in the cellar; no, he loves that to such a degree that he becomes furious if anyone would propose to him to occupy the bel étage which stands empty at his disposition—for in fact he is dwelling in his own house.

No, to be in error or delusion is (quite un-Socratically) the thing they fear the least. One may behold amazing examples which illustrate this fact on a prodigious scale. A thinker erects an immense building, a system, a system which embraces the whole of existence and world-history etc.—and if we contemplate his personal life, we discover to our astonishment this terrible and ludicrous fact, that he himself personally does not live in this immense high-vaulted palace, but in a barn alongside of it, or in a dog kennel, or at the most in the porter's lodge. If one were to take the liberty of calling his attention to this by a single word, he would be offended. For he has no fear of being under a delusion, if only he can get the system completed . . . by means of the delusion.

So then, the fact that the man in despair is unaware that his condition is despair, has nothing to do with the case, he is in despair all the same. If despair is bewilderment (*Forvildelse*), then the fact that one is unconscious of it is the additional aggravation of being at the same time under a delusion (*Vildfarelse*). Unconsciousness of despair is like unconsciousness of dread (cf. *The Concept of Dread* by Vigilius Haufniensis): the dread characteristic of spiritlessness is recognizable precisely by the spiritless sense of security; but nevertheless dread is at the bottom of it, and when the enchantment of illusion is broken, when existence begins to totter, then too does despair manifest itself as that which was at the bottom.

The despairing man who is unconscious of being in despair is, in comparison with him who is conscious of it, merely a negative step further from the truth and from salvation. Despair itself is a negativity, unconsciousness of it is a new negativity. But to reach truth one must pierce through every negativity. For here applies what the fairy-tale recounts about a certain enchantment: the piece of music must be played through backwards; otherwise the enchantment is not broken.[10] However, it is only in one sense, in a purely dialectical sense, that he who is unconscious of despair is further away from truth and salvation than the man who is conscious of his despair and yet remains in it. For in another sense, an ethical-dialectic sense, the despairing man who consciously remains in despair is further from salvation, since his despair is more intense. But unawareness is so far from removing despair, or of transforming despair into non-despair, that, on the contrary, it may be the most dangerous form of despair. By unconsciousness the despairing man is in a way secured (but to his own destruction) against becoming aware—that is, he is securely in the power of despair.

In unconsciousness of being in despair a man is furthest from being conscious of himself as spirit. But precisely the thing of not being conscious of oneself as spirit is despair, which is spiritlessness—whether the condition be that of complete deadness, a merely vegetative life, or a life of higher potency the secret of which is nevertheless despair. In the latter instance the man is like the sufferer from consumption: he feels well, considers himself in the best of health, seems perhaps to others to be in florid health, precisely when the sickness is most dangerous.

This form of despair (i.e. unconsciousness of it) is the commonest in the world—yes, in what people call the world, or, to define it more exactly, what Christianity calls "the world," i.e. paganism, and the natural man in Christendom. Paganism as it historically was and is, and paganism within Christendom, is precisely this sort of despair, it is despair but does not know it. It is true that a distinction is made also in paganism, as well as by the natural man, between being in despair and not being in despair; that is to say, people talk of despair as if only certain particular individuals were in despair. But this distinction is just as deceitful as that which paganism and the natural man make between love and self-love, as though all this love were not essentially self-love. Further, however, than this deceitful distinction it was impossible for paganism, including the natural man, to go; for the specific character of despair is precisely this: it is unconscious of being despair.

From this we can easily perceive that the aesthetic concept of spiritlessness by no means furnishes the scale for judging what is despair and what is not—which moreover is a matter of course; for since it is unable to define what spirit truly is, how could the aesthetical make answer to a question which does not exist for it at all? It would also be a prodigious stupidity to deny that pagan nations *en masse*, as well as individual pagans, have performed amazing exploits which have prompted and will prompt the enthusiasm of poets; to deny that paganism exhibits examples of achievement which aesthetically cannot be sufficiently admired. It would also be foolish to deny that in paganism lives have been led which were rich in aesthetic enjoyment, and that the natural man can lead such a life, utilizing every advantage offered with the most perfect good taste, even letting art and learning enhance, embellish, ennoble the enjoyment. No, it is not the aesthetic definition of spiritlessness which furnishes the scale for judging what is despair and what is not; the definition which must be used is the ethico-religious: either spirit/or the negative lack of spirit, spiritlessness. Every human existence which is not conscious of itself as spirit, or conscious of itself before God as spirit, every human existence which is not thus grounded transparently in God but obscurely reposes or terminates in some abstract universality (state, nation, etc.), or in obscurity about itself takes its faculties merely as active powers, without in a deeper sense being conscious whence it has them, which regards itself as an inexplicable something which is to be understood from without—every such existence, whatever it accomplishes, though it be the most amazing exploit, whatever it explains, though it were the whole of existence, however intensely it enjoys life aesthetically—every such existence is after all despair. It was this the old theologians meant when they talked about the virtues of the pagans being splendid vices.[11] They meant that the most inward experience of the pagan was despair, that the pagan was not conscious of himself before God as spirit. Hence it came about (to cite here an example which has at the same time a deeper relation to the whole study) that the pagans judged self-slaughter so lightly, yea, even praised it,[12] notwithstanding that for the spirit it is the most decisive sin, that to break out of existence in this way is rebellion against God. The pagan lacked the spirit's definition of the self, therefore he expressed such a judgment of *self*-slaughter—and this the same pagan did who condemned with moral severity theft, unchastity, etc. He lacked the point of view for regarding self-slaughter, he lacked the God-relationship and the self. From a purely pagan point of view self-slaughter is a thing indifferent, a thing every man may do if he likes, because it concerns nobody else. If from a pagan point of view one were to warn against self-slaughter, it must be by a long detour, by showing that it was breach of duty toward one's fellow-men. The point in self-slaughter, that it is a crime against God, entirely escapes the pagan. One cannot say, therefore, that the self-slaughter was despair, which would be a thoughtless hysteron proteron; one must say that the fact that the pagan judged self-slaughter as he did was despair.

Nevertheless there is and remains a distinction, and a qualitative one, between paganism in the narrowest sense, and paganism within Christendom. The distinction (as Vigilius Haufniensis has pointed out in relation to dread) is this, that paganism, though to be sure it lacks spirit, is definitely oriented in the direction of spirit, whereas paganism within Christendom lacks spirit with a direction away from it, or by apostasy, and hence in the strictest sense is spiritlessness.

(b). *The Despair which is Conscious of being Despair, as also it is Conscious of being a Self wherein there is after all something Eternal, and then is either in despair at not willing to be itself, or in despair at willing to be itself.*

A distinction of course must be made as to whether he who is conscious of his despair has the true conception of what despair is. Thus a man may be right, according to the conception he has, in asserting that he is in despair, it may be true that he is in despair, and yet this is not to say that he has the true conception of despair, it may be that one who contemplated this man's life in the light of the true conception would say, "You are far more in despair than you are aware, the despair lies far deeper." So with the pagan (to recall the foregoing instance), when in comparison with others he considered himself in despair, he doubtless was right in thinking that he was in despair, but he was wrong in thinking that the others were not; that is to say, he had not the true conception of despair.

So then, for conscious despair there is requisite on the one hand the true conception of what despair is. On the other hand, clearness is requisite about oneself—in so far, that is to say, as clearness and despair are compatible. How far complete clarity about oneself, as to whether one is in despair, may be united with being in despair, where this knowledge and self-knowledge might not avail precisely to tear a man out of his despair, to make him so terrified about himself that he would cease to be in despair—these questions we shall not decide here, we shall not even attempt to do so, since in the sequel we shall find a place for this whole investigation. But without pursuing the thought to this extremest point, we here merely call attention to the fact that, although the degree of consciousness as to what despair is may be very various, so also may be the degree of consciousness touching one's own condition, the consciousness that it is despair. Real life is far too multifarious to be portrayed by merely exhibiting such abstract contrasts as that between a despair which is completely unconscious, and one which is completely conscious of being such. Most frequently, no doubt, the condition of the despairing man, though characterized by multiform nuances, is that of a half obscurity about his own condition. He himself knows well enough in a way up to a certain point that he is in despair, he notices it in himself, as one notices in oneself that one is going about with an illness as yet unpronounced, but he will not quite admit what illness it is. At one moment it has almost become clear to him that he is in despair; but then at another moment it appears to him after all as though his indisposition might have another ground, as though it were the consequence of something external, something outside himself, and that if this were to be changed, he would not be in despair. Or perhaps by diversions, or in other ways, e.g., by work and busy occupations as means of distraction, he seeks by his own effort to preserve an obscurity about his condition, yet again in such a way that it does not become quite clear to him that he does it for this reason, that he does what he does in order to bring about obscurity. Or perhaps he even is conscious that he labors thus in order to sink the soul into obscurity, does this with a certain acuteness and shrew calculation, with psychological insight, but is not in a deeper sense clearly conscious of what he does, of how despairingly he labors etc. For in fact there is in all obscurity a dialectical interplay of knowledge and will, and in interpreting a man one may err, either by emphasizing knowledge merely, or merely the will.

But, as was pointed out above, the degree of consciousness potentiates despair. In the same degree that a man has a truer conception of despair while still remaining in it, and in the same degree that he is more conscious of being in despair, in that same degree is his despair more intense. He who with the consciousness that suicide is despair, and to that extent with the true conception of what despair is, then commits suicide—that man has a more intense despair than the man who commits suicide without having the true conception that suicide is despair; but, conversely, the less true his conception of suicide is, the less intense his despair. On the other hand, the clearer consciousness of himself (self-consciousness) a man has in committing suicide, the more intense is his despair, in comparison with that of the man whose soul, compared with his, is in a confused and obscure condition.

In what follows I shall go on to examine the two forms of conscious despair, in such a way as to display at the same time a heightening of the consciousness of what despair is, and of the consciousness of the fact that one's own condition is despair—or, what is the same thing and the decisive thing, a heightening of the consciousness of the self. But the opposite of being in despair is believing; hence we may perceive the justification for what was stated above (I.A) as the formula which describes a condition in which no despair at all exists, for this same formula is also the formula for believing: by relating itself to its own self, and by willing to be itself, the self is grounded transparently in the Power which constituted it.

(1). IN DESPAIR AT NOT WILLING TO BE ONESELF, THE DESPAIR OF WEAKNESS.

When this form of despair is called the despair of weakness, there is already contained in this a reflection upon the second form (2), the despair of willing despairingly to be oneself—defiance. So the contrast here is only relative. No despair is entirely without defiance: in fact defiance is implied in the very expression, "Not to will to be." On the other hand, even the extremest defiance of despair is after all never without some weakness. The difference is therefore only relative. The one form is, so to speak, the despair of womanliness, the other of manliness.*

*If psychologically one will take a look around in real life, one will from time to time have opportunity to convince oneself that this distinction, which is logically correct and so shall and must be pertinent, is in fact pertinent, and that this classification embraces the whole reality of despair. For so far as the child is concerned, one does not talk about despair but only about ill-temper, because one has only a right to assume that the eternal is present in the child κατά δύναμιν, and has never a right to demand it of the child, as one has a right to demand it of the grown man, to whom it applies that he *shall* have it. However, I do not by any means wish to deny that on the part of women there may occur forms of manly despair, and conversely forms of womanly despair on the part of men. But these are exceptions. And this is a matter of course, the ideal also is rare; and only in a purely ideal sense is this distinction between manly and womanly despair entirely true. Woman has neither the selfishly developed conception of the self nor the intellectuality of man, for all that she is his superior in tenderness and fineness of feeling. On the other hand, woman's nature is devotion (*Hengivenhed*), submission (*Hengivelse*), and it is unwomanly if it is not so. Strangely enough, no one can be so pert (a word which language has expressly coined for woman), so almost cruelly particular as a woman—and yet her nature is devotion, and yet (here is the marvel) all this is really the expression for the fact that her nature is devotion. For just because in her nature she carries the whole womanly devotion, nature has lovingly equipped her with an instinct, in comparison with which in point of delicacy the most eminently developed male reflection is as nothing. This devotion of woman, this (to speak as a Greek) divine dowry and riches, is too great a good to be thrown away blindly; and yet no clear-sighted manly reflection is capable of seeing sharply enough to be able to dispose of it rightly. Hence nature has taken care of her: instinctively she sees blindly with greater clarity than the most sharp-sighted reflection, instinctively she sees where it is she is to admire, what it is she ought to devote herself to. Devotion is the only thing woman has, therefore nature undertook to be her guardian. Hence it is too that womanliness first comes into existence through a metamorphosis; it comes into existence when the infinite pertness is transfigured in womanly devotion. But the fact that devotion is woman's nature comes again to evidence in despair. By devotion [the word literally means giving away] she has lost herself, and only thus is she happy, only thus is she herself; a woman who is happy without devotion, that is, without giving herself away (to whatever it may be she gives herself) is unwomanly. A man also devotes himself (gives himself away), and it is a poor sort of a man who does not do it; but his self

(i). *Despair over the earthly or over something earthly.*

This is pure immediacy, or else an immediacy which contains a quantitative reflection.—Here there is no infinite consciousness of the self, of what despair is, or of the fact that the condition is one of despair; the despair is passive, succumbing to the pressure of the outward circumstance, it by no means comes from within as action. It is, if I may say so, by an innocent misuse of language, a play upon words, as when children play at being soldiers, that in the language of immediacy such words as the self and despair occur.

The *immediate* man (in so far as immediacy is to be found without any reflection) is merely soulishly determined, his self or he himself is a something included along with "the other" in the compass of the temporal and the worldly, and it has only an illusory appearance of possessing in it something eternal. Thus the self coheres immediately with "the other," wishing, desiring, enjoying, etc., but passively; even in desiring, the self is in the dative case, like the child when it says "me" for I. Its dialectic is: the agreeable and the disagreeable; its concepts are: good fortune, misfortune, fate.

Now then there *happens*, befalls (falls upon) this immediate self something which brings it to despair; in no other way can this come about, since the self has no reflection in

---

is not devotion (this is the expression for womanly substantial devotion), nor does he acquire himself by devotion, as in another sense a woman does, he has himself; he gives himself away, but his self still remains behind as a sober consciousness of devotion, whereas woman, with genuine womanliness, plunges her self into that to which she devotes herself.—In such a way man does not devote himself; but the second form of despair expressed also the manly nature: in despair at willing to be oneself.

So far with respect to the relation between the manly and the womanly despair. It must be remembered, however, that we are not speaking here of devotion to God or of the God-relationship, which is not to be dealt with till we come to Part Second. In the relationship to God, where such a distinction as man/woman vanishes, it is true of man as of woman that devotion is the self, and that by devotion the self is acquired. This is true equally for man and woman, although most frequently in real life woman is related to God only through man.

itself, that which brings it to despair must come from without, and the despair is merely passive. That wherein immediacy has its being, or (supposing that after all it has a little bit of reflection in itself) that part thereof to which it especially clings, a man is deprived of by "a stroke of fate," in short, he becomes, as he calls it, unfortunate, that is, the immediacy in him receives such a shock that it cannot recover itself— he despairs. Or (to mention a case which is more rarely to be seen in real life, but which dialectically is entirely correct) this despair of immediacy occurs through what the immediate man calls an all-too-great good fortune; for it is a fact that immediacy as such is prodigiously fragile, and every *quid nimis* [excess] which demands of it reflection brings it to despair.

So then he despairs, that is to say, by a strangely preposterous attitude and a complete mystification with regard to himself, he calls this despair. But to despair is to lose the eternal —and of this he does not speak, does not dream. The loss of the earthly as such is not the cause of despair, and yet it is of this he speaks, and he calls it despairing. What he says is in a certain sense true, only it is not true in the sense in which he understands it; he stands with his face inverted, and what he says must be understood inversely; he stands and points at that which is not a cause of despair, and he declares that he is in despair, and nevertheless it is quite true that despair is going on behind him without his knowing it. It is as if one were to stand with one's back toward the City Hall and the Court House, and pointing straight before him were to say, "There is the City Hall and the Court House." The man is right, there it is . . . if he turns around. It is not true, he is not in despair, and yet he is right when he says it. But he calls himself "in despair," he regards himself as dead, as a shadow of himself. But dead he is not; there is, if you will, *life* in the characterization. In case everything suddenly changes, everything in the outward circumstances, and the wish is fulfilled, then life enters into him again, immediacy rises again, and he begins to live as fit as a fiddle. But this is the only way immediacy knows how to fight, the one thing it knows how to do: to despair and swoon—and yet it knows what despair is less than anything else. It despairs and swoons, and thereupon it lies quite still as if it were dead, like the childish play of "lying dead"; immediacy is like certain lower animals which have no other weapon or means of defense but to lie quite still and pretend they are dead.

Meanwhile time passes. If outward help comes, then life returns to the despairer, he begins where he left off; he had no self, and a self he did not become, but he continues to live on with only the quality of immediacy. If outward help does not come, then in real life something else commonly occurs. Life comes back into him after all, but "he never will be himself again," so he says. He now acquires some little understanding of life, he learns to imitate the other men, noting how they manage to live, and so he too lives after a sort. In Christendom he too is a Christian, goes to church every Sunday, hears and understands the parson, yea, they understand one another; he dies; the parson introduces him into eternity for the price of $10—but a self he was not, and a self he did not become.

This form of despair is: despair at not willing to be oneself; or still lower, despair at not willing to be a self; or lowest of all, despair at willing to be another than himself, wishing for a new self. Properly speaking, immediacy has no self, it does not recognize itself, so neither can it recognize itself again, it terminates therefore preferably in the romantic. When immediacy despairs it possesses not even enough self to wish or to dream that it had become what it did not become. The immediate man helps himself in a different way: he wishes to be another. Of this one may easily convince oneself by observing immediate men. At the moment of despair no wish is so natural to them as the wish that they had become or might become another. In any case one can never forbear to smile at such a despairer, who, humanly speaking, although he is in despair, is so very innocent. Commonly such a despairer is infinitely comic. Think of a self (and next to God there is nothing so eternal as a self), and then that this self gets the notion of asking whether it might not let itself become or be made into another . . . than itself. And yet such a despairer, whose only wish is this most crazy of all transformations, loves to think that this change might be accomplished as easily as changing a coat. For the immediate man does not recognize his self, he recognizes himself only by his dress, he recognizes (and here again appears the infinitely comic trait) he recognizes that he has a self only by externals. There is no more ludicrous confusion, for a self is just infinitely different from externals. When then the whole of existence has been altered for the immediate man and he has fallen into despair, he goes a step further, he thinks thus, this has become his wish: "What if I were to become another, were to get myself a new self?" Yes, but if he did become another, I wonder if he would recognize himself again! It is related of a peasant who came cleanly shaven to the Capital, and had made so much money that he could buy himself a pair of shoes and stockings and still had enough left over to get drunk on—it is related that as he was trying in his drunken state to find his way home he lay down in the middle of the highway and fell asleep. Then along came a wagon, and the driver shouted to him to move or he would run over his legs. Then the drunken peasant awoke, looked at his legs, and since by reason of the shoes and stockings he didn't recognize them, he said to the driver, "Drive on, they are not my legs." So in the case of the immediate man when he is in despair it is impossible to represent him truly without a touch of the comic; it is, if I may say so, a clever trick to talk in this jargon about a self and about despair.

When *immediacy is assumed to have self-reflection*, despair is somewhat modified; there is somewhat more consciousness of the self, and therewith in turn of what despair is, and of the fact that one's condition is despair; there is some sense in it when such a man talks of being in despair: but the despair is essentially that of weakness, a passive experience; its form is, in despair at not wanting to be oneself.

The progress in this case, compared with pure immediacy, is at once evident in the fact that the despair does not always come about by reason of a blow, by something that happens, but may be occasioned by the mere reflection within oneself, so that in this case despair is not a purely passive defeat by outward circumstances, but to a certain degree is self-activity, action. Here there is in fact a certain degree of self-reflection, and so a certain degree of observation of oneself. With this certain degree of self-reflection begins the act of discrimination whereby the self becomes aware of itself as something essentially different from the environment, from externalities and their effect upon it. But this is only to a certain degree. Now when the self with a certain degree of self-reflection wills to accept itself, it stumbles perhaps upon one difficulty or another in the composition of the self. For as no human body is perfection, so neither is any self. This difficulty, be it what it may, frightens the man away shudderingly. Or something happens to him which causes within him a breach with immediacy deeper than he has made by reflection. Or his imagination discovers a possibility which, if it were to come to pass, would likewise become a breach with immediacy.

So he despairs. His despair is that of weakness, a passive suffering of the self, in contrast to the despair of self-assertion; but, by the aid of relative self-reflection which he has, he makes an effort (which again distinguishes him from the purely immediate man) to defend his self. He understands that the thing of letting the self go is a pretty serious business after all, he is not so apoplectically muddled by the blow as the immediate man is, he understands by the aid of reflection that there is much he may lose without losing the self; he makes admissions, is capable of doing so—and why? Because to a certain degree he has dissociated his self from external circumstances, because he has an obscure conception that there may even be something eternal in the self. But in vain he struggles thus; the difficulty he stumbled against demands a breach with immediacy as a whole, and for that he has not sufficient self-reflection or ethical reflection; he has no consciousness of a self which is gained by the infinite abstraction from everything outward, this naked, abstract self (in contrast to the clothed self of immediacy) which is the first form of the infinite self and the forward impulse in the whole process whereby a self infinitely accepts its actual self with all its difficulties and advantages.

So then he despairs, and his despair is: not willing to be

himself. On the other hand, the ludicrous notion of wanting to be another never occurs to him; he maintains the relationship to his self—to that extent reflection has identified him with the self. He then is in just such a situation with regard to the self as a man may be with regard to his dwelling-place. The comic feature is that a self certainly does not stand in such a casual relation to itself as does a man to his dwelling-place. A man finds his dwelling-place distasteful, either because the chimney smokes, or for any other reason whatsoever; so he leaves it, but he does not move out, he does not engage a new dwelling, he continues to regard the old one as his habitation; he reckons that the offense will pass away. So it is with the despairer. As long as the difficulty lasts he does not dare to come to himself (as the common phrase expresses it with singular pregnancy), he does not want to be himself—but that surely will pass by, perhaps things will change, the dark possibility will surely be forgotten. So meanwhile he comes to himself only once in a while, as it were on a visit, to see whether the change has not occurred, and so soon as it has occurred he moves home again, "is again himself," so he says. However, this only means that he begins again where he left off; he was to a certain degree a self of a sort, and he became nothing more.

But if no change occurs, he helps himself in another way. He swings away entirely from the inward direction which is the path he ought to have followed in order to become truly a self. The whole problem of the self in a deeper sense becomes a sort of blind door in the background of his soul behind which there is nothing. He accepts what in his language he calls his self, that is to say, whatever abilities, talents, etc. may have been given him; all this he accepts, yet with the outward direction toward what is called life, the real, the active life; he treats with great precaution the bit of self-reflection which he has in himself, he is afraid that this thing in the background might again emerge. So little by little he succeeds in forgetting it; in the course of years he finds it almost ludicrous, especially when he is in good company with other capable and active men who have a sense and capacity for real life. *Charmant!* He has now, as they say in romances, been happily married for a number of years, is an active and enterprising man, a father and a citizen, perhaps even a great man; at home in his own house the servants speak of him as "himself"; in the city he is among the *honoratiores*; his bearing suggests "respect of persons," or that he is to be respected as a person, to all appearance he is to be regarded as a person. In Christendom he is a Christian (quite in the same sense in which in paganism he would have been a pagan, and in England an Englishman), one of the cultured Christians. The question of immortality has often been in his mind, more than once he has asked the parson whether there really was such an immortality, whether one would really recognize oneself again—which indeed must have for him a very singular interest, since he has no self.

It is impossible to represent truly this sort of despair without a certain admixture of satire. The comical thing is that he will talk about having been in despair; the dreadful thing is that after having, as he thinks, overcome despair, he is then precisely in despair. It is infinitely comic that at the bottom of the practical wisdom which is so much extolled in the world, at the bottom of all the devilish lot of good counsel and wise saws and "wait and see" and "put up with one's fate" and "write in the book of forgetfulness"—that at the bottom of all this, ideally understood, lies complete stupidity as to where the danger really is and what the danger really is. But again this ethical stupidity is the dreadful thing.

Despair over the earthly or over something earthly is the commonest sort of despair, especially in the second form of immediacy with a quantitative reflection. The more thoroughly reflected the despair is, the more rarely it occurs in the world. But this proves that most men have not become very deep even in despair; it by no means proves, however, that they are not in despair. There are very few men who live even only passably in the category of spirit; yea, there are not many even who merely make an attempt at this life, and most of those who do so, shy away. They have not learned to fear, they have not learned what "must" means, regardless, infinitely regardless of what it may be that comes to pass. Therefore they cannot endure what even to them

seems a contradiction, and which as reflected from the world
around them appears much more glaring, that to be concerned for one's own soul and to want to be spirit is a waste
of time, yes, an inexcusable waste of time, which ought if
possible to be punishable by law, at all events is punished
by contempt and ridicule as a sort of treason against men,
as a froward madness which crazily fills up time with nothing. Then there is a period in their lives (alas, their best
period) when they begin after all to take the inward direction.
They get about as far as the first difficulties, there they veer
away; it seems to them as though this road were leading to
a disconsolate desert—*und rings umher liegt schöne grüne
Weide*[13] [and all about lie beautiful green pastures]. So they
are off, and soon they forget that best period of theirs; and,
alas, they forget it as though it were a bit of childishness. At
the same time they are Christians, tranquilized by the parson
with regard to their salvation. This despair, as I have said, is
the commonest, it is so common that only thereby can one
explain the rather common opinion in common intercourse
that despair is something belonging to youth, which appears
only in youthful years, but is not to be found in the settled
man who has come to the age of maturity and the years of
wisdom. This is a desperate error, or rather a desperate mistake, which overlooks (yes, and what is worse, it overlooks
the fact that what it overlooks is pretty nearly the best
thing that can be said of a man, since far worse often occurs)
—it overlooks the fact that the majority of men do never
really manage in their whole life to be more than they were
in childhood and youth, namely, immediacy with the addition of a little dose of self-reflection. No, despair verily is
not something which appears only in the young, something
out of which one grows as a matter of course—"as one grows
out of illusion." But neither is illusion something one grows
out of, though people are foolish enough to think so. On
the contrary, one encounters grown men and women and
aged persons who have as much childish illusion as any youth.
People overlook the fact that illusion has essentially two
forms: that of hope, and that of recollection. But just because the older person is under illusion, he has also an en-

tirely onesided conception of what illusion is, thinking that
it is only the illusion of hope. And this is natural. The older
man is not plagued by the illusion of hope, but he is on the
other hand by the whimsical idea of looking down at the
illusion of youth from a supposedly superior standpoint which
is free from illusion. The youth is under illusion, he hopes
for the extraordinary from life and from himself. By way of
compensation one often finds in an older man illusion with
respect to the recollections of his youth. An elderly woman
who has now supposedly given up all illusions is often found
to be as fantastic in her illusion as any young girl, with
respect to how she remembers herself as a girl, how happy
she once was, how beautiful, etc. This *fuimus*[14] [we have
been] which is so often heard from old people is fully as
great an illusion as the futuristic illusion of the youth. They
both of them are lying or poetizing.

But far more desperate than this is the mistake that despair belongs only to youth. In the main it is a great folly,
and precisely it is a lack of sense as to what spirit is, and
moreover it is failure to appreciate that man is spirit, not
merely an animal, when one supposes that it might be such
an easy matter to acquire faith and wisdom which come with
the years as a matter of course, like teeth and a beard and
such like. No, whatever it may be that a man as a matter of
course comes to, and whatever it may be that comes to a
man as a matter of course—one thing it is not, namely,
faith and wisdom. But the thing is this: with the years man
does not, spiritually understood, come to anything; on the
other hand, it is very easy with the years to go from something. And with the years one perhaps goes from the bit of
passion, feeling, imagination, the bit of inwardness, which
one had, and goes as a matter of course (for such things go
as a matter of course) under triviality's definition of understanding of life. This . . . improved condition, which true
enough has come about with the years, he now in despair
regards as a good, he readily assures himself (and in a certain
satirical sense there is nothing more sure) that it now never
could occur to him to despair—no, he has assured himself
against this, yet he *is* in despair, spiritually in despair. Why

I wonder did Socrates love youths—unless it was because he knew men!

And if it does not so happen that a man with the years sinks into the most trivial kind of despair, from this it does not by any means follow that despair might belong only to youth. If a man really develops with the years, if he ripens into essential consciousness of the self, he may perhaps despair in a higher form. And if he does not essentially develop with the years, nor yet sink into sheer triviality, that is to say, if he remains pretty much a young man, a youth, although he is mature, a father and gray-haired, retaining therefore something of the good traits of youth, then indeed he will be exposed also to the possibility of despairing as a youth over the earthly or over something earthly.

So a difference there may well be between the despair of an older man and a youth, but no essential difference, only a fortuitous one. The youth despairs over the future, as a present tense *in futuro;* there is something in the future he is not willing to accept, with this he will not be himself. The older man despairs over the past, as a present *in praeterito,*[15] which refuses to become more and more past—for so desperate he is not that he entirely succeeds in forgetting it. This past is perhaps something even which repentance should have taken in hand. But if repentance were to emerge, one would first have to despair completely, to despair out and out, and then the spirit-life might break through from the very bottom. But desperate as he is, he dare not let the thing come to such a pass. So there he remains standing, time goes on— unless he succeeds, still more desperately, by the help of forgetfulness, in healing it, so that instead of becoming a repenter, he becomes his own healer [or accomplice, as the word would be more commonly understood]. But such despair, whether it be of the youth or of the man, is essentially the same, it does not reach any metamorphosis in which the consciousness of the eternal in the self breaks through, so that the battle might begin which either potentiates despair to a higher power or leads to faith.

But is there no essential difference between the two expressions hitherto used as identical: to despair over the earthly (the determinant of totality), and to despair over something earthly (the particular)? Indeed there is. When with infinite passion the self by means of imagination despairs over something earthly, this infinite passion transforms this particular, this something, into the earthly *in toto*, that is to say, the determinant of totality inheres in and belongs to the despairer. The earthly and temporal as such are precisely what falls apart into the particular. It is impossible actually to lose or be deprived of all that is earthly, for the determinant of totality is a thought-determinant. So the self first increases infinitely the actual loss, and then it despairs over the earthly *in toto*. But so soon as this distinction (between despairing over the earthly and over something earthly) is essentially affirmed there is also an essential advance made in the consciousness of the self. This formula, "to be in despair over the earthly" is a dialectic first expression for the next form of despair.

(ii). *Despair about the eternal or over oneself.*

Despair over the earthly or over something earthly is really despair also about the eternal and over oneself, in so far as it is despair, for this is the formula for all despair.* But the despairer, as he was depicted in the foregoing, did not observe

*Therefore it is linguistically correct to say, "in despair over the earthly" (the occasion), and "about the eternal," but "over oneself," because this is again another expression for the occasion of despair, which in its concept is always about the eternal, whereas that over which one despairs may be of the most various sorts. One despairs over that which fixes one in despair, over one's misfortune, for example, over the earthly, over the loss of one's fortune, but about that which, rightly understood, releases one from despair, therefore about the eternal, about one's salvation, about one's own power, etc. In relation to the self one employs both words: to despair over and about oneself, because the self is doubly dialectic. And herein consists the obscurity, especially in all lower forms of despair, and in almost all despairers, that with such passionate clearness a man sees and knows over what he is in despair, but about what it is escapes his notice. The condition requisite for healing it always this about-face, and from a purely philosophical point of view it might be a subtle question whether it is possible for one to be in despair with full consciousness of what it is about which one despairs.

what was happening behind him, so to speak; he thinks he is in despair over something earthly and constantly talks about what he is in despair over, and yet he is in despair about the eternal; for the fact that he ascribes such great value to the earthly, or, to carry the thought further, that he ascribes to something earthly such great value, or that he first transforms something earthly into everything earthly, and then ascribes to the earthly such great value, is precisely to despair about the eternal.

This despair is now well in advance. If the former was the despair of *weakness*, this is *despair over his weakness*, although it still remains as to its nature under the category "despair of weakness," as distinguished from defiance in the next section. So there is only a relative difference. This difference consists in the fact that the foregoing form has the consciousness of weakness as its final consciousness, whereas in this case consciousness does not come to a stop here but potentiates itself to a new consciousness, a consciousness of its weakness. The despairer understands that it is weakness to take the earthly so much to heart, that it is weakness to despair. But then, instead of veering sharply away from despair to faith, humbling himself before God for his weakness, he is more deeply absorbed in despair and despairs over his weakness. Therewith the whole point of view is inverted, he becomes now more clearly conscious of his despair, recognizing that he is in despair about the eternal, he despairs over himself that he could be weak enough to ascribe to the earthly such great importance, which now becomes his despairing expression for the fact that he has lost the eternal and himself.

Here is the scale of ascent. First, in consciousness of himself: for to despair about the eternal is impossible without having a conception about the self, that there is something eternal in it, or that it has had something eternal in it. And if a man is to despair over himself, he must indeed be conscious also of having a self; that, however, is the thing over which he despairs—not over the earthly or over something earthly, but over himself. Moreover there is in this case a greater consciousness of what despair is; for despair is precisely to have lost the eternal and oneself. As a matter of course there is greater consciousness of the fact that one's condition is that of despair. Furthermore, despair in this case is not merely passive suffering but action. For when the earthly is taken away from the self and a man despairs, it is as if despair came from without, though it comes nevertheless always from the self, indirect-directly from the self, as counter-pressure (reaction), differing in this respect from defiance, which comes directly from the self. Finally, there is here again, though in another sense, a further advance. For just because this despair is more intense, salvation is in a certain sense nearer. Such a despair will hardly forget, it is too deep; but despair is held open every instant, and there is thus possibility of salvation.

For all that, this despair is to be referred to the formula: in despair at not willing to be oneself. Just as a father disinherits a son, so the self is not willing to recognize itself after it has been so weak. In its despair it cannot forget this weakness, it hates itself in a way, it will not humble itself in faith under its weakness in order to gain itself again; no, in its despair it will not hear of itself, so to speak, will not know anything about itself. But there can be no question of being helped by forgetfulness, no question of slipping by the aid of forgetfulness under the determinant of selflessness, and so being a man and a Christian like other men and Christians; no, for this the self is too much a self. As it often was the case with the father who disinherited his son that the outward fact was of little avail to him, he did not by this get free of his son, at least his thought did not; as is often the case with the lover's curse upon the hated one (i.e. the loved one) that it does not help much, it almost imprisons him the more—so it is in the case of the despairing self with relation to itself.

This despair is one quality deeper than the foregoing and is a sort which rarely is met with in the world. That blind door behind which there was nothing is in this case a real door, a door carefully locked to be sure, and behind it sits as it were the self and watches itself, employed in filling up time with not willing to be itself, and yet is self enough to love itself. This is what is called *introversion*.[16] And from now on we shall be dealing with introversion, which is the direct opposite to immediacy and has a great contempt for it, in the sphere of thought more especially.

But does there then in the realm of reality exist no such self? Has he fled outside of reality to the desert, to the cloister, to the mad-house? Is he not a real man, clothed like others, or like others clad in the customary outer-garments? Yes, certainly there is! Why not? But with respect to this thing of the self he initiates no one, not a soul, he feels no urge to do this, or he has learnt to suppress it. Hear how he talks about it.[17] "After all it's only the purely immediate men—who so far as spirit is concerned are about at the same point as the child in the first period of earliest infancy when with a thoroughly endearing nonchalance it lets everything pass out— it's the purely immediate men who can't retain anything. It is this sort of immediacy which often with great pretentiousness proclaims itself 'truth,' that one is 'a true man and just like people generally are'—which is just as true as it is untrue that a grown man as soon as he feels a corporal need at once yields to it. Every self which is even a little bit reflective has surely a notion of what it is to repress the self." And our despairer is introverted enough to be able to keep every intruder (that is, every man) at a distance from the topic of the self, whereas outwardly he is completely "a real man." He is a university man, husband and father, an uncommonly competent civil functionary even, a respectable father, very gentle to his wife and carefulness itself with respect to his children. And a Christian? Well, yes, he is that too after a sort; however, he preferably avoids talking on the subject, although he willingly observes and with a melancholy joy that his wife for her edification engages in devotions. He very seldom goes to church, because it seems to him that most parsons really don't know what they are talking about. He makes an exception in the case of one particular priest of whom he concedes that he knows what he is talking about, but he doesn't want to hear him for another reason, because he has a fear that this might lead him too far. On the other hand, he often feels a need of solitude, which for him is a vital necessity—sometimes like breathing, at other times like sleeping. The fact that he feels this vital necessity more than other men is also a sign that he has a deeper nature. Generally the need of solitude is a sign that there is spirit in a man after all, and it is a measure for what spirit there is. The purely twaddling inhuman and too-human men are to such a degree without feeling for the need of solitude that like a certain species of social birds (the so-called love birds) they promptly die if for an instant they have to be alone. As the little child must be put to sleep by a lullaby, so these men need the tranquilizing hum of society before they are able to eat, drink, sleep, pray, fall in love, etc. But in ancient times as well as in the Middle Ages people were aware of the need of solitude and had respect for what it signifies. In the constant sociability of our age people shudder at solitude to such a degree that they know no other use to put it to but (oh, admirable epigram!) as a punishment for criminals. But after all it is a fact that in our age it is a crime to have spirit, so it is natural that such people, the lovers of solitude, are included in the same class with criminals.

The introverted despairer thus lives on *horis succesivis* [successive hours], through hours which, though they are not lived for eternity, have nevertheless something to do with the eternal, being employed about the relationship of one's self to itself—but he really gets no further than this. So when this is done, when the need for solitude is satisfied, he goes outside as it were—even when he goes in to converse with wife and children. That which as a husband makes him so gentle and as a father so careful is, apart from his good-nature and his sense of duty, the admission he has made to himself in his most inward reserve concerning his weakness.

If it were possible for anyone to be privy to his introversion and were to say to him, "This is in fact pride, thou art proud of thyself," he would hardly be likely to admit it to another. When he was alone with himself he would likely admit that there was something in it; but the passionateness with which his self had pictured his weakness would quickly make him believe again that it could not possibly be pride, for it was in fact precisely over his weakness he was in despair—just as if it were not pride which attached such prodigious weight to weakness, just as if it were not because he wanted to be proud of himself that he could not endure this consciousness of weakness.—If one were to say to him, "This is a strange complication, a strange sort of knot; for the whole misfortune consists in the way thought is twined; otherwise the direction is quite normal, it is just this path you must travel through the despair of the self to faith. It is true enough about the weakness, but it is not over this you must despair; the self must be broken in order to become a self, so cease to despair over it." If one were to talk to him thus, he would perhaps understand it in a dispassionate moment, but soon passion would again see falsely, and so again he takes the wrong turn into despair.

As I have said, such despair is rather rare. If it does not stay at that point, merely marking time, and if on the other hand there does not occur a radical change in the despairer so that he gets on the right path to faith, then such despair will either potentiate itself to a higher form and continue to be introversion, or it breaks through to the outside and demolishes the outward disguise under which the despairing man has been living in his incognito. In the latter case such a despairer will then plunge into life, perhaps into the distractions of great undertakings, he will become a restless spirit which leaves only too clear a trace of its actual presence, a restless spirit which wants to forget, and inasmuch as the noise within is so loud stronger means are needed, though of a different sort, than those which Richard III. employs in order not to hear his mother's curses.[18] Or he will seek forgetfulness in sensuality, perhaps in debauchery, in desperation he wants to return to immediacy, but constantly with consciousness of the self, which he does not want to have. In the first case, when despair is potentiated it becomes defiance, and it now becomes manifest how much truth there was in this notion of weakness, it becomes manifest how dialectically correct it is to say that the first expression of defiance is precisely despair over one's weakness.

However, let us in conclusion take another little look at the introvert who in his introversion marks time on the spot. If this introversion is absolutely maintained, *omnibus numeris absoluta* [perfect in every respect], then suicide will be the danger nearest to him. The common run of men have of course no presentiment of what such an introvert is capable of bearing; if they were to come to know it, they would be astonished. If on the other hand he talks to someone, if to one single man he opens his heart, he is in all probability strained to so high a tension, or so much let down, that suicide does not result from introversion. Such an introvert with one person privy to his thought is a whole tone milder than the absolute case. He probably will shun suicide. It may happen, however, that he falls into despair just for the fact that he has opened his heart to another; it may be that he thinks it would have been infinitely preferable to maintain silence rather than have anyone privy to his secret. There are examples of introverts who are brought to despair precisely because they have acquired a confidant. So after all suicide may be the consequence. Poetically the catastrophe (assuming *poetice* that the protagonist was e.g. a king or emperor) might be fashioned in such a way that the hero had the confidant put to death. One could imagine such a demoniacal tyrant who felt the need of talking to a fellow-man about his torment, and in this way consumed successively a whole lot of men; for to be his confidant was certain death.—It would be the task for a poet to represent this agonizing self-contradiction in a demoniac man who is not able to get along without a confidant, and not able to have a confidant, and then resolving it in such a way as this.[19]

(2). THE DESPAIR OF WILLING DESPAIRINGLY TO BE ONESELF—DEFIANCE.

As it was shown that one might call the despair dealt with in section 1 the despair of womanliness, so one might call the despair now to be considered the despair of manliness. In connection with the kind just described it may be called: despair viewed under the determinant of spirit. But this manliness belongs more precisely under the determinant of spirit, and womanliness is a lower synthesis.

The despair described in section 1 (ii) was despair over one's weakness, the despairer does not want to be himself. But if one goes one single dialectical step further, if despair thus becomes conscious of the reason why it does not want to be itself, then the case is altered, then defiance is present, for then it is precisely because of this a man is despairingly determined to be himself.

First comes despair over the earthly or something earthly, then despair over oneself about the eternal. Then comes defiance, which really is despair by the aid of the eternal, the despairing abuse of the eternal in the self to the point of being despairingly determined to be oneself. But just because it is despair by the aid of the eternal it lies in a sense very close to the true, and just because it lies very close to the true it is infinitely remote. The despair which is the passageway to faith is also by the aid of the eternal: by the aid of the eternal the self has courage to lose itself in order to gain itself. Here on the contrary it is not willing to begin by losing itself but wills to be itself.

In this form of despair there is now a mounting consciousness of the self, and hence greater consciousness of what despair is and of the fact that one's condition is that of despair. Here despair is conscious of itself as a deed, it does not come from without as a suffering under the pressure of circumstances, it comes directly from the self. And so after all defiance is a new qualification added to despair over one's weakness.

In order to will in despair to be oneself there must be consciousness of the infinite self. This infinite self, however, is really only the abstractest form, the abstractest possibility of the self, and it is this self the man despairingly wills to be, detaching the self from every relation to the Power which posited it, or detaching it from the conception that there is such a Power in existence. By the aid of this infinite form the self despairingly wills to dispose of itself or to create itself, to make itself the self it wills to be, distinguishing in the concrete self what it will and what it will not accept. The man's concrete self, or his concretion, has in fact necessity and limitations, it is this perfectly definite thing, with these faculties, dispositions, etc. But by the aid of the infinite form, the negative self, he wills first to undertake to refashion the whole thing, in order to get out of it in this way a self such as he wants to have, produced by the aid of the infinite form of the negative self—and it is thus he wills to be himself. That is to say, he is not willing to begin with the beginning but "in the beginning."[20] He is not willing to attire himself in himself, nor to see his task in the self given him; by the aid of being the infinite form he wills to construct it himself.

If one would have a common name for this despair, one might call it Stoicism—yet without thinking only of this philosophic sect. And to illuminate this sort of despair more sharply one would do well to distinguish between the active and the passive self, showing how the self is related to itself when it is active, and how it is related to itself in suffering when it is passive, and showing that the formula constantly is: in despair to will to be oneself.

If the despairing *self* is *active*, it really is related to itself only as experimenting with whatsoever it be that it undertakes, however great it may be, however astonishing, however persistently carried out. It acknowledges no power over it, hence in the last resort it lacks seriousness and is able only to conjure up a show of seriousness when the self bestows upon its experiments its utmost attention. Like the fire which Prometheus stole from the gods, so does this mean to steal from God the thought which is seriousness, that God is regarding one, instead of which the despairing self is content with regarding itself, and by that it is supposed to bestow upon its undertakings infinite interest and importance, whereas it is precisely this which makes them mere experiments. For though this self were to go so far in despair that it becomes an experimental god, no derived self can by regarding itself give itself more than it is: it nevertheless remains from first to last the self, by self-duplication it becomes neither more nor less than the self. Hence the self in its despairing effort to will to be itself labors itself into the direct opposite, it becomes really no self. In the whole dialectic within which it acts there is nothing firm, what the self is does not for an instant stand firm, that is, eternally firm. The negative form of the self exercises quite as much the power of loosing as of binding, every instant it can quite arbitrarily begin all over again, and however far a thought may be pursued, the whole action is within a hypothesis. It is so far from being true that the self succeeds more and more in becoming itself, that in fact it merely becomes more and more manifest that it is a hypothetical self. The self is its own lord and master, so it is said, absolutely its own lord, and precisely this is despair, but it also is what it regards as its pleasure and enjoyment. However, by closer inspection one easily ascertains that this ruler is a king without a country, he rules really over nothing; his condition, his dominion, is subjected to the dialectic that every instant revolution is legitimate. For in the last resort this depends arbitrarily upon the self.

So the despairing self is constantly building nothing but castles in the air, it fights only in the air. All these experimented virtues make a brilliant showing; for an instant they are enchanting like an oriental poem: such self-control, such firmness, such ataraxia, etc., border almost on the fabulous. Yes, they do to be sure; and also at the bottom of it all there is nothing. The self wants to enjoy the entire satisfaction of making itself into itself, of developing itself, of being itself; it wants to have the honor of this poetical, this masterly plan according to which it has understood itself. And yet in the last resort it is a riddle how it understands itself; just at the instant when it seems to be nearest to having the fabric finished it can arbitrarily resolve the whole thing into nothing.[21]

If the despairing self is a passive sufferer, we have still the same formula: in despair at willing to be oneself. Perhaps such an experimenting self which in despair wills to be itself, at the moment when it is making a preliminary exploration of its concrete self, stumbles upon one or another hardship of the sort that the Christian would call a cross, a fundamental defect, it matters not what. The negative self, the infinite form of the self, will perhaps cast this clean away, pretend that it does not exist, want to know nothing about it. But this does not succeed, its virtuosity in experimenting does not extend so far, nor does its virtuosity in abstraction; like Prometheus the infinite, negative self feels that it is nailed to this servitude. So then it is a passively suffering self. How then does the despair which despairingly wills to be itself display itself in this case?

Note that in the foregoing the form of despair was represented which is in despair over the earthly or over something earthly, so understood that at bottom this is and also shows itself to be despair about the eternal, i.e. despair which wills not to let itself be comforted by the eternal, which rates the earthly so high that the eternal can be of no comfort. But this too is a form of despair: not to be willing to hope that an earthly distress, a temporal cross, might be removed. This is what the despair which wills desperately to be itself is not willing to hope. It has convinced itself that this thorn in the flesh[22] gnaws so profoundly that he cannot abstract it— no matter whether this is actually so or his passion makes it true for him,* and so he is willing to accept it as it were eternally. So he is offended by it,[23] or rather from it he takes occasion to be offended at the whole of existence, in spite of it he would be himself, not despitefully be himself without it (for that is to abstract from it, and that he cannot do, or that would be a movement in the direction of resignation); no, in spite of or in defiance of the whole of

---

*From this standpoint, it is well to note here, one will see also that much which is embellished by the name of resignation is a kind of despair, that of willing despairingly to be one's abstract self, of willing despairingly to be satisfied with the eternal and thereby be able to defy or ignore suffering in the earthly and temporal sphere. The dialectic of resignation is commonly this: to will to be one's eternal self, and then with respect to something positive wherein the self suffers, not to will to be oneself, contenting oneself with the thought that after all this will disappear in eternity, thinking itself therefore justified in not accepting it in time, so that, although suffering under it, the self will not make to it the concession that it properly belongs to the self, that is, it will not humble itself under it in faith. Resignation regarded as despair is essentially different from the form, "in despair at not willing to be oneself," for it wills desperately to be itself—with exception, however, of one particular, with respect to which it wills despairingly not to be itself.

existence he wills to be himself with it, to take it along, almost defying his torment. For to hope in the possibility of help, not to speak of help by virtue of the absurd, that for God all things are possible—no, that he will not do. And as for seeking help from any other—no, that he will not do for all the world; rather than seek help he would prefer to be himself—with all the tortures of hell, if so it must be.

And of a truth it is not quite so true after all when people say that "it is a matter of course that a sufferer would be so glad to be helped, if only somebody would help him"—this is far from being the case, even though the opposite case is not always so desperate as this. The situation is this. A sufferer has one or more ways in which he would be glad to be helped. If he is helped thus, he is willing to be helped. But when in a deeper sense it becomes seriousness with this thing of needing help, especially from a higher or from the highest source—this humiliation of having to accept help unconditionally and in any way, the humiliation of becoming nothing in the hand of the Helper for whom all things are possible, or merely the necessity of deferring to another man, of having to give up being oneself so long as one is seeking help —ah, there are doubtless many sufferings, even protracted and agonizing sufferings, at which the self does not wince to this extent, and which therefore at bottom it prefers to retain and to be itself.

But the more consciousness there is in such a sufferer who in despair is determined to be himself, all the more does despair too potentiate itself and become demoniac. The genesis of this is commonly as follows. A self which in despair is determined to be itself winces at one pain or another which simply cannot be taken away or separated from its concrete self. Precisely upon this torment the man directs his whole passion, which at last becomes a demoniac rage. Even if at this point God in heaven and all his angels were to offer to help him out of it—no, now he doesn't want it, now it is too late, he once would have given everything to be rid of this torment but was made to wait, now that's all past, now he would rather rage against everything, he, the one man in the whole of existence who is the most unjustly treated, to whom it is especially important to have his torment at hand, important that no one should take it from him—for thus he can convince himself that he is in the right. This at last becomes so firmly fixed in his head that for a very peculiar reason he is afraid of eternity—for the reason, namely, that it might rid him of his (demoniacally understood) infinite advantage over other men, his (demoniacally understood) justification for being what he is. It is himself he wills to be; he began with the infinite abstraction of the self, and now at last he has become so concrete that it would be an impossibility to be eternal in that sense, and yet he wills in despair to be himself. Ah, demoniac madness! He rages most of all at the thought that eternity might get it into its head to take his misery from him!

This sort of despair is seldom seen in the world, such figures generally are met with only in the works of poets, that is to say, of real poets, who always lend their characters this "demoniac" ideality (taking this word in the purely Greek sense). Nevertheless such a despairer is to be met with also in real life. What then is the corresponding outward mark? Well, there is no "corresponding" mark, for in fact a corresponding outward expression corresponding to close reserve is a contradiction in terms; for if it is corresponding, it is then of course revealing. But outwardness is the entirely indifferent factor in this case where introversion, or what one might call inwardness with a jammed lock, is so much the predominant factor. The lowest forms of despair, where there really was no inwardness, or at all events none worth talking about, the lowest forms of despair one might represent by describing or by saying something about the outward traits of the despairer. But the more despair becomes spiritual, and the more inwardness becomes a peculiar world for itself in introversion, all the more is the self alert with demoniac shrewdness to keep despair shut up in close reserve, and all the more intent therefore to set the outward appearance at the level of indifference, to make it as unrevealing and indifferent as possible. As according to the report of superstition the troll disappears through a crack which no one can perceive, so it is for the despairer all the more important to dwell in an exterior semblance behind which it ordinarily would never occur to anyone to look for it. This hiddenness is precisely something spiritual and is one of the safety-devices for assuring oneself of having as it were behind reality an enclosure, a world for itself locking all else out, a world where the despairing self is employed as tirelessly as Tantalus in willing to be itself.

We began in section 1 (ii) with the lowest form of despair, which in despair does not will to be itself. The demoniac despair is the most potentiated form of the despair which despairingly wills to be itself. This despair does not will to be itself with Stoic doting upon itself, nor with self-deification, willing in this way, doubtless mendaciously, yet in a certain sense in terms of its perfection; no, with hatred for existence it wills to be itself, to be itself in terms of its misery; it does not even in defiance or defiantly will to be itself, but to be itself in spite; it does not even will in defiance to tear itself free from the Power which posited it, it wills to obtrude upon this Power in spite, to hold on to it out of malice. And that is natural, a malignant objection must above all take care to hold on to that against which it is an objection. Revolting against the whole of existence, it thinks it has hold of a proof against it, against its goodness. This proof the despairer thinks he himself is, and that is what he wills to be, therefore he wills to be himself, himself with his torment, in order with this torment to protest against the whole of existence. Whereas the weak despairer will not hear about what comfort eternity has for him, so neither will such a despairer hear about it, but for a different reason, namely, because this comfort would be the destruction of him as an objection against the whole of existence. It is (to describe it figuratively) as if an author were to make a slip of the pen, and that this clerical error became conscious of being such—perhaps it was no error[24] but in a far higher sense was an essential constituent in the whole exposition—it is then as if this clerical error would revolt against the author, out of hatred for him were to forbid him to correct it, and were to say, "No, I will not be erased, I will stand as a witness against thee, that thou art a very poor writer."

PART SECOND

Despair Is Sin

I. DESPAIR IS SIN

Sin is this: *before God, or with the conception of God, to be in despair at not willing to be oneself, or in despair at willing to be oneself.* Thus sin is potentiated weakness or potentiated defiance: sin is the potentiation of despair. The point upon which the emphasis rests is *before God*, or the fact that the conception of God is involved; the factor which dialectically, ethically, religiously, makes "qualified" despair (to use a juridical term) synonymous with sin is the conception of God.

Although in this Second Part, and especially in this section, there is no place or occasion for psychological description, there here may be introduced, as the most dialectical borderline between despair and sin, what one might call a poet-existence in the direction of the religious,[25] an existence which has something in common with the despair of resignation, only that the conception of God is involved. Such an existence (as is to be seen from the conjunction and position of the categories) will be the most eminent poet-existence. From a Christian standpoint such an existence (in spite of all aesthetic) is sin, it is the sin of poetizing instead of being, of standing in relation to the Good and the True through imagination instead of being that, or rather existentially striving to be it. The poet-existence here in question is distinguished from despair by the fact that it includes the conception of God or is before God; but it is prodigiously dialectical, and is in an impenetrable dialectical confusion as to how far it is conscious of being sin. Such a poet may have a very deep religious need, and the conception of God is included in his despair. He loves God above everything, God is for him the only comfort in his secret torment, and yet he loves the torment, he will not let it go. He would so gladly be himself before God, but not with respect to this fixed point where the self suffers, there despairingly he will not be himself; he hopes that eternity will remove it, and here in the temporal, however much he suffers under it, he cannot will to accept it, cannot humble himself under it in faith. And yet he continues to hold to God, and this is his only happiness, for him it would be the greatest horror to have to do without God, "it would be enough to drive one to despair"; and yet he permits himself commonly, but perhaps unconsciously, to poetize God, making him a little bit other than He is, a little bit more like a loving father who all too much indulges the child's "only wish." He who became unhappy in love, and therefore became a poet, blissfully extolls the happiness of love—so he became a poet of religiousness, he understands obscurely that it is required of him to let this torment go, that is, to humble himself under it in faith and to accept it as belonging to the self—for he would hold it aloof from him, and thereby precisely he holds it fast, although doubtless he thinks (and this, like every other word of despair, is correct in the opposite sense and therefore must be understood inversely) that this must mean separating himself from it as far as possible, letting it go as far as it is possible for a man to do so. But to accept it in faith, that he cannot do, or rather in the last resort he will not, or here is where the self ends in obscurity.[26] But like that poet's description of love, so this poet's description of the religious possesses an enchantment, a lyrical flight, such as no married man's description has, nor that of his Reverence. What he says is not untrue, by no means, his representation reflects his happier, his better ego. With respect to the religious he is an unhappy lover, that is, he is not in a strict sense a believer, he has only the first prerequisite of faith, and with that an ardent longing for the religious. His collision is essentially this: is he the elect, is the thorn in the flesh the expression for the fact that he is to be employed as the extraordinary, is it before God quite as it should be with respect to the extraordinary figure he has become? or is the thorn in the flesh the experience he must humble himself under in order to attain the universal human?[27] But enough of this. I can say with the emphasis of truth, "To whom am I talking?" Who will bother about such psychological investigations carried to the *n*th power? The Nüremburg Picture Books painted by priests are easily understood; one and all, they resemble, deceptively, people as they generally are, and, spiritually understood, nothing.

1. Gradations in the Consciousness of the Self
(The Qualification "before God")

In the foregoing there is steadily pointed out a gradation in the consciousness of the self: first came unconsciousness of being an eternal self (III.B a), then a knowledge of having a self in which there is after all something eternal (III.B b), and under this (1 i and ii, 2) there were again pointed out gradations. This whole situation must now be turned about and viewed in a new way. The point is this. The gradations in the consciousness of the self with which we have hitherto been employed are within the definition of the human self, or the self whose measure is man. But this self acquires a new quality or qualification in the fact that it is the self directly in the sight of God. This self is no longer the merely human self but is what I would call, hoping not to be misunderstood, the theological self, the self directly in the sight of God. And what an infinite reality this self acquires by being before God! A herdsman who (if this were possible) is a self only in the sight of cows is a very low self, and so also is a ruler who is a self in the sight of slaves—for in both cases the scale or measure is lacking. The child who hitherto has had only the parents to measure himself by, becomes a self when he is a man by getting the state as a measure. But what an infinite accent falls upon the self by getting God as a measure! The measure for the self always is that in the face of which it is a self; but this does not define what "measure" is. As one can add up only magnitudes of the same order, so each thing is qualitatively that by which it is measured; and that which is qualitatively its measure (*Maalestok*) is ethically its goal (*Maal*); and the measure and goal are qualitatively that which something is— with exception of the relation which obtains in the world of freedom, where a man by not being qualitatively that which is his goal and his measure must himself have deserved this disqualification, so that the goal and the measure remains the same . . . condemningly, making manifest what it is he is not: that, namely which is his goal and his measure.

It was a very just thought to which the older dogmatic[28] frequently recurred, whereas a later dogmatic[29] so often censored it for lack of understanding and a proper sense of its meaning —it was a very just thought, although sometimes a wrong application was made of it: the thought that what makes sin so frightful is that it is before God. From this the theologians proved the eternity of hell-punishment. Subsequently they became shrewder and said, "Sin is sin; sin is not greater because it is against God or before God." Strange! For even the jurists talk about "qualified" crimes and extenuating circumstances, even the jurists make distinction with regard to a crime, inquiring, for example, whether it is committed against a public functionary or a private person, they prescribe a different punishment for the murder of a father and an ordinary murder.

No, the earlier dogmatic was right in asserting that the fact that the sin was before God infinitely potentiated it. Their fault lay in regarding God as something external, and in assuming that it was only now and then men sinned against God. But God is not something external in the sense that a policeman is. What we need to emphasize is that the self has the conception of God, and that then it does not will as He wills, and so is disobedient. Nor is it only now and then one sins before God; for every sin is before God, or rather it is this which properly makes human guilt to be sin.[30]

Despair is potentiated in proportion to consciousness of self; but the self is potentiated in the ratio of the measure proposed for the self, and infinitely potentiated when God is the measure. The more conception of God, the more self; the more self, the more conception of God. Only when the self as this definite individual is conscious of existing before God, only then is it the infinite self; and then this self sins before God. The selfishness of paganism, therefore, in spite of all that can be said about it, is not nearly so "qualified" as that of Christendom, in so far as here also there is selfishness; for the pagan did not possess his self directly in the face of God. The pagan and the natural man have as their measure the merely human self. One may be right therefore from a higher stand-point in regarding paganism as lying in sin, but properly the sin of paganism was the despairing unawareness of God, un-awareness of existing before God; this means to be "without God in the world."[31] On the other hand, it is for this reason true that the pagan did not sin in the strictest sense, for he did not sin before God. Moreover, it is also in a sense quite certain that many a time a pagan is enabled in a way to slip through the world irreproachably precisely because his light-minded Pelagian interpretation saved him; but then his sin is a different one, namely, this light-minded interpretation. On the other hand and in a different aspect it is quite certain that just by being brought up strictly in Christianity a man has in a certain sense been plunged into sin, because the whole Christian view was too serious for him, especially in an earlier period of his life;[32] but then in another sense this is again of some help to him, this deeper apprehension of what sin is.

Sin is: before God in despair not to will to be oneself, or before God in despair to will to be oneself. But is not this definition, even though in other aspects it may be conceded to have advantages (and among them this which is the weightiest of all, that it is the only Scriptural definition, for the Scripture always defines sin as disobedience), is it not after all too spiritual? To this one must first of all make answer that a definition of sin can never be too spiritual (unless it becomes so spiritual that it does away with sin); for sin is precisely a determinant of spirit. And in the next place, why should it then be too spiritual? Because it does not talk about murder, theft, unchastity, etc.? But does it not talk of them? Is it not also self-assertion against God when one is disobedient and de-fies His commandment? But on the other hand, when in talk-ing about sin one talks only of such sins, it is so easily forgotten that in a way it may be all right, humanly speaking, with re-spect to all such things up to a certain point, and yet the whole life may be sin, the well-known kind of sin: glittering vices, wilfulness, which either spiritlessly or impudently continues to be or wills to be unaware in what an infinitely deeper sense a human self is morally under obligation to God with respect to every most secret wish and thought, with respect to quickness in comprehending and readiness to follow every hint of God as to what His will is for this self. The sins of the flesh are the self-assertion of the lower self; but how often one devil is cast out by the devil's help, and the last state becomes worse than the first. For so it is with men in this world: first a man sins from frailty and weakness; and then—yes, then perhaps he learns to flee to God and to be helped by faith which saves from all sin; but of this we are not talking here—then he despairs over his weakness and becomes, either a Pharisee who in despair manages to attain a certain legal righteousness, or he despairs and plunges again into sin.

The definition therefore certainly embraces every conceivable and actual form of sin; it certainly throws into relief the decisive fact that sin is despair (for sin is not the wildness of flesh and blood, but it is the spirit's consent thereto), and it is . . . before God. As a definition it is algebraic. In this little work it would be out of place, and an effort moreover which perhaps would not succeed, were I to begin by describing the particular sins. The principal thing here is that the definition like a net must embrace all forms. And that it does, as can be seen when one tests it by setting up the opposite, namely, the definition of faith, by which I steer my course in the whole of this work, as by a sure mariners' mark. Faith is: that the self in being itself and in willing to be itself is grounded transparently in God.

But too often it has been overlooked that the opposite of sin is not *virtue*, not by any manner of means. This is in part a pagan view which is content with a merely human measure and properly does not know what *sin* is, that all sin is before God. No, *the opposite of sin is faith*, as is affirmed in Rom. 14:23, "whatsoever is not of faith is sin." And for the whole of Christianity it is one of the most decisive definitions that the opposite of sin is not virtue but faith.

THAT THE DEFINITION OF SIN CONTAINS
THE POSSIBILITY OF THE OFFENSE
—A GENERAL OBSERVATION ABOUT OFFENSE

The opposition sin/faith is the Christian one, which in a Christian way transforms the definition of all ethical concepts, giving them one distillation the more. At the bottom of this opposition lies the decisive Christian concept, "before God," a determinant which in turn stands in relation to the decisive criterion of Christianity: the absurd, the paradox, the possibility of offense.[33] And that this should be indicated in every definition of Christianity is of the utmost importance, for the offense is Christianity's defense against all speculation. In this instance where is the possibility of the offense? It lies in the fact that a man, as a particular individual, should have such a reality as is implied by existing directly in the sight of God; and then again, and as a consequence of this, that a man's sin should concern God. This notion of the particular man . . . before God speculative philosophy never gets into its head, it can only universalize the particular man fantastically. It was just for this reason also that an incredulous Christianity made out that sin is sin, no matter whether it is directly in the sight of God or not. That is to say, they wanted to do away with the determinant "before God," and to this end they discovered a higher wisdom—which, however, strangely enough, was neither more nor less than what the higher wisdom no doubt generally is . . . the old paganism.

There is so much said now about people being offended at Christianity because it is so dark and gloomy, offended at it because it is so severe, etc. It is now high time to explain that the real reason why man is offended at Christianity is because it is too high, because its goal is not man's goal, because it would make of a man something so extraordinary that he is unable to get it into his head. A perfectly simple psychological investigation of what offense is will explain this, and at the same time it will show how infinitely silly their behavior has been who defended Christianity by taking away the offense, how stupidly or impudently they have ignored Christ's own instruction, who often and with such deep concern warns against the offense, that is, intimates that the possibility of the offense is present, and must be ever-present; for if it is not present, if it is not an eternally essential constituent of Christianity, it is nonsense, humanly speaking, for Christ, instead of taking it away, to be distressed about it and to give warning against it.

If I were to imagine to myself a day-laborer and the mightiest emperor that ever lived, and were to imagine that this mighty Emperor took a notion to send for the poor man, who never had dreamed, "neither had it entered into his heart to believe," that the Emperor knew of his existence, and who therefore would think himself indescribably fortunate if merely he was permitted once to see the Emperor, and would recount it to his children and children's children as the most important event of his life—but suppose the Emperor sent for him and informed him that he wished to have him for his son-in-law . . . what then? Then the laborer, humanly, would become somewhat or very much puzzled, shame-faced, and embarrassed, and it would seem to him, quite humanly (and this is the human element in it), something exceedingly strange, something quite mad, the last thing in the world about which he would say a word to anybody else, since he himself in his own mind was not far from explaining it by supposing (as his neighbors would be busily doing as soon as possible) that the Emperor wanted to make a fool of him, so that the poor man would be the laughing-stock of the whole town, his picture in the papers, the story of his espousal to the Emperor's daughter the theme of ballad-mongers. This thing, however, of becoming the Emperor's son-in-law might readily be subjected to the tests of reality, so that the laborer would be able to ascertain how far the Emperor was serious in this matter, or whether he merely wanted to make fun of the poor fellow, render him unhappy for the rest of his life, and help him to find his way to the mad-house; for the *quid nimis* is in evidence, which with such infinite ease can turn into its opposite. A small expression of favor the laborer would be able to get through his head; it would be understood in the market-town[34] by "the highly respected cultured public," by all ballad-mongers, in short, by the 5 times 100,000 persons who dwelt in that market-town, which with respect to its population was even a very big city, but with respect to possessing understanding of and sense for the extraordinary was a very small market-town—but this thing of becoming the Emperor's son-in-law was far too much. And suppose now that this was not an external reality but an inward thing, so that factual proofs could not help the laborer to certitude, but faith itself was the facticity, and so it was all left to faith whether he possessed humble courage enough to dare to believe it (for impudent courage cannot help one to *believe*) —how many laboring men were there likely to be who possessed this courage? But he who had not this courage would be offended; the extraordinary would seem to him almost like mockery of him. He would then perhaps honestly and plainly admit, "Such a thing is too high for me, I cannot get it into my head; it seems to me, if I may blurt it straight out, foolishness."

And now for Christianity! Christianity teaches that this particular individual, and so every individual, whatever in other respects this individual may be, man, woman, serving-maid, minister of state, merchant, barber, student, etc.—this individual exists *before* God—this individual who perhaps would be vain for having once in his life talked with the King, this man who is not a little proud of living on intimate terms with that person or the other, this man exists before God, can talk with God any moment he will, sure to be heard by Him; in short, this man is invited to live on the most intimate terms with God! Furthermore, for this man's sake God came to the world, let himself be born, suffers and dies; and this suffering God almost begs and entreats this man to accept the help which is offered him! Verily, if there is anything that would make a man lose his understanding, it is surely this! Whosoever has not the humble courage to dare to believe it, must be offended at it. But why is he offended? Because it is too high for him, because he cannot get it into his head, because in the face of it he cannot acquire frank-heartedness, and therefore must have it done away with, brought to naught and nonsense, for it is as though it would stifle him.

For what is offense? Offense is unhappy admiration. It is therefore akin to envy, but it is an envy which is turned against oneself, or, more exactly, envy which is worst of all against one-self. The narrow-mindedness of the natural man cannot wel-come for itself the extraordinary which God has intended for him; so he is offended.

The degree of the offense depends upon what passion a man has for admiration. The more prosaic men, devoid of imagina-tion and passion, and who therefore are not apt to admire, they too may be offended, but they confine themselves to say-ing, "Such a thing I can't get through my head, I let it alone." These are the sceptics. But the more passion and imagination a man has, the nearer consequently he is in a certain sense (that is, in possibility) to being able to become a believer— *nota bene!* by adoringly humbling himself under the extraor-dinary—all the more passionate is the offense, which at last cannot be contented with less than getting this thing rooted out, annihilated and trodden in the dust.

If one would learn to understand offense, let him study human envy, a subject which I offer as an extra course, plum-ing myself upon having studied it profoundly. Envy is con-cealed admiration. An admirer who feels that he cannot be happy by surrendering himself elects to become envious of that which he admires. So he speaks another language, and in that language of his the thing which he really admires is called a stupid, insipid and queer sort of thing. Admiration is happy self-surrender; envy is unhappy self-assertion.

So also it is with offense: that which in the relation between man and man is known as admiration/envy, in the relation between man and God is adoration/offense. The *summa sum-marum* of all human wisdom is this "golden,"[35] or perhaps more properly the gilded, *ne quid nimis* [nothing to excess], too much or too little spoils the broth. This is given and taken between man and man as wisdom and is honored by admira-tion, its quotation never fluctuates, the whole of humanity guarantees its value. So if once in a while there lives a genius who goes a little bit beyond it, he is declared mad . . . by the wise. But Christianity takes a prodigious giant-stride be-yond this *ne quid nimis*, a stride into the absurd—there Christianity begins . . . and the offense.

One sees now how extraordinarily (that there might be

something extraordinary left)—how extraordinarily stupid it is to defend Christianity, how little knowledge of men this betrays, and how truly, even though it be unconsciously, it is working in collusion with the enemy, by making of Christianity a miserable something or another which in the end has to be rescued by a defense. Therefore it is certain and true that he who first invented the notion of defending Christianity in Christendom is *de facto* Judas No. 2; he also betrays with a kiss, only his treachery is that of stupidity. To defend anything is always to discredit it. Let a man have a storehouse full of gold, let him be willing to dispense every ducat to the poor—but let him besides that be stupid enough to begin this benevolent undertaking with a defense in which he advances three reasons to prove that it is justifiable—and people will be almost inclined to doubt whether he is doing any good. But now for Christianity! Yea, he who defends it has never believed in it. If he believes, then the enthusiasm of faith is . . . not defense, no, it is attack and victory. The believer is a victor.

Thus it stands with Christianity and the offense. The possibility of the offense is quite rightly included in the Christian definition of sin—in this phrase, "before God." A pagan, the natural man, is very willing to admit that sin exists, but this "before God," which really is what makes sin to be sin, is for him too much, it seems to him (though in a different sense from that pointed out here) to make too much of what it is to be a man; a little less, and then he is willing to agree to it—"but too much is too much."

2. The Socratic Definition of Sin

Sin is ignorance. This is the well-known Socratic definition of sin, which, like everything Socratic, is an opinion always worthy of attention. However, with respect to this Socratic position, as with respect to many other Socratic positions, how many men have felt a need of going further? What an innumerable number have felt the need of going further than the Socratic ignorance—presumably because they felt that it was impossible for them to stay there; for in every generation how many men are there that are capable, even for only a month, of

enduring and existentially expressing ignorance about everything?

Therefore I do not by any means intend to dispose of the
Socratic definition on the ground that one cannot stop with it;
but, having the Christian definition *in mente* [in mind], I
would make use of it to bring the other out sharply (just because the Socratic definition is so genuinely Greek), so that
here as always the hollowness of every other definition which
is not in the strictest sense Christian (that is, of every partial
definition) may become manifest.

The difficulty with the Socratic definition is that it leaves
undetermined how ignorance itself is to be more precisely
understood, the question of its origin, etc. That is to say, even
if sin be ignorance (or what Christianity would perhaps prefer
to call stupidity), which in one sense cannot be denied, we
have to ask, is this an original ignorance, is it always the case
that one has not known and hitherto could not know anything
about the truth, or is it a superinduced, a subsequent ignorance? If it is what the last question implies, then sin must
properly have its ground in something else, it must have its
ground in the activity with which a man has labored to obscure his intelligence. But also when this is assumed, the stiff-
necked and tough-lived difficulty returns, prompting the question whether at the instant a man began to obscure his intelligence he was distinctly conscious of what he was doing. If he
was not distinctly conscious of this, then his intelligence was
already somewhat obscured before he began, and the question
merely returns again. If it is assumed on the contrary that
when he began to obscure his intelligence he was distinctly
conscious of it, then sin (even though it be unconsciousness,
seeing that this was an induced state) would not lie in the intelligence but in the will, and the question which must be
raised is about the relation of the intelligence and the will to
one another. With such questions as these (and one might
continue to augment them for many a day) the Socratic definition does not deal. Socrates was certainly an ethical teacher
(the Classical age claims him absolutely as the discoverer of
ethics), he was the first one, as he is and remains the first in
his class; but he begins with ignorance. Intellectually, it is to-

ward ignorance he tends, toward the position of knowing nothing. Ethically, he understands by ignorance quite a different thing, and so he begins with that.

But on the other hand, as a matter of course, Socrates is not an essentially religious ethicist, still less a dogmatic one, as the Christian ethicist is. Hence he does not really enter into the whole investigation with which Christianity begins, into the *prius* [before] in which sin presupposes itself, and which is Christianly explained by the doctrine of original sin—a dogma to the border of which only we come in this investigation.

Socrates therefore never really gets to the determinant we know as sin, which is surely a defect in a definition of sin. Why is this? For if sin is indeed ignorance, then sin properly does not exist, since sin is definitely consciousness. If sin consists in being ignorant of what is right, so that one consequently does what is wrong, sin does not exist. If this is sin, then it must be assumed, as Socrates also assumed, that the case does not occur of a man knowing what is right and doing what is wrong, or knowing that a thing is wrong and doing the wrong. So then, if the Socratic definition is correct, sin does not exist. But, lo, precisely this is, Christianly understood, just as it should be, in a deeper sense it is quite correct, in the interest of Christianity it is *quod erat demonstrandum*. Precisely the concept by which Christianity distinguishes itself qualitatively and most decisively from paganism is the concept of sin, the doctrine of sin; and therefore Christianity also assumes quite consistently that neither paganism nor the natural man knows what sin is; yea, it assumes that there must be a revelation from God to make manifest what sin is. For it is not true, as a superficial view assumes, that the doctrine of the atonement is the qualitative difference between paganism and Christianity. No, the beginning must be made far deeper, with sin, with the doctrine of sin, as Christianity also does. What a dangerous objection therefore against Christianity if paganism had a definition of sin which Christianity must admit is correct!

What determinant is it then that Socrates lacks in determining what sin is? It is will, defiant will. The Greek intellectualism was too happy, too naïve, too aesthetic, too ironical, too witty . . . too sinful to be able to get it into its head that a person knowingly could fail to do the good, or knowingly, with knowledge of what was right, do what was wrong. The Greek spirit proposes an intellectual categorical imperative.

The truth in this definition must by no means be overlooked, and it needs to be enforced in times such as these which have gone astray in so much flatulent and unfruitful knowledge, so that doubtless now, just as in Socrates' age, only much more, it is advisable that people should be starved a little bit Socratically. It is enough to provoke both laughter and tears—not only all these protestations about having understood and comprehended the highest thought, but also the virtuosity with which many know how to present it *in abstracto,* and in a certain sense quite correctly—it is enough to provoke both laughter and tears when one sees then that all this knowing and understanding exercises no influence upon the lives of these men, that their lives do not in the remotest way express what they have understood, but rather the contrary. One involuntarily exclaims at the sight of a disproportion at once so sorrowful and so ludicrous. But how in the world is it possible that they have understood it? And is it true that they have understood? Here the ancient ironist and ethicist makes answer: "My dear man, never believe it, for if they truly had understood, their lives also would have expressed it, they would have done what they understood."

To understand/and to understand are therefore two things? Certainly they are; and he who has understood this (but not, be it noted, in the sense of the first sort of understanding) is initiated into all the secret mysteries of irony. It is with this contradiction irony is properly employed. To perceive the comic in the fact that a person is actually ignorant of something means a very low sort of comic, beneath the dignity of irony. There is properly no profound comic in the fact that people once lived who assumed that the earth stands still—when nobody knew any better. The same thing will presumably befall our age in contrast with an age which knows more of physical law. The contradiction is one between two different ages, there is lacking a deeper point of coincidence; such a contradiction is not essential, and hence neither is it essentially comic. No, but that a man stands up and says the right thing . . . and so has understood it, and then when he has to act does the wrong thing . . . and so shows that he has not understood it—yes, that is comic. It is infinitely comic that a man, moved unto tears, so much moved that not only tears but sweat trickle from him, can sit and read, or hear, representations of self-denial, of the nobility of sacrificing one's life for the truth—and then the next instant—one, two, three, slap-dash, almost with the tears still in his eyes—is in full swing, in the sweat of his brow, with all his might and main, helping falsehood to conquer. It is infinitely comic that an orator, with truth in his voice and in the expression of his features, profoundly touched and profoundly touching, can present the truth in a heart-rending way, can tread all evil and all the powers of hell under his feet, with an aplomb in his attitude, an assurance in his glance, a resoluteness in his step, which is altogether admirable—it is infinitely comic that almost at the same moment, almost "with his dressing-gown still on,"[86] he can run cowardly and timidly out of the way of the least inconvenience. It is infinitely comic that a man can understand the whole truth about how wretched and petty this world is, etc.—that he can understand this, and then cannot recognize again what he understood; for almost in the same moment he himself goes off and takes part in the same pettiness and wretchedness, takes glory in it and receives glory from it, that is, accepts it. O when one beholds a man who protests that he has entirely understood how Christ went about in the form of a lowly servant, poor, despised, and, as the Scripture says, spat upon—when I see the same man so careful to betake himself thither where in a worldly sense it is good to be, and accommodate himself there in the utmost security, when I see him apprehensive of every puff of wind from right or left, as though his life depended upon it, and so blissful, so utterly blissful, so awfully glad—yes, to make the thing complete, so awfully glad that he is able to thank God for it—glad that he is held in honor by all men—then I have often said to myself and by myself, "Socrates, Socrates, Socrates, can it be possible that this man has understood what he says he has understood?" So I have said, and at the same time I have wished that Socrates might be right. For it seemed to me after all as though Christianity were too severe, nor can I bring it into accord with my experience to treat such a man as a hypocrite. No, Socrates, thee I can understand; thou dost treat him as a wag, as a sort of merry Andrew, thou dost treat him as a butt for laughter, thou hast no objection, it has even thine approval, that I prepare and serve him up as a comic dish—provided I do it well.

Socrates, Socrates, Socrates! Yes, one may well call thy name thrice, it would not be too much to call it ten times, if that would do any good. People think that the world needs a republic, and they think that it needs a new social order, and a new religion—but it never occurs to anybody that what the world now needs, confused as it is by much knowing, is a Socrates. But that is perfectly natural, for if anybody had this notion, not to say if many were to have it, there would be less need of a Socrates. What a delusion most needs is the very thing it least thinks of—naturally, for otherwise it would not be a delusion.

So then, such an ironic-ethical correction might very well be what our age needs, and perhaps the only thing it really needs; for it is evident that this is the thing it least thinks of. It is highly important that, instead of going further than Socrates, we simply return to the Socratic dictum that to understand/and to understand are two things—not returning to it as a result [once for all acquired], for in the end that only helps men into the deepest wretchedness, since it simply abolishes the distinction between understanding/and understanding, but returning to it as the ethical interpretation of every-day life.

The Socratic definition helps itself out as follows. When a person doesn't do the right thing; why then, neither has he understood it; his understanding is a vain conceit, his assertion that he has understood it is a false indication of the way, his repeated assertion that the devil take him if he has not understood it is a prodigious remoteness along the greatest possible detour. But then indeed the definition is correct. If a man does the right thing, then surely he doesn't sin; and if he doesn't do the right thing, then neither has he understood it; if in truth he had understood it, this would at once have moved him to do it, would at once make him an echo of his understanding—ergo sin is ignorance.

But where does the difficulty lie? It is to be ascribed to a fact of which the Socratic view itself was aware (though only to a certain degree) and sought to remedy, that it lacks a dialectical determinant for the transition from having understood something to the doing of it. In this transition Christianity makes its start; by proceeding along this path it proves that sin lies in the will, thus attaining the concept of defiance; and then, in order to make the end thoroughly fast,[37] it adjoins to this the dogma of original sin—for, alas, the secret of Speculation's success in comprehending is just this, of sewing without making the end fast and without knotting the thread, and therefore it can marvellously keep on sewing, i.e. keep on pulling the end through. Christianity, on the contrary, fastens the end by means of the paradox.

In pure ideality, where there is no question of the real individual man, the transition is accomplished by necessity (in the System indeed everything comes about by necessity), in other words, there is no difficulty at all connected with the transition from understanding to doing. This is purely in the Greek spirit—yet not Socratic, for Socrates was too much of an ethicist for that. And quite the same thing is really the secret of the whole of recent philosophy: *cogito ergo sum*, to think is to be. The Christian motto, on the contrary, is: As thou believest, so it comes to pass; or As thou believest, so art thou; to believe is to be. So one can see that modern philosophy is neither more nor less than paganism. But this is not the worst, to be akin to Socrates is not the meanest position. But the entirely unsocratic trait of modern philosophy is that it wants to make itself and us believe that it is Christianity.

In the world of reality, on the other hand, where it is a question of the individual man, there is this little tiny transition from having understood to doing; it is not always *cito citissime* [as quickly as possible], not *geschwind wie der Wind* [fast as the wind], if I may speak German for lack of philosophic terms. On the contrary, here begins a very prolix story.

In the life of spirit, on the other hand, there is no stopping

[*Stilstand*] (nor in reality is there any condition [*Tilstand*], everything is actuality): in case then a man the very same second he has known what is right does not do it—well then, first of all, the knowledge stops boiling. And next comes the question how the will likes this thing that is known. If it does not like it, it does not follow that the will goes ahead and does the opposite of that which the intelligence understood, such strong contrasts occur doubtless rather seldom; but the will lets some time pass, there is an interim, that means, "We'll see about that to-morrow." All this while the intelligence becomes more and more obscured, and the lower nature triumphs more and more. For, alas, the good must be done at once—at once, the moment it is known (and hence the transition goes so easily in the pure ideality where everything is "at once"), but the strength of the lower nature consists in dragging a thing out. The will has no particular objection to it—so it says with its fingers crossed. And then when the intelligence has become duly darkened, the intelligence and the will can understand one another better; at last they agree entirely, for now the intelligence has gone over to the side of the will and acknowledges that the thing is quite right as it would have it. And so there live perhaps a great multitude of men who labor off and on to obscure their ethical and religious understanding which would lead them out into decisions and consequences which the lower nature does not love, extending meanwhile their aesthetic and metaphysical understanding, which ethically is a distraction.

However, with all this we have not yet got any further than the Socratic position; for, as Socrates would say, if this comes about, then it only shows that such a man had not understood what is right. That is to say, the Greek spirit had not the courage to assert that a man knowingly does what is wrong, with knowledge of the right does what is wrong; so Socrates comes to its aid and says, When a man does wrong, he has not understood what is right.

Quite correct, and further than that no man can go: no man by himself and of himself can explain what sin is, precisely because he is in sin. All his talk about sin is at bottom palliation for sin, an excuse, a sinful mitigation. Hence

Christianity begins also in another way, by declaring that there must be a revelation from God in order to instruct man as to what sin is, that sin does not consist in the fact that man has not understood what is right, but in the fact that he will not understand it, and in the fact that he will not do it.

With respect to the distinction between not being *able* to understand/and not being *willing* to understand, even Socrates furnishes no real enlightenment, whereas he is Grand Master above all ironists in operating by means of the distinction between understanding/and understanding. Socrates explains that he who does not do the right thing has not understood it; but Christianity goes a little further back and says, it is because he will not understand it, and this in turn is because he does not will the right. And in the next place, describing what properly is defiance, it teaches that a man does wrong although he understands what is right, or forbears to do right although he understands what is right; in short, the Christian doctrine of sin is pure impertinence against man, accusation upon accusation; it is the charge which the Deity as prosecutor takes the liberty of lodging against man.

But can anyone comprehend this Christian doctrine? By no means—this too is Christian, and so is an offense. It must be believed. Comprehension is conterminous with man's relation to the human, but faith is man's relation to the divine. How then does Christianity explain this incomprehensible? Quite consistently, in an equally incomprehensible way, by means of the fact that it is revealed.

So then, Christianly understood, sin lies in the will, not in the intellect; and this corruption of the will goes well beyond the consciousness of the individual. This is the perfectly consistent declaration, for otherwise the question how sin began must arise with respect to each individual.

Here again we have the criterion of the offense. The possibility of the offense consists in the fact that there has to be a revelation from God to enlighten man as to what sin is and how deep it lies. The natural man, the pagan, thinks thus: "O well, I admit that I have not understood everything in heaven and earth; if there is to be a revelation, let it inform us about the heavenly; but that there should be a revelation to explain what sin is, that is the most preposterous thing of all. I don't pretend to be a perfect man, far from it, but I know and I am willing to concede how far I am from perfection—ought I not then to know what sin is?" But Christianity makes answer, "No, that is what you know least about, how far you are from perfection, and what sin is." Behold, in this sense, in a Christian sense, sin doubtless is ignorance, it is ignorance of what sin is.

The definition of sin which was given in the preceding chapter therefore still needs to be completed: sin is, after having been informed by a revelation from God what sin is, then before God in despair not to will to be oneself, or before God in despair to will to be oneself.

3. Sin Is Not a Negation but a Position

For the truth of this affirmation the orthodox dogmatic as a whole has constantly contended, and it has rejected as pantheistic every definition of sin which makes it something negative—weakness, sensuality, finiteness, ignorance, etc. Orthodoxy has perceived very rightly that here is where the battle has to be fought, or (to recall the foregoing) that it is here the end must be made fast, that here is the place to put up resistence. Orthodoxy has rightly perceived that, if sin is defined negatively, all of Christianity totters. Therefore orthodoxy insists that there must be a revelation from God in order to teach fallen men what sin is, a revelation which, quite consistently, must be believed, since it is a dogma. And naturally paradox, faith, dogma, these three determinants, form an alliance and accord which is the firmest support and bulwark against pagan wisdom.

So it is with orthodoxy. By a strange misunderstanding, a so-called speculative dogmatic,[38] which certainly has suspicious dealings with philosophy, has entertained the notion that it is able to comprehend this definition of sin as a position.[39] But if this is true, then sin is a negation. The secret of all comprehending is that the very act of comprehension is higher than every position which it posits. The concept posits a position, but the fact that it is comprehended means precisely that it is negated. The speculative dogmatic, being itself aware of this to a certain degree, has known no other way to help itself but by the maneuver, not very seemly in a philosophic science, of throwing out a detachment of asseverations at the point where a movement is being made. One asseverates, each time more solemnly than the last, and with more and more oaths and curses, that sin is a position, that to say that it is merely a negation is pantheism and rationalism, and God knows what all, but altogether something which the speculative dogmatic renunciates and abhors —and then one goes on to comprehend what it means that sin is a position. That is to say that after all it is a position only up to a certain degree, not any more so than that one can after all comprehend it.

And the same duplicity of speculation is manifested also at another point, which is, however, related to the same subject. The interpretation of sin, or the way sin is defined, is decisive for the interpretation of repentance. Then since this thing of negating a negation is so speculative, there is nothing else to be done, repentance must be a negation of the negation—and so sin becomes the negation.

However, it is certainly very much to be desired that a sober thinker would for once explain how far this purely logical process, which recalls the grammatical rule that two negatives make an affirmative, and the mathematical rule that two minuses are a plus—how far, I say, this logical process is valid in the world of reality, in the world of qualities; whether after all the qualities are not subject to a different dialectic; whether in this case "transition" does not play a different rôle. *Sub specie aeterni, aeterno modo, etc.* the element of time is lacking in which things can be spaced out, hence everything *is*, and there is no transition at all. In this abstract medium to posit is *eo ipso* the same thing as to cancel or "resolve." But to regard reality in the same way is pretty close to madness. One can say also *in abstracto* that the perfect tense follows the imperfect. But if in the world of reality a man were to infer that it followed by itself and followed at once, that a work he had not completed (the imperfect) became complete (the perfect)—he surely would be crazy. But so it is too with the so-called "position" of sin when the medium in which it is posited is pure thinking; that medium is far too unstable to insure that this assertion that sin is a position can be taken seriously.

However, all such questions are aside from the issue which immediately concerns me here. I am merely keeping a steady hold upon the Christian dogma that sin is a position—not, however, as though it could be comprehended, but as a paradox which must be believed. To my way of thinking, this is the correct thing. If only one can get it made manifest that all attempts at comprehending are self-contradictory, then the thing assumes the correct position, and then it becomes clear that it must be left to faith whether one will believe or not.

I can well comprehend (this being not too divine a matter to be comprehended) that one who just simply has to comprehend, and only can think of such matters as offer themselves to comprehension, may find this material very scanty. But in case the whole of Christianity hinges upon this, that it must be believed, not comprehended, that it *either* must be believed or one must be offended at it—is it then so meritorious to be determined to comprehend it? Is it meritorious, or is it not rather insolence or thoughtlessness, to will to comprehend that which is not willing to be comprehended? When a King takes the notion of wishing to be entirely incognito, to be treated in all respects as a simple man, is it then, just because in general it seems to men a greater distinction to do him royal homage, is it then the correct thing to do it? Or is it not precisely to assert oneself and one's own way of thinking directly in opposition to the King's will? Is it not to do as one wilfully prefers to do, instead of deferring to the King's will? Or would it, I wonder, give pleasure to the King in proportion as such a man was more ingenious in displaying toward him the proper reverence of a subject when the King does not wish to be treated in that way—that is to say, the more ingenious such a man might be in acting contrary to the King's will?

So let others admire and extoll him who claims to be able

to comprehend Christianity—I regard it as a plain ethical duty, which perhaps demands no little self-denial in such speculative times when all "the others" are busy about comprehending—I regard it then as a plain duty to admit that one neither can nor shall comprehend it. Just this, however, is doubtless what the age, what Christendom, needs, namely, a little Socratic ignorance in relation to Christianity—but I say emphatically *Socratic* ignorance. Let us never forget (yet after all how many are there that ever have known it or thought of it?)—let us never forget that the ignorance of Socrates was a kind of godly fear and divine worship, that his ignorance was the Greek rendering of the Jewish perception that the fear of God is the beginning of wisdom. Let us never forget that precisely out of reverence for the Deity he was ignorant, that, so far as a pagan could be, he kept watch as a *judge* on the border between God/and man, watching out to see that the deep gulf of qualitative distinction be firmly fixed between them, between God/and man, that God/and man may not in a way, *philosophice*, *poetice*, etc., coalesce into one. Lo, for this reason Socrates was the ignorant man, and for this reason the Deity recognized him as the most knowing.—But Christianity teaches that everything Christian exists only for faith; for this reason precisely it wills to be a Socratic, a Godfearing ignorance, which by ignorance defends faith against speculation, keeping watch to see that the deep gulf of qualitative distinction between God/and man may be firmly fixed, as it is in the paradox and in faith, lest God/and man, still more dreadfully than ever it occurred in paganism, might in a way, *philosophice*, *poetice*, etc., coalesce into one . . . in the System.

Only from one side can there be any question here of illuminating the fact that sin is a position. In the foregoing description of despair attention was constantly directed to an ascending scale. The expression for the scale was in part potentiation of consciousness of the self, in part potentiation as from passive suffering to conscious action. Both expressions in combination are in turn the expression for the fact that despair does not come from without but from within. And in the same degree despair is more and more positive [*ponerende*]. But according to the definition of sin we have formulated, a constituent of sin is the self as infinitely potentiated by the conception of God, and thus in turn it is the greatest possible consciousness of sin as a deed. This is the expression for the fact that sin is a position; the positive factor in it is precisely this, that it is *before* God.

Moreover, the determination of sin as a position involves also, in an entirely different sense, the possibility of offense, the paradox. For the paradox results from the doctrine of the atonement. First Christianity goes ahead and establishes sin so securely as a position that the human understanding never can comprehend it; and then it is the same Christian doctrine which in turn undertakes to do away with this position so completely that the human understanding never can comprehend it. Speculation, which chatters itself away from the paradoxes, lops a little bit off at both ends, and so it goes easier: it does not make sin so entirely positive—and in spite of this it cannot get it through its head that sin should be entirely forgotten.[40] But Christianity, which is the first discoverer of the paradoxes, is in this case also as paradoxical as possible; it works directly against itself when it establishes sin so securely as a position that it seems a perfect impossibility to do away with it again—and then it is precisely Christianity which, by the atonement, would do away with it so completely that it is as though drowned in the sea.

APPENDIX TO I

BUT THEN IN A CERTAIN SENSE DOES NOT SIN BECOME A GREAT RARITY? (THE MORAL)

It was remarked in Part First that the more intense despair becomes, the more rare it is in the world. But now, as we have seen, sin is that despair which has been still further potentiated and qualitatively potentiated, and so this surely must be exceedingly rare! Marvellous objection! Christianity has concluded all under sin; we have endeavored to represent the Christian position as rigorously as possible—and from this results the strange conclusion that sin is not to be found at all in paganism, but only in Judaism and Christianity, and there again only very rarely!

And yet this is (but only in one sense) perfectly correct. "After having been informed by a revelation from God what sin is, then before God in despair not to will to be oneself, or before God in despair to will to be oneself," is to sin—and certainly it is rare for a man to be so developed, so transparent to himself, that this can fit his case. But what logically follows from this? Yea, one may well take heed of this, for here there is a peculiar dialectical turn. From the fact that a man is not in a more intense despair it did not follow that he is not in despair. On the contrary, it was proved precisely that most men, by far the majority of men, are in despair, despair in a lower form. There is no merit in being in despair in a higher degree. Aesthetically it is an advantage, for aesthetically one has regard merely to strength; but ethically the more intense kind of despair is further from salvation than is the lower.

And so it is also in the case of sin. The lives of most men, being determined by a dialectic of indifference, are so remote from the good (faith) that they are almost too spiritless to be called sin, yes, almost too spiritless to be called despair.

To be in the strictest sense a sinner is again very far from being meritorious. But then on the other hand how on earth can one expect to find an essential consciousness of sin (and after all that is what Christianity wants) in a life which is so retarded by triviality, by a chattering imitation of "the others," that one hardly can call it sin, that it is too spiritless to be so called, and fit only, as the Scripture says, to be "spewed out"?

But this is not the end of the matter, for the dialectic of sin merely catches one in another way. For how does it come about that a man's life becomes so spiritless that it is as if Christianity could not be brought into relation to it, as when a jack-screw (and like a jack-screw is the uplifting power of Christianity) cannot be employed because there is no solid ground but only moss and bog? Is this something that befalls a man? No, it is man's own fault. No man is born with spiritlessness, and however many there be who in death bring with them this as the only acquisition of their lives—this is not the fault of life.

But it must be said, and as outspokenly as possible, that the so-called Christendom (in which after a sort all men are Christians in a way, so that there are just as many, precisely as many Christians as there are men)—it must be said that not only is it a wretched edition of Christianity, full of misprints disturbing to the sense, and of senseless omissions and additions, but that it has abusively taken Christianity's name in vain.[41] In a small country there are born hardly three poets in every generation, but of priests there are a plenty, many more than can get appointments. With regard to a poet people speak of his having a call; but as for becoming a priest, it seems enough to the generality of men (and that means of Christians) that one has taken an examination. And yet, alas, a true priest is even more rare than a true poet, and the word "call" originally was used in a religious sense. But with respect to being a poet people still retain a notion that it is something, and that there is something in it that a man is called. On the other hand, to be a priest is in the eyes of the generality of men (and so also of Christians) a thing bereft of every uplifting conception, lacking the least trace of the mysterious, *in puris naturalibus* [i.e., without mincing words] it is a career. "Call" means a benefice; people talk about getting a call; but about having a call—O yes, they talk about being "called" for trumps.

And, alas, the fate of this word in Christendom is like a motto for Christianity as a whole. The misfortune is not that Christian truth is never uttered (just as it is not the misfortune that there are not priests enough), but that it is uttered in such a way that at last the generality of men attach to it no significance whatever (just as the generality of men attach to being a priest no other significance than that which goes with the week-day occupations of a merchant, attorney, book-binder, veterinary, etc.), so that the highest things make no impression at all, but sound out and are heard as something which somehow, God knows how, has become use and wont, like so many other things. What wonder then that certain people, instead of finding their own conduct indefensible, find it incumbent upon them to defend Christianity.

After all, a priest surely ought to be a believer. And think what a believer is! A believer is surely a lover, yea, of all lovers the most in love. With respect to enthusiasm a lover is after all only a stripling in comparison with a believer. Think now of a lover. He would be capable, would he not, day in and day out, as long as it was day and well into the night, of talking about his love. But dost thou believe it could occur to him, dost thou believe it would be possible for him, dost thou not believe that it would be an abomination to him, to talk in such a way as to try to prove by three reasons that there is after all something in this thing of being in love?—pretty much as when the parson proves by three reasons that it is profitable to pray, so that this thing of prayer has sunk so low in price that there must be three reasons alleged to bring it a little bit into repute. Or as when the parson (and this is the same thing, only still more laughable) proves by three reasons that to pray is a bliss surpassing all understanding. Oh, priceless anticlimax! The fact that something surpasses all understanding is proved by three . . . reasons, which, whatever else they may be good for, surely do not surpass the understanding, but precisely on the contrary make it evident to the understanding that this bliss does not surpass the understanding; for, after all, reasons certainly lie within the compass of the understanding. No, for that which surpasses the understanding, and for him who believes in it, the three reasons signify no more than three bottles or three red deer!—And now further. Dost thou believe it would occur to a lover to put up a defense for his love, that is, to admit that to him it was not the absolute, unconditionally the absolute, but that he thinks this thought of love along with objections against it, and from this proceeds the defense; that is to say, dost thou believe that he could or would concede that he was not in love, denounce himself as not being a lover? And in case a man were to propose to a lover to talk thus, dost thou not believe that he would regard that man as mad? And in case, besides being in love, he was something of an observer, dost thou not believe that he would suspect that the man who made to him this proposal had never known what it is to be in love, or would like to get him to betray and deny his love . . . by defending it?—Is it not evident that it could never occur to one who really is in love to want to prove it by three reasons or to defend it? For in fact he himself is that which is more than all reasons and more than every defense—he is a lover. And he who does this is not in love, he merely gives himself out [*udgiver*] to be that, and unfortunately—or fortunately—he does it so stupidly that he merely denounces [*angiver*] himself as one who is not in love.

But this is just the way Christianity is talked about . . . by believing priests. They either "defend" Christianity, or they translate it into "reasons"—if they are not at the same time dabbling in "comprehending" it speculatively. This is what is called preaching, and it is regarded in Christendom as already a big thing that such preaching is done and that some hear it. And it is precisely for this reason that Christendom (here is the proof of it) is so far from being what it calls itself that the lives of most men are, Christianly understood, too spiritless even to be called in a strictly Christian sense sin.

Every state or condition in sin is new sin, or, as it might be more exactly expressed and as it will be expressed in the following, the state of being in sin is the new sin, is emphatically the sin. This seems perhaps to the sinner an exaggeration; he at the most recognizes every actual sin as a new sin. But eternity which keeps his accounts must register the state of being in sin as a new sin. It has only two rubrics, and "everything which is not of faith is sin"; every unrepented sin is a new sin, and every moment it is unrepented is new sin. But how rare is the man who possesses continuity with respect to his consciousness of himself! Generally men are only momentarily conscious, conscious in the great decisions, but the daily things are not computed at all; such men are spirit (if this word may be applied to them) once a week for one hour —of course that is a pretty bestial way of being spirit. Eternity, however, is essential continuity and requires this of man, or requires that he shall be conscious of himself as spirit and shall have faith. The sinner on the other hand is so thoroughly in the power of sin that he has no conception of its totalitarian character, or that he is in the byway of perdition. He takes into account only each individual new sin by which he acquires new headway onward along the path of perdition, just as if the previous instant he were not going with the speed of the previous sins along that same path. So natural has sin become to him, or sin has so become his second nature, that he finds the daily continuance quite a matter of course, and it is only when by a new sin he acquires as it were new headway that for an instant he is made aware. By perdition he is blinded to the fact that his life, instead of possessing the essential continuity of the eternal by being before God in faith, has the continuity of sin.

But, "The continuity of sin!" Is not sin precisely the discontinuous?[42] Lo, here we have again the notion that sin is merely a negation to which one can acquire no title, as one can acquire no title to stolen property, a negation, an impotent attempt to give itself consistency, which nevertheless,

suffering as it does from the torture of impotence in the defiance of despair, it is not able to do. Yes, so it is speculatively;
but Christianly sin is (and this has to be believed, it is indeed
the paradox which no man can comprehend)—sin is a position which out of itself develops a more and more positive
[*ponerende*] continuity.

And the law for the growth of this continuity is moreover
different from the law which applies to a debt or to a negation. For a debt does not grow because it is not paid, it grows
every time it is added to. But sin grows every instant one does
not get out of it. It is as far as possible from being true
that the sinner is right in only regarding every new sin as an
increase of sin—so far from being true that, Christianly understood, the state of remaining in sin is really a greater sin.
We have even a proverb which says that to sin is human, but
to remain in sin is devilish. But Christianly this proverb must
be understood in a rather different sense. The merely desultory way of conceiving the case, which has regard only to the
new sin and passes over the intermediate state, the interval
between the particular sins, is just as superficial a way of
conceiving it as it would be to assume that the railway train
moved only when the locomotive puffed. No, this puffing
and the onrush which succeeds it is really not the thing that
has to be considered, but rather the even momentum with
which the locomotive proceeds and which occasions the
puffing. And so it is with sin. The state of remaining in sin
is in the deepest sense sin, the particular sins are not the
continuation of sin, but they are the expression for the continuation of sin; in the particular new sins the momentum of
sin merely becomes more observable.

The state of being in sin is a worse sin than the particular
sins, it is the sin emphatically, and thus understood it is true
that the state of remaining in sin is the continuation of sin,
is a new sin. Generally one understands this differently, one
understands that the one sin gives birth to new sin. But this
has a far deeper ground for the fact that the state of being in
sin is new sin. Psychologically it is a masterly stroke of
Shakespeare to let Macbeth say (Act iii, Scene 2),
"*Sündentsprossne Werke erlangen nur durch Sünde Kraft und*

Stärke."[43] That is to say, sin is within itself a consistency, and in this consistency of evil within itself it possesses a certain power. But one never reaches such a point of view when one considers merely the particular sins.

Doubtless most men live with far too little consciousness of themselves to have a conception of what consistency is; that is to say, they do not exist *qua* spirit. Their lives (either with a certain childish and lovable naïveté or in sheer banality) consist in some act or another, some occurrence, this or that; and then they do something good, then in turn something wrong, and then it begins all over again; now they are in despair, for an afternoon, perhaps for three weeks, but then they are jovial again, and then again they are a whole day in despair. They take a hand in the game of life as it were, but they never have the experience of staking all upon one throw, never attain the conception of an infinite self-consistency. Therefore among themselves their talk is always about the particular, particular deeds, particular sins.

Every existence which is under the rubric of spirit (even if it is such only on its own responsibility and at its own peril) has essentially consistency within itself, and consistency in something higher, at least in an idea. But again such an existence fears infinitely every inconsistency, because it has an infinite conception of what the consequence may be, that because of it one might be wrenched out of the totality in which one has one's life. The least inconsistency is a prodigious loss, for with that a man in fact loses consistency; that same instant the charm is perhaps broken, the mysterious power which bound all powers in harmony is enfeebled, the spring loses its tension, the whole machinery is a chaos where the forces fight in rebellion against one another, to the injury of the self, and therein there is no accord with oneself, no momentum, no impetus. The prodigious machine which in consistency was so compliant with its iron strength, so pliable with all its power, is in disorder; and the more excellent the machine was, all the more frightful is the confusion.—The believer, who reposes in and has his strength in the consistency of the good, has an infinite fear of even the least sin, for he stands to lose infinitely. The immediate men—the childlike or the childish—have no totality to lose, they constantly lose and win only the particular thing and in the particular instance.

But as with the believer, so it is also with his counterpart, the demoniac man, with respect to the consistency of sin in itself. As the drunkard steadily keeps up the intoxication from day to day, for fear of the languor which would ensue from arresting it, and the possible consequences if for one day he were to remain entirely sober—so it is with the demoniac. Yea, just as the good man, if one were to approach him temptingly, picturing sin in one or another alluring form, would bid him, "tempt me not," so one has instances of exactly the same thing on the part of the demoniac. Face to face with one who is stronger than he in the good, the demoniac, when one would picture to him the good in its blissful sublimity, might beg for himself, beg him with tears in his eyes, that he would not talk to him, would not, as he expresses it, make him weak. Just because the demoniac is consistent in himself and in the consistency of evil, just for this cause he also has a totality to lose. A single instant outside of his consistency, one single dietetic imprudence, one single glance aside, one instant when the whole thing, or at least a part thereof, is seen and understood in a different way— and with that, he would never more be himself, he says. That is, he has given up the good in despair, it could not help him anyway, he says, but it well might disturb him, make it impossible for him ever again to acquire the full momentum of consistency, make him weak. Only in the continuation of sin he is himself, only in that does he live and have an impression of himself. What does this mean? It means that the state of being in sin is that which, in the depth to which he has sunk, holds him together, impiously strengthening him by consistency; it is not the particular new sin which (crazy as it sounds to say it) helps him, but the particular new sin is merely the expression for the state of being in sin which properly is the sin.

By "the continuation in sin," which is the theme we now have to deal with, we are to think not so much of the particular new sins as of the state of being in sin, which in turn becomes the potentiation of sin in itself, an abiding in the state of sin with consciousness thereof, so that the law for the movement in potentiation is, here as everywhere, in the inward direction, in more and more intense consciousness.

1. The Sin of Despairing over One's Sin

Sin is despair, the potentiation of this is the new sin of despairing over one's sin. It can easily be seen moreover that this is characterized as potentiation. It is not a new sin in the sense of repetition, as in the case of a man who once stole $100 and another time steals $1,000. No, it is not a question of particular acts of sin; the state of sin is sin, and this is potentiated in a new consciousness.

Despairing over one's sin is the expression for the fact that sin has become or would become consistent in itself. It will have nothing to do with the good, will not be weak enough to harken once in a while to another sort of talk. No, it will hear only itself, have to do only with itself, shut itself in with itself, yea, enclose itself within one enclosure more and by despair over its sin secure itself against every assault of the good or every aspiration after it. It is conscious of having cut the bridge behind it and so of being inaccessible to the good as the good is to it, so that though in a weak moment it were to will the good, this would nevertheless be impossible. Sin itself is detachment from the good, but despair over sin is a second detachment. This of course tortures out of sin its utmost demoniac powers, bestowing upon it the ungodly hardiness or obduracy which must constantly regard everything which is of the nature of repentance and everything which is of the nature of grace not only as empty and meaningless but as its foe, as the thing which most of all it has to guard against, quite in the same way as the good guards itself against temptation. So understood, it is rightly said by Mephistopheles in *Faust*[44] that nothing is more miserable than a devil who despairs; for by despairing must here be understood unwillingness to hear anything about repentance and grace. To indicate the character of this potentiation from sin to despair over sin one might say that the

former is the breach with the good, the latter is the breach
with repentance.

Despair over sin is an attempt to maintain oneself by sinking still deeper. As one who ascends in a balloon rises by
casting weights from him, so does the despairing man sink
by casting from him the good (for the weight of the good is
uplift), he sinks, doubtless he thinks he is rising—he does
indeed become lighter. Sin itself is the struggle of despair;
but then when strength is exhausted there must needs be
a new potentiation, a new demoniacal introversion, and this
is despair over one's sin. This is a step in advance, an ascent
in the demoniacal, but of course it means sinking deeper in
sin. It is an attempt to impart to sin as a positive power
firmness and interest, by the fact that now it is eternally decided that one will hear nothing about repentance, nothing
about grace. Nevertheless despair over sin is conscious of its
own emptiness, conscious of the fact that it has nothing whatever to live on, not even a lofty conception of one's own self.
Psychologically it is a masterly line Macbeth utters after the
murder when he is in despair over his sin (Act ii, Scene 3):

For, from this instant,
There's nothing serious in mortality:
All is but toys: renown and grace is dead.

The masterly double stroke is in the last words, "*renown
and grace.*" By sin, that is to say, by despairing over his sin,
he has lost every relation to grace—and to himself at the same
time. His selfish self culminates in ambition. Now he has indeed become king, and yet, by despairing over his sin, and
about the reality of repentance, about grace, he has also lost
himself, he cannot even maintain himself in his own eyes, and
he is precisely as far from being able to enjoy his own self
in ambition as he is from grasping grace.

In real life (in so far as despair over sin actually occurs in
life—but there occurs at all events something they call such)
people generally have a mistaken notion of despair over sin,
presumably because in the world one generally has to do with
levity, thoughtlessness and pure prattle, and therefore be-

comes quite solemn and reverently lifts the hat before every
expression of something deeper. Either in confused obscurity
about oneself and one's significance, or with a trace of hy-
pocrisy, or by the help of cunning and sophistry which is
present in all despair, despair over sin is not indisposed to bestow upon itself the appearance of something good. So it is
supposed to be an expression for a deep nature which thus
takes its sin so much to heart. I will adduce an example.
When a man who has been addicted to one sin or another, but
then for a long while has withstood temptation and conquered
—if he has a relapse and again succumbs to temptation, the
dejection which ensues is by no means always sorrow over sin.
It may be something else, for the matter of that it may be ex-
asperation against providence, as if it were providence which
had allowed him to fall into temptation, as if it ought not to
have been so hard on him, since for a long while he had
victoriously withstood temptation. But at any rate it is woman-
ish without more ado to regard this sorrow as good, not to be
in the least observant of the duplicity there is in all passionateness, which in turn has this ominous consequence that at
times the passionate man understands afterwards, almost to
the point of frenzy, that he has said exactly the opposite of
that which he meant to say. Such a man asseverated with
stronger and stronger expressions how much this relapse tortures and torments him, how it brings him to despair, "I can
never forgive myself for it," he says. And all this is supposed to
be the expression for how much good there dwells within him,
what a deep nature he is. In this representation I intentionally
introduced the catchword, "I can never forgive myself for it,"
precisely the word which is commonly used in such a connection. And precisely by this catchword one can orient oneself dialectically. He can never forgive himself for it—but now
in case God would forgive him for it, he might well have the
kindness to forgive himself. No, his despair over sin, and all
the more, the more it storms in the passion of expression,
whereby without being aware of it in the least he informs
against himself when he "never can forgive himself" that he
could sin thus (for this sort of talk is pretty nearly the opposite of penitent contrition which prays God for forgiveness)

—this despair is far from being a characteristic of the good, rather it is a more intensive characterization of sin, the intensity of which is a deeper sinking into sin. The fact is that during the time he victoriously withstood temptation he was in his own eyes better than he actually was, he was proud of himself. It is now in the interest of pride that the past should be something entirely left behind. But in the relapse the past suddenly becomes again entirely present. This reminder his pride cannot endure, and hence the deep distress etc. But the direction of this distress is evidently away from God, manifesting a hidden self-love and pride—instead of humbly beginning by thanking God humbly for helping him so long to withstand temptation, acknowledging before God and before himself that this after all is much more than he had deserved, and so humbling himself under the remembrance of what he had been.

In this instance as usual the explanation given in the old works of edification[45] is so profound, so understanding, so instructive. They teach that God sometimes permits the believer to stumble and fall into one temptation or another—precisely to humble him and thereby confirm him the more in the good; the contrast between the relapse and the perhaps considerable progress in the good is so humiliating, the identity with himself so painful. The better a man is, the more dangerous, in case he does not make the right turn, is even the least little bit of impatience. He may perhaps for sorrow sink into the darkest melancholy—and a fool of a pastor may not be far from admiring his deep soul and the power of good which is in him . . . as though this were the good. And his wife, yea, she feels herself deeply humbled in comparison with such an earnest and holy man who can thus sorrow for his sin. Perhaps his talk is still more deceptive, he perhaps does not say, I can never forgive myself for it (as if before he had forgiven himself for his sins—a blasphemy), no, he talks about God never forgiving him for it. And, alas, this is only a mystification. His sorrow, his concern, his despair, is selfish (like the dread of sin which at times almost frightens a man into sin) because it is self-love which would like to be proud of itself, like to be without sin—and consolation is what he is least in need of, wherefore also the prodigious quantity of consoling thoughts the physicians of the soul prescribe only make the sickness worse.

2. The Sin of Despairing of* the Forgiveness of Sins (Offense)

The potentiation in consciousness of the self is in this instance knowledge of Christ, being a self face to face with Christ. First there came (in Part First) ignorance of having an eternal self; then knowledge of having a self wherein there is after all something eternal. Thereupon (as a transition to Part Second) it was shown that this distinction is referable to the self which has a human conception of itself or whose goal is man. The contrast to this was a self face to face with God, and this was taken as the basis of the definition of sin.

Now comes a self face to face with Christ—a self which nevertheless in despair will not be itself, or in despair will be itself. For despair of the forgiveness of sins must be related to one or the other formula of despair: that of weakness, or that of defiance; that of weakness which being offended does not dare to believe, or that of defiance which being offended will not believe. Only in this case (since here it is not a question about being oneself simply, but about being oneself qua sinner, consequently oneself as characterized by one's imperfection) weakness and defiance are the converse of what they ordinarily are. Ordinarily weakness is: in despair not to will to be oneself.[46] Here this is defiance; for here it is clearly defiance not to will to be the man one is, a sinner, and for this reason to will to dispense with the forgiveness of sins. Ordinarily defiance is: in despair to will to be oneself. Here this is weakness: in despair to will to be oneself, a sinner, in such wise that there is no forgiveness.

A self face to face with Christ is a self potentiated by the prodigious concession of God, potentiated by the prodigious emphasis which falls upon it for the fact that God also for the sake of this self let Himself to be born, became man, suffered,

*Mark the distinction between despairing *over* one's sin, and despairing *of* the forgiveness of sins.

died. As was said in the foregoing, "the more conception of God, the more self," so here it is true that the more conception of Christ, the more self. A self is qualitatively what its measure is. That Christ is the measure is on God's part attested as the expression for the immense reality a self possesses; for it is true for the first time in Christ that God is man's goal and measure, or measure and goal.—But the more self, the more intense the sin.

There is also another side from which the potentiation in sin can be shown. In the first instance we considered that sin was despair, its potentiation was despair over sin. But now God offers reconciliation in the forgiveness of sins. Yet the sinner despairs, and despair acquires a still deeper expression. It now relates itself after a sort to God, but precisely thereby it is still further away, still more deeply sunken in sin. When the sinner despairs of the forgiveness of sins it is almost as if he were directly picking a quarrel with God, it sounds in fact like a rejoinder when he says, "No, there is not any forgiveness of sins, it is an impossibility"; this looks like a hand-to-hand scuffle. But yet a man must remove himself to a qualitative distance from God in order to be able to say this and in order that it may be heard, and in order to fight *cominus* he must be *eminus*;[47] so strangely constructed in an acoustic sense is the world of spirit, so strangely are the relationships of distance arranged. A man must be as far as possible removed from God for that "No" to be heard, while yet in a way he wants to pick a quarrel with God. The greatest possible nearness to God, actually treading on His toes, means to be far off. In order to behave forwardly toward God one must retire far backward; if one is nearer, one cannot be forward, and if one is forward, this signifies *eo ipso* that one is far off. O human impotence in the face of God! When one behaves forwardly toward a man of high station, one may perhaps as a punishment be cast far away from him; but to behave forwardly toward God one must retire backward far from Him.[48]

In real life the sin of despairing of the forgiveness of sins is generally misunderstood, especially now that they have done away with the ethical, so that one seldom or never hears a sound ethical word. Aesthetic-metaphysically it is honored as a sign of a deep nature that one despairs of the forgiveness of sins, pretty much as if one were to regard it as a sign of a deep nature in a child that it is naughty. On the whole it is unbelievable what confusion has invaded the religious sphere since in man's relationship to God there has been abolished the "Thou shalt," which is the only regulative principle. This "Thou shalt" ought to be a part of every definition of the religious; instead of which people have employed fantastically conceptions of God as an ingredient in human self-importance, so as to be self-important over against God. As in political life one becomes important by belonging to the Opposition, and in the last resort may well wish that there should be a government so that one might at least have something to oppose; so in the last resort one does not wish to abolish God—if merely with a view to becoming still more self-important by being the Opposition. And all that which in the old days was regarded with horror as the expression of impious insubordination has now become spirited, the sign of a deep nature. "Thou shalt *believe*," that is what was said in the old days, as soberly as possible and in so many words—now it is spirited and the sign of a deep nature not to be able to do so. "Thou shalt believe in the forgiveness of sins," was what they said, and as the only commentary to this text it was said, "It will go ill with thee if thou canst not, for what one shall do, one can do"—now it is spirited and the sign of a deeper nature not to be able to believe it. Splendid result attained by Christendom! If not a word about Christianity were heard, men would not be so conceited (as paganism never has been at any time); but by the help of the fact that Christian conceptions are unchristianly floating in the air they are employed in the interest of this most potentiated impertinence, in so far as they are not misused in another and equally shameless way. For it surely is very epigrammatic that swearing was after all not customary in paganism but on the other hand is properly at home in Christendom; that paganism generally uttered the name of God with great solemnity, with a certain horror, with a dread of the mysterious, whereas in Christendom the name of God is surely the word which occurs most frequently in daily speech and is absolutely the word to which one attaches the least meaning and uses most carelessly, because this poor revealed God (who was so imprudent and unwise as to become revealed instead of keeping Himself hidden as superior persons always do) has become a personage all too well known by the whole population, to whom one renders an exceedingly great service by going once in a while to church, where one is praised for it by the parson, who on God's behalf thanks one for the honor of the visit, confers upon one the title of pious, and on the other hand taunts a bit those who never do God the honor of going to church.

The sin of despairing of the forgiveness of sins is offense. The Jews were quite right in being offended at Christ because He would forgive sins. It requires a singularly high degree of dullness (that is to say, the sort ordinarily found in Christendom) in case a man is not a believer (and if he is, then he believes that Christ is God) not to be offended at the fact that a man would forgive sins. And in the next place it requires an equally singular degree of dullness not to be offended at the assertion that sin can be forgiven. This is for the human understanding the most impossible thing. Not that I would extoll it as a sign of genius that one is unable to believe this, for it *shall* be believed.

In paganism of course this sin did not exist. If the pagan might have the true conception of sin (but even this he could not have because he lacked the conception of God), he could not get further than to despair over his sin. Yea, what is more (and herein lies all the concession one can make to human understanding and human thinking), one might praise the pagan who really managed to despair, not over the world, not over himself in general, but over his sin.* Humanly speaking,

---

*One will observe that despair over sin is here dialectically conceived in the direction toward faith. That there is this dialectical possibility must never be forgotten, even though this work only deals with despair as sin. This dialectical possibility is due to the fact that despair is also the first factor in faith. On the other hand, when the direction is away from faith, away from the God-relationship, despair over sin is the new sin. In the life of spirit everything is dialectical. Offense is thus, as a possibility annulled, a factor in faith; but offense with a direction away from faith is sin. One can reproach a man for not even being offended at Christianity. When one speaks

both depths of understanding and ethical definitions are requisite for this. No man as such can get further, and seldom does one get so far. But Christianly everything is altered, for thou shalt believe in the forgiveness of sins.

And where does Christendom find itself with reference to the forgiveness of sins? Indeed, the situation of Christendom is really despair over the forgiveness of sins. This, however, must be understood in the sense that Christendom is so backward that it is not even manifest that the situation is such. People have not even reached the consciousness of sin, they know only the kind of sin which paganism also knew, and they live on happily in pagan security. But by the fact that they live in Christendom they go further than paganism, they go on to imagine that this security is . . . consciousness of the forgiveness of sins. Indeed how can it be otherwise in Christendom? In this the parsons confirm the congregation.

The fundamental misfortune of Christendom is really Christianity, the fact that the doctrine of the God-Man (the Christian understanding of which, be it noted, is secured by the paradox and the possibility of offense) is taken in vain, the qualitative distinction between God and man is pantheistically abolished—first speculatively with an air of superiority, then vulgarly in the streets and alleys. Never anywhere has any doctrine on earth brought God and man so near together as has Christianity; neither could anyone else do it, only God Himself can, every human invention remains after all a dream, an uncertain imagination. Neither has any doctrine ever so carefully defended itself against the most shocking of all blasphemies, that after God had taken this step it then should be taken in vain, as though God and man coalesced in one and the same thing—never has any doctrine ever defended itself against this as Christianity has, which defends itself by the help of the offense. Woe unto the slack orators, woe unto the loose thinkers, and woe, woe unto all the adherents who have learnt from them and extolled them!

If order is to be maintained in existence—and that after all is what God wills, for He is not a God of confusion—first and

---

thus, one speaks of being offended as something good, and on the other hand one may say that to be offended is sin.

foremost it must be remembered that every man is an individual man, is himself conscious of being an individual man. If once men are permitted to coalesce into what Aristotle[49] calls "the multitude," a characteristic of beasts, this abstraction (instead of being regarded as less than nothing, as in fact it is, less than the lowliest individual man) will be regarded as something, and no long time will elapse before this abstraction becomes God. And then, why then in fact it corresponds *philosophice* with the God-Man. Then as people in the various nations have learnt that the multitude overawes the King and the daily papers overawe the Privy Council,[50] so then at last they discover that the *summa summarum* of all men overawes God. This then is called the doctrine of the God-Man or the doctrine that God and men are *idem per idem* [identical]. Naturally several of the philosophers who took part in spreading this doctrine of the preponderance of the generations of mankind over the individual now turn away in disgust when their doctrine has sunk so low that the mob is God. But these philosophers forget that after all this was their doctrine, they overlook the fact that it was not more true when the superior men accepted it, when the élite of the superior class or an elect circle of philosophers was the Incarnation.

This means that the doctrine of the God-Man has made Christendom impudent. It almost appears as if God had been too weak. It is as though it had come to pass with Him as with the good-natured man who makes too great a concession and is rewarded by ingratitude. It was God who discovered the doctrine of the God-Man, and now Christendom has got the thing turned topsy-turvy and imputes to God consanguinity, so that the concession God has made means pretty much what in these times it means when a king grants a freer constitution—and one knows well enough what that means, "He pretty well had to." It is as though God had got Himself into an embarrassing situation; it is as though the shrewd man were in the right if he were to say to God, "It is Thine own fault. Why hast Thou put Thyself upon such familiar terms with man? It never would have occurred to anyone, never have entered into any man's heart, that there might be likeness between God and man. It was Thou Thyself that had this proclaimed, now Thou art reaping the fruits."

Yet Christianity has secured itself from the very beginning. It begins with the doctrine of sin. The category of sin is the category of the individual. Speculatively sin cannot be thought at all. The individual man is subsumed under the concept; one cannot think an individual man but only the concept man.— Hence it is that Speculation at once reaches the doctrine of the preponderance of the generations over the individual; for it is not to be expected that Speculation should recognize the *impotence* of the concept in relation to reality.—But as one cannot think an individual man, so neither can one think an individual sinner; one can think sin (then it becomes negative), but not an individual sinner. Just for this reason, however, there can be no seriousness about sin when it is merely thought. For seriousness is precisely the fact that thou and I are sinners. Seriousness is not sin in general, but the emphasis of seriousness falls upon the sinner who is an individual. In relation to "the individual man" Speculation, if it is consistent, must think very scornfully of what it is to be an individual or that it is something which cannot be thought. If it would do anything in this line, it must say to the individual, "Is that anything to waste time on? Above all try to forget it, to be an individual man is not to be anything—think, and then thou art the whole of humanity, *cogito ergo sum*." This, however, might perhaps be a lie, and the individual might be the highest. Yet suppose it is so. But to be entirely consistent Speculation must also say, "The thing of being an individual sinner, that's not to be anything, it is subsumed under the concept, waste no time on it etc." And then what further? Is one perhaps to think sin instead of being an individual sinner?—just as one was exhorted to think the concept of man instead of being the individual man. And then what further? Does a man become himself "sin" by thinking sin? *Cogito ergo sum.* A capital proposal! However, one does not even in this case need to be afraid of becoming sin . . . the pure sin, for sin cannot be thought. This after all Speculation itself might concede, since sin is in fact a falling away from the concept. But not to dispute any longer *e concessis*, the principal difficulty is another. Speculation does not take heed of the fact that in relation to sin the ethical has its place, which employs an emphasis which is the converse of that of Speculation and accomplishes the opposite development; for the ethical does not abstract from reality but goes deeper into reality, operating essentially by the aid of the category of the individual, which is the category overlooked and despised by Speculation. Sin is a characteristic of the individual; it is frivolity and a new sin to act as if it were nothing to be an individual sinner. Here Christianity is in place. It marks a cross before Speculation. It is as impossible for Speculation to get out of this difficulty as for a sailing vessel to sail directly against a contrary wind. The seriousness of sin is its reality in the individual, whether it be thou or I. Speculatively one has to look away from the individual. So it is only frivolously one can talk speculatively about sin. The dialectic of sin is directly contrary to that of Speculation.

Here Christianity begins with the doctrine of sin, and therefore with the individual.* For it is Christianity to be sure

---

*The doctrine of the sin of the human race has often been misused because it has not been noticed that sin, common though it is to all, does not gather men together in a common concept, into a society or a partnership ("any more than out in the churchyard the multitude of the dead constitute a society"), but it splits men into individuals and holds every individual fast as a sinner—a splitting which in another sense is both in correspondence with and teleologically in the direction of the perfection of existence. This men have not observed, and so they have let the fallen race become once for all good again in Christ. And so in turn they have saddled God with an abstraction which, as an abstraction, presumes to claim kinship with Him. But this is a false pretext which only makes men insolent. For if the individual is to feel himself akin to God (and this is the doctrine of Christianity), the whole weight of this falls upon him in fear and trembling, and he must discover (if it were not an old discovery) the possibility of offense. But if the individual is to attain this glory through an abstraction, the thing becomes too easy, and essentially it is taken in vain. The individual does not in this case get the prodigious weight of God, which by humiliation presses down as deeply as it uplifts; the individual imagines that he possesses everything as a matter of course by participating in this abstraction. Being a man is not like being an animal, where the specimen is always less than the species. Man is distinguished from other animals not only by the advantages which are commonly enumerated, but qualitatively by the fact that the individual is more than the species. And this characteristic is again dialectical, it

which has taught this about the God-Man, about the likeness between God and man, but Christianity is a great hater of wanton and impertinent forwardness. By the help of the doctrine of sin and of the individual sinner God and Christ have been secured once for all, and far better than any king, against the nation, the people, the crowd, etc., *item* against every demand for a freer constitution. All these abstractions are before God nonexistent, before God in Christ there live only individual men (sinners)—yet God can well oversee the whole, He can care for the sparrows too. God is wholly a friend of order, and to that end He is Himself present at every point, in every instant, He is omnipresent—which is specified in the text-books as one of the titles by which God is called, which men once in a while think about a little but surely never try to think every instant. His concept is not like that of man under which the individual is subsumed as a thing which cannot be absorbed by the concept, His concept comprises everything, and in another sense He has no concept. God does not help Himself by an abbreviation, He comprehends (*comprehendit*) reality itself, all the individuals; for Him the individual is not subsumed under the concept.

The doctrine of sin, the doctrine that we are sinners, thou and I, which absolutely disperses the "crowd," fixes then the qualitative distinction between God and man more deeply than ever it was fixed anywhere—for again this God alone can do, sin is in fact *before* God etc. In no respect is a man so different from God as in the fact that he is a sinner, as every man is, and is a sinner "before God," whereby indeed the opposites are held together in a double sense: they are held together (*continentur*), not allowed to separate from one another; but by being thus held together the differences display themselves all the more strikingly, as when one speaks of holding colors together, *opposita juxta se posita magis illucescunt*. Sin is the only thing universally predicated of man which cannot in any way, either via *negationis* or via *eminentia*, be affirmed of God.[50a] It may be affirmed of God that He is not

---

means that the individual is a sinner, but then again that it is perfection to be the individual.

finite as man is, and so, *via negationis*, that He is infinite; but to affirm of God that He is not a sinner is blasphemy. As a sinner man is separated from God by a yawning qualitative abyss. And obviously God is separated from man by the same yawning qualitative abyss when He forgives sins. In case it were possible by a converse kind of accommodation to transfer the divine attributes to a human being, in one respect man will never in all eternity come to resemble God, namely, in forgiving sins.

Here then lies the utmost concentration of the offense, which precisely that doctrine has found necessary which teaches the likeness between God and man.

But offense is the most decisive determinant of subjectivity, of the individual man, the most decisive it is possible to think of. Doubtless to think of offense without thinking the offended man is not so impossible as to think of the music of the flute without thinking the flute-player;[51] but after all even thought must admit that offense even more than love is an unreal concept which only becomes real when there is an individual who is offended.

So then offense is related to the individual. And therewith Christianity begins, by making every man an individual, an individual sinner; and now everything that heaven and earth can manage to raise up by way of the possibility of offense (God alone disposing of it) is concentrated in one place—and that is Christianity. Then it says to every individual, "Thou shalt believe," i.e. thou shalt either be offended or thou shalt believe. Not one word more. There is nothing more to add. "Now I have spoken," says God, "in eternity we shall speak together again. In the meanwhile thou canst do what thou wilt, but the Judgment is to come."

What, a judgment! Why, we men have learned, indeed experience teaches, that when there is a mutiny aboard ship or in an army, the guilty are so numerous that the punishment cannot be applied; and when it is a question of the public, "the highly respected cultured public," then not only is there no crime, but, according to the newspapers, upon which one can rely as upon the Gospel or divine revelation, this is the will of God. Why is this? The reason for it is that the concept of judgment corresponds to the individual, one does not pronounce a judgment *en masse*; one can put the people to death *en masse*, play the hose on them *en masse*, flatter them *en masse*, in fine can treat the people in many ways like beasts, but to hold judgment over the people as beasts one cannot do, for one cannot hold judgment over beasts; even though ever so many are judged, if there is to be any seriousness and truth in the judgment, it is each individual who is judged.* Now when the guilty are so numerous it is not humanly possible to do this, therefore one must give the whole thing up, one perceives that there can be no question of any judgment, they are too numerous to be judged, one cannot make them or in any way manage to make them individuals, so one must give up holding judgment.

And since now in our enlightened age when people find all anthropomorphic and anthropathic conceptions of God improper, yet do not find it improper to think of God as a judge in likeness of an ordinary civil judge or solicitor general who cannot get at the rights of such a prolix affair—they conclude then that it will be exactly so in eternity. Therefore only let us hold together and secure ourselves by seeing to it that the parson preachifies in this way. And if there should be an individual who ventured to talk differently, an individual who was foolish enough to make his own life anxious and responsible in fear and trembling, and should then want also to worry others —then let us secure ourselves by regarding him as mad, or, if need be, by putting him to death. If only there are many of us engaged in it, it is not wrong, what the many do is the will of God. To this wisdom, as we know by experience—for we are not inexperienced youths, we do not throw out ill considered words, we talk as men of experience—all men hitherto have submitted, kings and emperors and their excellencies. By the aid of this wisdom all our cattle have been bred up—and, by Jove, God shall also have to submit to it. The thing to do is to become many, a whole lot of us, if we do that, then we are secured against the judgment of eternity.

*Lo, for this reason God is "the Judge" because before him there is no crowd but only individuals.

Yes, doubtless they are secured if it was only in eternity they became individuals. But they were and are before God constantly individuals. A man seated in a glass case is not put to such embarrassment as is a man in his transparency before God. This is the factor of conscience. By the aid of conscience things are so arranged that the judicial report follows at once upon every fault, and that the guilty one himself must write it. But it is written with sympathetic ink and only becomes thoroughly clear when in eternity it is held up to the light, while eternity holds audit over the consciences. Substantially everyone arrives in eternity bringing with him and delivering the most accurate account of every least insignificance which he has committed or has left undone. Therefore to hold judgment in eternity is a thing a child could manage; there is really nothing for a third person to do, everything, even to the most insignificant word is counted and in order. The case of the guilty man who journeys through life to eternity is like that of the murderer who with the speed of the railway train fled from the place where he perpetrated his crime. Alas, just under the railway coach where he sat ran the electric telegraph[52] with its signal and the order for his apprehension at the next station. When he reached the station and alighted from the coach he was arrested. In a way he had himself brought the denunciation with him.

So then despair of the forgiveness of sins is offense. And offense is the potentiation of sin. Generally one hardly thinks of this as sin at all; it is likely that people hardly account offense a sin, and of that therefore they do not talk, but rather of sins, among which offense has no place. Still less do they interpret offense as the potentiation of sin. This is due to the fact that they do not Christianly construct the opposition sin/faith, but sin/virtue.

3. The Sin of Abandoning Christianity *Modo Ponendo*,[53] of Declaring It Falsehood

This is sin against the Holy Ghost. The self is here most despairingly potentiated; it not merely casts away from itself the whole of Christianity, but it makes it a lie and a falsehood.

What a prodigiously despairing conception of itself that self must have!

The potentiation of sin is clearly shown when it is apprehended as a war between man and God where the tactics are changed; the potentiation ascends from the defensive to the offensive. Sin is despair: here one fights by evading. Then came despair over one's sin: here one still is fighting by evasion or by fortifying oneself in the position to which one has retired, but constantly *pedem referens* [foot backwards]. Now the tactic is changed: notwithstanding that sin becomes more and more absorbed in itself, and so withdraws, yet in another sense it comes nearer, becomes more and more decisively itself. Despair of the forgiveness of sins is a definite position directly in the face of the offer of God's compassion; sin is now not entirely in flight, not merely on the defensive. But the sin of abandoning Christianity as a falsehood and a lie is offensive warfare. All the foregoing forms of despair conceded in a way that the adversary is the stronger, but now sin is aggressive.

Sin against the Holy Ghost is the positive form of offense.

The doctrine of Christianity is the doctrine of the God-Man, of kinship between God and men, but in such a way, be it noted, that the possibility of offense is, if I may dare to express it thus, the guarantee whereby God makes sure that man cannot come too near to Him. The possibility of offense is the dialectical factor in everything Christian. Take that away, and then Christianity is not simply paganism but something so fantastic that paganism might well declare it bosh. To be so near to God as Christianity teaches that man can come to Him, and dare come to Him, and shall come to Him in Christ, has never entered into any man's head. If this then is to be understood bluntly, just as a matter of course, without the least reservation, to be taken quite unconcernedly and flippantly—then, if paganism's poetic fiction about the gods might be called human craziness, Christianity might be the invention of a crazy god; such a doctrine could only occur to a god who had lost his wits—so a man must judge who had kept his wits. The incarnate God, if man wanted to be as it were a chum of His, would be an apt counterpart to Prince Henry in Shakespeare.

God and man are two qualities between which there is an infinite qualitative difference. Every doctrine which overlooks this difference is, humanly speaking, crazy; understood in a godly sense, it is blasphemy. In paganism man made God a man (the Man-God); in Christianity God makes Himself man (the God-Man)—but in the infinite love of His compassionate grace He made nevertheless one stipulation, He can do no other. This precisely is the sorrow in Christ: "He can do no other";[54] He can humble Himself, take the form of a servant, suffer and die for man, invite all to come unto Him, sacrifice every day of His life and every hour of the day, and sacrifice His life—but the possibility of the offense He cannot take away. Oh, unique work of love! Oh, unfathomable sorrow of love! that God Himself cannot, as in another sense He does not will, cannot will it, but, even if He would, He could not make it impossible that this work of love might not turn out to be for a person exactly the opposite, to be the extremest misery! For the greatest possible human misery, greater even than sin, is to be offended in Christ and remain offended. And Christ cannot, "Love" cannot render this impossible. Lo, for this reason He says, "Blessed is he who shall not be offended in me." More He cannot do. So then He may (that is possible), He may by His love have the effect of making a man more miserable than ever in any other way he could become. Oh, unfathomable contradiction in love! But for all that, in love, He cannot find the heart to leave unfinished the work of love. Alas, if then this were to make a man more miserable than ever in any other way he could become!

Let us talk of this quite humanly.[55] Ah, wretched is the man who never has felt the compelling urge of love to sacrifice everything out of love, and who accordingly has not been able to do it! But then when he discovered that precisely this sacrifice of his out of love might possibly occasion the other, the loved one, the greatest unhappiness—what then? Then either love within him lost its resilience, from being a life of power collapsed into the introverted rumination of a sad sentiment, he was a deserter to love, he did not venture to perform this work of love, himself sinking down, not under this work, but under the weight of this possibility. For just as a weight is infinitely heavier when it is attached to the end of a rod and the man who lifts it has to hold the opposite end, so every work becomes infinitely harder when it becomes dialectic, so that what love prompts one to do for the beloved, care for the beloved seems again in another sense to dissuade from doing.—Or else love conquered, and he ventured to do this work out of love. Oh, but in the joyfulness of love (as love always is joyful, especially when it sacrifices all) there was nevertheless a deep sorrow—for this sad result indeed was possible! Behold, he therefore brought to completion this work of love, he offered the sacrifice (in which for his part he exulted), but not without tears. Over this—what shall I call it?—historical painting of inward life there hovered that dark possibility. And yet, if this had not hovered over it, his work would not have been that of true love—O my friend, what hast thou maybe attempted to do in life? Tax thy brain, tear off every covering and lay bare the *viscera* of feeling in thy breast, surmount every barrier which separates thee from him of whom thou readest, and then read Shakespeare—and thou shalt shrink from the collisions. But Shakespeare himself seems to have shrunk back from the genuinely religious collisions. Perhaps these can only be expressed in the language of the gods. And this language no man can speak; for, as a Greek[56] already has said so beautifully, "From men man learns to speak, from the gods to keep silent."

That there is an infinite difference of quality between God and man is the possibility of offense which cannot be taken away. Out of love God becomes man; He says, "Look what it is to be a man"; but He adds, "O take heed, for at the same time I am God—blessed is he who shall not be offended in me." As man He assumes the lowly form of a servant. He expresses what it is to be a lowly man, to the intent that no one shall think himself excluded, or think that it is human prestige or prestige among men which brings one nearer to God. No, he is the lowly man. "Look hither," He says, "and learn what it is to be a man; O but take heed, for at the same time I am God—blessed is he who shall not be offended in me." Or conversely, "I and the Father are one, and yet I am this particular lowly man, poor, forsaken, delivered into the hands of men—blessed is he who shall not be offended in me. I, this lowly man, am He who maketh the deaf to hear, the blind to see, the lame to walk, the leper to be cleansed, the dead to rise up—blessed is he who shall not be offended in me."

Under accountability to the highest seat of authority I therefore make bold to say that these words, "blessed is he who shall not be offended in me," belong essentially to the preaching about Christ, if not in the same way as the words of institution at the Holy Communion, yet at least like the words, "let every man examine himself." They are Christ's own words, and they must (especially in Christendom) be again and again enjoined, repeated, addressed to every man severally. Everywhere* where these words do not resound, or at least wherever the statement of Christianity is not at every point permeated by this thought—there Christianity is blasphemy. For without a bodyguard, without servants who might prepare His way and make men attentive to who it was that came, Christ walked here upon earth in the lowly form of a servant. But the possibility of offense (O how great a sorrow this was to Him in His love!) defended Him and defends Him, fixes a yawning abyss between Him and the man who was closest to Him and stood nearest.

For he who is not offended worships in faith. But to worship (which is the expression of faith) is to express the consciousness that the infinite yawning abyss of quality is fixed between them. For in faith again the possibility of offense is the dialectical factor.†

*And such is now the case almost everywhere in Christendom, which, as it seems, either entirely ignores the fact that Christ Himself it is who so frequently and with such heartfelt emphasis warned against offense, even at the end of His life, and even when He addressed His faithful Apostles who had followed Him from the beginning and for His sake had forsaken all—or maybe silently regards this as an extravagant apprehension on the part of Christ, inasmuch as the experience of thousands and thousands proves that one can have faith in Christ without having noticed the least trace of the possibility of offense. But this might be a mistake which surely will be made evident when the possibility of offense shall judge Christendom.

†Here is a little task for acute observers. In case one assumes that all the many parsons here and in foreign lands who deliver and

But the sort of offense here in question is *modo ponendo*, it affirms of Christianity that it is a falsehood and a lie, and therefore affirms the same of Christ.

To illustrate this sort of offense it is best to pass in review the various forms of offense which are fundamentally related to the paradox (Christ), and then with every definition to come back to the Christian conception, for every such definition is related to Christ, has Christ *in mente*.

The lowest form of offense, that which, humanly speaking, is the least guilty, is to let the whole question about Christ remain undecided and to judge in this fashion: "I do not presume to pass any judgment; I do not believe, but I pass no judgment." That this is a form of offense escapes the attention of most men. The fact is that people have clean forgotten the Christian "thou shalt." Therefore it is that they do not perceive that this is offense, this thing of treating Christ as a matter of indifference. The fact that Christ is preached to thee signifies that thou shalt have an opinion about Christ. The judgment that He is, or that He exists, or that He has existed, is the decision for the whole of existence. If Christ is preached to thee, it is offense to say, "I will have no opinion about it."

This however must be understood with a certain qualification in these times, inasmuch as Christianity is so poorly preached as it now is. There doubtless are living thousands of men who have heard Christ preached and have never heard a word about this "shall." But he who has heard it and says, "I will have no opinion about it," is offended. For he denies the

---

write sermons are believing Christians, how can it be explained that one never hears or reads a prayer which in our time especially is so pertinent: "God in heaven, I thank Thee that Thou hast not required it of man that he should comprehend Christianity; for if that were required, I should be of all men the most miserable. The more I seek to comprehend it, the more incomprehensible it appears to me, and the more I discover merely the possibility of offense. Therefore I thank Thee that Thou dost only require faith, and I pray Thee to increase it more and more." This prayer would from the point of view of orthodoxy be entirely correct, and, assuming that it is true in the man who prays, it at the same time would be correct as irony upon Speculation as a whole. But is faith I wonder to be found on earth?

divinity of Christ when he denies that it has a right to require
a man to have an opinion. It is of no avail for such a man to
say, "I do not affirm anything about Christ, either yes or no";
for then one has only to ask, "Hast thou then no opinion as to
whether thou shalt have an opinion about this or not?", and
if he replies, "Well, yes," he has trapped himself; and if he
replies, "No," then Christianity condemns him all the same,
requiring that he shall have an opinion about Christianity and
also about Christ, that no one shall presume to treat Christ as
a curiosity. When God lets Himself be born and becomes man,
this is not an idle notion of His, something that occurs to Him
as a way of undertaking something to put an end after all to
the boredom which people have been impudent enough to
say must be associated with being God—it is not for the
interest of an adventure. No, when God does this it is the
seriousness of existence. And the seriousness in this seriousness
is that every one *shall* have an opinion about it. When a king
visits a provincial town he regards it as an affront if without
sufficient excuse an office-bearer in the town fails to do him
homage. But what I wonder would he judge if one were to
ignore entirely the fact that the King was in town, were to
behave as a private person who on such an occasion "doesn't
care a fig for His Majesty and the royal law"? And so it is
also when it pleases God to become man—that then it pleases
a man (and what the office-bearer is to the King, that is every
man before God) to say of it, "Well, that's something about
which I don't wish to have any opinion." So it is one speaks
superciliously of that upon which one essentially looks down—
and so one superciliously looks down upon God.

The next form of offense is the negative but passive form.
It feels to be sure that it is not able to ignore Christianity, it
is not capable of letting all that about Christ remain in doubt,
and then being for the rest busy about life. But neither does
it believe; it continues to stare at one and the same point, the
paradox. To that extent it honors Christianity after all, it gives
expression to the conviction that the question, "What think
ye of Christ?", is the most decisive question. Such an offended
man lives on like a shadow; his life is consumed because in his
inmost soul he is constantly preoccupied with this decision.

And thus he attests (as the suffering of unhappy love attests the reality of love)—he attests what a reality Christianity possesses.

The last form of offense is that about which we are speaking in this chapter, the positive form. It declares that Christianity is a falsehood and a lie, it denies Christ (that He existed and that He is what He claimed to be) either docetically or rationalistically, so that Christ either does not become a particular man except apparently, or He becomes only a particular man, so that He either becomes docetically, poetry and mythology which make no claim to reality, or rationalistically, a reality which makes no claim to be divine. In this denial of Christ as the paradox there is naturally implied the denial of everything Christian: sin, the forgiveness of sins, etc.

This form of offense is sin against the Holy Ghost. As the Jews said of Christ that He cast out devils by the help of the devil, so does this form of offense make of Christ an invention of the devil.

This offense is the highest potentiation of sin, which is a fact people generally overlook inasmuch as they do not Christianly construct the opposition sin/faith.

On the other hand, this opposition is affirmed in the whole of this work, which straightway in the first section (I.A) constructed the formula for the situation where no offense at all is to be found: "By relating itself to its own self and by willing to be itself, the self is grounded transparently in the Power which constituted it." And this formula again, as has often been noted, is the definition of faith.

(I am indebted for most of these notes to the editors of the Danish edition of S.K.'s Complete Works.)

1 The story of Tarquin's son at Gabii is told in the Introduction.

2 The Preface is aimed especially at Martensen's review of J. L. Heiberg's "Introductory Lectures to Speculative Logic," *Danske Maanedskrift*, No. 16 for 1836, pp. 515ff.

3 Descartes is mentioned here because Martensen made appeal to him in the article mentioned in the preceding note.

4 Remembering, however, as I have already said, that the natural light is to be trusted only in so far as nothing to the contrary is revealed by God Himself. . . . Moreover, it must be fixed in one's memory as the highest rule, that what has been revealed to us by God is to be believed as the most certain of all things; and even though the light of reason should seem most clearly to suggest something else, we must nevertheless give credence to the divine authority only, rather than to our own judgment. (*Principia philosophiae, pars prima* 28 and 76.)

5 Let no one think that I am here about to propound a method which everyone ought to follow in order to govern his reason aright; for I have merely the intention of expounding the method I myself have followed. . . . But no sooner had I finished the course of study at the conclusion of which one is ordinarily adopted into the ranks of the learned, than I began to think of something very different from that. For I became aware that I was involved in so many doubts, so many errors, that all efforts to learn were, as I saw it, of no other help to me than that I might more and more discover my ignorance (*Dissertatio de methodo*, pp. 2 and 3).

6 Martensen gave such "promises" in the article referred to in notes 2 and 3.

7 S.K.'s contemptuous way of referring to the *Berlingske Tidende*, a newspaper owned and edited by his *bête noire*, the wholesale merchant Nathanson. This advertisement attracted particular attention because the enterpris-

ing young gardener accompanied it with a sketch of himself in the ingratiating attitude here described.

8 In J. L. Heiberg's *The Reviewer and the Beast*, Trop tears his own tragedy, *The Destruction of the Human Race*, into two equal pieces, remarking, "Since it doesn't cost more to preserve good taste, why shouldn't we do it?"

9 Only three years before this the first omnibus was seen in Copenhagen.

10 One might blamelessly be in doubt how to translate this title (as the four translators into German, French and English have been) had not S.K. himself indicated (IV B 81) that he here uses the word *Stemning* in the sense of προοιμιον, the Greek word which gives us proem. I have preferred to use the word prelude because it will be more commonly understood. Cf. IV A 93.

11 Genesis, Chapter 22.

12 Judith 10:11. S.K. quotes this passage in the *Postcript*. Cf. III A 197.

13 Alluding to various passages in Homer (e.g. *Iliad* III 381) where a divinity saves a hero by enveloping him in a cloud and carrying him away. We discover additional pathos in this picture of the "lover" when we remember that at the end of *The Point of View* (pp. 62f. and 100ff.) S.K. looks for the coming of his poet, his lover.

14 It is evident from the sequel that Jeremiah is meant.

15 Here we have a glimpse of "repetition."

16 Cf. Plato's *Phaedrus*, 22 and 37.

17 In Oelenschläger's play *Aladdin* the hero is contrasted with Noureddin the representative of darkness.

18 Isaiah 26:18.

19 Themistocles, as related in Plutarch's *Themistocles*, 3, 3.

20 Eleven months later (with only one pseudonymous work intervening) S.K. published *The Concept of Dread*, and this remained one of his most distinctive categories. Although all have agreed to use the word "dread," no one can think it adequate as a translation of *Angst*. For though it denotes the presentiment of evil it does not sufficiently emphasize the anguish of the experience.

21 The connection requires a masculine pronoun, but Regina is meant, and she must have known it, for such were her words when she refused to give Kierkegaard back his freedom.

22 As Professor Martensen had claimed to do (*Danske Maanedskrift*, No. 16 referred to in note 2 above. Cf. I A 328, p. 130). But Sibbern too claimed for Heiberg that he "goes beyond Hegel" (the same review, No. 10, year 1838, p. 292).

23 Quoted from Horace's *Letters*, I, 18, 84: "It's your affair when the neighbor's house is afire."

24 The reader may need to be apprised that Johannes de silentio is in that religious stage which by Johannes Climacus in the *Postscript* is called "religiousness A," the basis of all religiousness, but therefore not the distinctively Christian position, which here is called "religiousness B," or the paradoxical religiousness which is characterized by faith in the strictest sense.

25 This is decidedly autobiographical.

26 S.K. attributed his spinal curvature to a fall from a tree when he was a child.

27 The reader who has not heard or has not heeded S.K.'s warning not to attribute to him personally a single word the pseudonyms say may need here to be reminded that it is not S.K. who reiterates so insistently that he cannot understand Abraham. It is Johannes de silentio who says this, and the purpose of it is to emphasize the fact that the paradoxical religiousness (religiousness B) is and remains a paradox to everyone who stands on a lower plane, even to one who has got so high as to be able to make the movement of infinite resignation, so long as his religion is in the sphere of immanence.

28 Introduced about 1840 in Cophenhagen.

29 The "princess" is of course the most obvious analogue to Regina, and one which she could not fail to discover; but every other reader may need the hint that in this whole paragraph S.K. describes his own act of resignation.

30 At the time of his engagement S.K. registered in his Journal the observation that certain insects die the instant they fertilize their mate, and he repeated this in the sixth Diapsalm of *Either/Or*.

31 "A blissful leap into eternity."

32 Cf. what is said in *Repetition* about the young man who "recollects" his love as soon as he is engaged. It is quoted in my *Kierkegaard*, p. 212.

33 It seems clear enough that this passage was written after

S.K. learned of Regina's engagement, and the tone of it suggests that he had had time to repent of the very different language he used when he rewrote *Repetition*. It is therefore an additional argument for the view that this book was written later than the other.

34 "The pre-established harmony" was a fundamental concept of Leibnitz's philosophy.

35 See *Magyarische Sagen* by Johan Graf Mailáth (Stuttgart u. Tübingen 1838), Vol. II, p. 18. Cf. *Journal* II A 449.

36 An entry in the *Journal* (IV A 107) dated May 17 [1843], at the time, that is, when he was composing these two works in Berlin, S.K. says: "If I had had faith, I would have remained with Regina." He was then only a knight of infinite resignation, but he was in the way of becoming a knight of faith.

37 It would have been well had I remarked earlier that the Danish words *resignere* and *Resignation* have a more active sense than we attach to the word "resignation," that they imply an act rather than a passive endurance of a situation, and therefore could be translated by "renounce," "renunciation"—yet it would not do to dub our knight the knight of renunciation.

38 See Rosenkranz, *Erinnerungen an Karl Daub* (Berlin 1837), p. 2. Cf. *Journal* IV A 92.

39 S.K. liked to be called "Master of Irony" in view of the big book on *The Concept of Irony* by which he won his degree of Master of Arts.

40 A Greek word meaning end or goal—which S.K. writes with Greek letters but I transliterate because it is of such common occurrence, and also because it is in the way of becoming an English word.

41 This is the conception of the ethical which is stressed in the Second Part of *Either/Or*. Perhaps Schrempf is right in affirming that what caused S.K. unnecessary agony was his acceptance of the Hegelian notion of the relation between the universal and the particular.

42 Cf. *Philosophie des Rechts*, 2nd ed. (1840) §§129–141 and Table of Contents p. xix.

43 The Trojan war. When the Greek fleet was unable to set sail from Aulis because of an adverse wind the seer Calchas announced that King Agamemnon had offended Artemis

and that the goddess demanded his daughter Iphigenia as a sacrifice of expiation.

44 See Euripides, *Iphigenia in Aulis*, v. 448 in Wilster's translation. Agamemnon says, "How lucky to be born in lowly station where one may be allowed to weep." The confidants mentioned below are Menelaus, Calchas and Ulysses. Cf. v. 107.

45 Jephtha. Judges 11:30–40.

46 The sons of Brutus, while their father was Consul, took part in a conspiracy to restore the king Rome had expelled, and Brutus ordered them to be put to death.

47 This is temptation in the sense we ordinarily attach to the word. For temptation in a higher sense (*Anfaegtelse*) I have in the translation of other books used the phrase "trial of temptation." Professor Swenson, in an important passage in the *Postscript*, preferred to use the German word *Anfechtung*. In this work I have used "temptation" and added the German word in parentheses. The distinction between the two sorts of temptation is plainly indicated by S.K. in this paragraph.

48 This is the Scriptural word which we translate by "offense" or "stumbling block." Only Mr. Dru has preferred to use the identical word "scandal."

49 *Docents* and *Privatdocents* (both of them German titles for subordinate teachers in the universities) were very frequently the objects of S.K.'s satire. He spoke more frequently of "the professor" after Martensen had attained that title.

50 It would be interesting and edifying to make an anthology of the passages in which S.K. speaks of the Blessed Virgin; for surely no Protestant was ever so much engrossed in this theme, and perhaps no Catholic has appreciated more profoundly the unique position of Mary.

51 In *Auszüge aus den Literatur-Briefen*, 81st letter, in Maltzahn's ed. Vol. vi, pp. 205ff.

52 E.g. Hegel's *Logik*, ii, Book 2, Sect. 3, Cap. C (*Werke* IV, pp. 177ff.; *Encyclopedie* I §140 (*Werke* VI, pp. 275ff.).

53 It appears from the *Journal* (I A 273) that S.K. had in mind Schleiermacher's "Theology of Feeling," and also (with not so obvious a justification) the dogmatists of the

Hegelian school. The Danish editors refer to Marheineke, *Dogmatik*, 2nd ed. §§70, 71, 86.

54 Unexpected.

55 In this particular instance S.K. could define precisely what he understood by Isaac, that is, Regnia; and the formlessness of this sentence was intentional—it is a smoke-screen.

56 The Danish editors refer to Bretschneider's Lexicon; but no language lacks "exegetical aids" which serve the purpose of emasculating the New Testament. In this instance the absolute word "hate" is weakened successively by each term used to define it: "feel dislike," "love less," "put in a subordinate place," "show no reverence," "regard as naught."

57 The Hebrew consonants *yodh* and *vav* originally indicated vowel sounds, and when the vowel sounds came to be written below the consonants these letters became superfluous in this respect and were said to repose (*hvile*) in the vowel. So S.K. understood the situation in his *Journal* II A 406, but here he has inverted it.

58 Fabius Maximus who in 217 B.C. conducted the war against Hannibal and received the appellation of Cunctator for his successful strategy of delay or procrastination.

59 Public property.

60 A play by Olussen, which in Act ii, Scene 10 and elsewhere speaks of "two witnesses" but not of beadles (*Stokkemændene*) i.e. four men appointed to attend legal proceedings as witnesses.

61 The corresponding passages are Deut. 13:6f. and 33:9; Matt. 10:37; 19:29. In the manuscript 1 Cor. 7:11 is spoken of as a "similar" passage, but not with good reason.

62 Two parts of the myth, viz. change and recognition, have to do with this [about which he has been talking].

63 The word is literally "carrom." The Danish editors explain that it means here to coincide at the same instant. Thus Oedipus by "recognizing" who he is brings about a "change" in his fortune.

64 Oedipus in Sophocles' tragedy of that name.

65 Iphigenia in Euripides' *Iphigenia in Tauris*.

66 In his *Natural History*, V, 4, 7. Cf. *Journal* IV A 36.

67 Book viii (5), Cap. 3, 3.

68 Title of a Roman priesthood, which S.K. (I know not for what reason) applies here to the Greek soothsayers.

69 Vol. I, §§1 and 2—p. 10 in Maltzahn's ed.

70 Theology of pilgrims—contrasted with *theologia beatorum*, an ancient division no longer in vogue.

71 It is to be remembered that S.K. believed his marriage was prohibited by a "divine veto." Hence the prospective bridegroom of Delphi presents the closest analogy to his situation. In fact, the *Journal* shows that every line of conduct contemplated in this passage was seriously considered by S.K.—even the possibility of a "romantic union" without marriage. But it was the second line of conduct he chose.

72 Axel and Valborg are the pair of unhappy lovers most celebrated in Danish literature. Because of their close consanguinity the Church forbade their marriage.

73 This in fact was S.K.'s position.

74 Cf. Lessing, *Hamburgische Dramaturgie*, Vol. I, art. 22 (in Maltzahn's ed. VII, p. 96).

75 Nowhere, not even in the *Journal*, has S.K. so perfectly described the modest confidence with which Regina committed herself to him.

76 It is found in the fairy tale of "Beauty and the Beast" (Molbeck, No. 7), but not in the legend of "Agnes and the Merman."

77 Cf. the *Stages*, pp. 193ff.

78 S.K. uses here the word "emotion," but it is clear that he has in mind what a modern psychology has called *libido*.

79 Letter of credit on happiness. See Schiller's "Resignation," 3rd strophe (*Gedichte, 2te Periode*).

80 For no one ever has escaped from love or ever will so long as there be beauty and eyes to see with. Longus, *Daphnis and Chloë*. Introduction, §4. Cf. *Journal* IV A 30.

81 Unfortunately the Danish word *bedrage* means to defraud as well as to deceive. I seek to straddle both meanings (imperfectly) by using the word "cheat."

82 So it was S.K. was accustomed to think of himself. How ingenious of him to make this story fit his case by the device of "supposing" Sarah was a man!

83 *The Jew*, a play by Cumberland which was many times presented at the Royal Theater in Copenhagen between 1795 and 1834 and was published in a Danish translation

in 1796. Scheva the Jew every one regarded as a miser and a usurer, but in secret he did great works of beneficence.

84 In *Kirkegaarden in Sobradise* (Danske Værker, I, p. 282).

85 There never was great genius without some madness. As quoted by Seneca (*de tranquilitate animi*, 17, 10) from Aristotle the phrase is: *sine mixtura dementiae*. S.K. quoted it in his *Journal* (IV A 148) at a time when he was anxiously inquiring whether his state of mind might not be close to madness.

86 If before the beginning of this century S.K. had been widely known in Europe, we would trace to him rather than to Dostoevski or any other the modern preoccupation with such topics.

87 It is to be remembered that in his university days S.K. was absorbingly interested in the legends of Faust, Don Juan, and Ahsverus (the Wandering Jew), which he took to be typical of doubt, sensuality and despair. The following footnote deals with other themes which interested him at the same time. He wrote a big book (his dissertation for the master's degree) on *The Concept of Irony*, and he made preparation for a work on satire.

88 In one financial crisis S.K.'s father increased his fortune by investing in bonds issued by the Crown (i.e. on the credit of the absolute sovereign), and in a later crisis S.K. lost much of his by investing in the same security.

89 The honor of destroying. Herostratus, to make his name immortal, burnt the temple of Artemis at Ephesus in the year 356 B.C.

90 Executioner of infants. This name was given to this Augustinian monk (who was Professor in the University of Paris and died in 1358) because he maintained the view that unbaptized infants went to hell—instead of the limbo to which the common Catholic view consigned them. *Tortor heroum* means torturer (executioner) of heroes.

91 Holberg's *Erasmus Montanus*, Act i, Scene 3: Peter Deacon says (about bargaining for the price of a grave), "I can say to a peasant, 'Will you have fine sand or simple earth?' "

92 *Werke* (2nd ed.), VIII, pp. 195ff; X, 1, pp. 84ff.; XIV, pp. 53ff.; XVI, pp. 486ff.

93 Adherents of Grundtvig who advocated his doctrine of the Church.

94 This is S.K.'s word, and here it means, leaping from one point to another so as to illuminate the subject from all sides, or in order that the unintelligibility might be broken down into its several parts.

95 Shakespeare's *King Richard III*, Act II, Scene 1.

96 Plato's *Apology*, Cap. 25. The best texts now read "thirty votes," but in the older editions "three" was commonly read.

97 "The Tailor in Heaven," one of Grimm's *Fairy Tales*. But according to Grimm the tailor was really dead (2nd German ed., I, p. 177).

98 Cf. the *Journal*, IV A 58.

1 In Danish the verb *ville* always implies volition more clearly than the verb "will" in English, and here the notion of volition is prominent, so that the sense might be rendered by the half colloquial expression, to want to be (or not to want to be) one's own self, or even by a stronger expression of resolute choice. But though this phrase recurs many times throughout the book it may suffice to apprise the reader once for all of the significance of it. In all these definitions the *self* is so emphatic that it might be better to say one's self, but I stick to the common idiom.

The abstract definitions of the self contained in this first section (A) are crucial for the understanding of the whole work—and they are indeed a crux for the translator. When I quoted them in my *Kierkegaard* I translated *forholde sig til* by "relate oneself to." Professor Swenson chided me for that. He asserted that the verb was neither reflexive nor active and therefore wrote "is related to." Because a passive sense did not seem to me in place here I used throughout this book the quasi active expression "stands related to." But then there came along a Danish lady, who herself had translated this whole work, and urged on by Professor Reinhold Niebuhr she tried in many letters to convince me of my mistake. She asserted that Swenson and I were equally wrong and totally wrong. Finally the question was decided by an umpire whom we both considered competent, Dr. Alfred T. Dorf, Pastor of the Danish Church of Our Saviour in Brooklyn. After consultation with other eminent Danish authorities he decided against the objector—but also against Swenson. His translation was, "relate oneself to." Such are the tribulations of a conscientious translator. It is much easier, as Dr. Dorf remarked, to do as many German translators do . . . "skip the difficult passages." In this case I do not repine at the criticism which liberated me from the inferiority complex which compelled me to compromise, nor did I grudge the pains I was put to in altering the phrase throughout my manuscript. Dr. Dorf's translation of the "formula" in the last sentence of this section is: "by relating itself to its own self and by maintaining its identity the self has its clarified formulation in the power which established it." This is a paraphrase which may perhaps help the reader to a clearer understanding of this important formula, but in the text I prefer as usual to stick to a more literal rendering.

2 Anti-Climacus doubtless refers here to Johannes Climacus the pseudonymous author of the *Fragments*, p. 60.

3 *Aut Caesar aut nullus* was the motto of Caesar Borgia.

4 The reference is to Fichte's doctrine of the *productive Einbildungskraft* in which he sought the conception of an environing world, the "not-I," and also the necessary forms of thought (the categories) etc. Cf. *Grundriss des Eigenthümlichen der Gewissenschaftslehre*, in the *Werke*, I, 1, pp. 386ff.

5 An orchestra of sixty men, each with a horn which produced only one note.

6 The quotation marks here are more significant than might appear at first sight, for the lines put in the mouth of the man in despair are in fact quoted from S.K.'s *Journal* where they were registered to characterize his own despair when he had reached the limit of the aesthetic life. The reader may need to be apprised at this point that this treatise, which is so objective in form, is an exquisitely personal document, in large part an analysis of the author's own experience. In his melancholy more than one form of despair was exhibited (or rather concealed). Hence his competence as a psychologist of despair.

7 There was at least one moment in his life when S.K. had a poignant experience of this form of despair. That was when he learned of Regina's engagement to another. After the desperate breach of his engagement to her he had in some measure succeeded in "procuring possibility by the inventiveness of human imagination" (to employ a phrase found here in the next paragraph but one). This effort is exhibited in his first three works: *Either/Or*, *Repetition*, and *Fear and Trembling*. But now it was proved to him that "the sum and substance of his sentiment was bosh" (to quote words he registered at that time in his *Journal*); and he describes his situation vividly in the last chapter of *The Concept of Dread*,

entitled "Dread as a means of salvation in conjunction with faith," from which I have quoted the most pertinent paragraph on pp. 261f. of my *Kierkegaard*. In that passage he dwells not so much upon the terrible experience of despair through loss of possibility, as upon the salvation which may be wrought from and by despair. One can be sure that what he writes here in the following paragraphs (whether it be about the horror of despair, or about salvation by faith that with God all things are possible) reflects his own experience. Precisely with respect to those passages in this book which deal with his own experience the reader will not be inclined to judge that "the form of exposition is too strict to be edifying."

8 Truth is the criterion of itself and of falsehood—quoted loosely from Spinoza's *Ethics*, Propositio 11, Scholium 43.

9 Cf. Diogenes Laertius, 2, 5, 31.

10 That is to say, the piece of music by which the enchantment was wrought. Cf. Grimm's *Irische Elfenmärchen*, p. xxxiii. S.K. frequently refers to this tale. In the first instance he registered it in his *Journal* at the time of his conversion, applying it to his own sorry plight when he found himself obliged to retrace as it were the path he had trod in his dissolute youth. His aesthetical works were his effort to play the music backwards.

11 Augustine, *De civitate Dei*, 19, 25.

12 This applies to the Stoics, but Plato, like S.K., regarded suicide as rebellion against God.

13 Goethe's *Faust*, I, 1479.

14 Virgil's *Aeneid*, 2, 325.

15 S.K. often used the technical terms of Latin grammar which was a favorite study in his youth.

16 *Indeslutethed*. There is no English word which adequately translates this, therefore I have often translated it in other works inadequately as "close reserve," and sometimes diffidently by the modern term introversion. Since others have adopted this latter word, I make bold (though it is an evident anachronism) to employ it here and in the sequel.

17 It may be well to apprise the reader beforehand that this is the way (precisely with such baffling complications of thought) young Kierkegaard talked in the days of his despair, as we hear him for example talking through the

mouth of the "young friend" of the Judge in the Second Part of *Either/Or*.

18 Shakespeare's *Richard III*, Act iv, Scene 4. He ordered the trumpets to be blown.

19 S.K. was such a man: he was unable to get along without a confidant, but was equally unable to confide in anyone. Like his melancholy father he felt the need of a "good old father-confessor," but even when his melancholy was relieved he could make confession to no one but God—except as he did it anonymously (and copiously) through the mouths of his pseudonyms.

20 Gen. 1:1.

21 In terms substantially equivalent S.K. describes himself in the character of the "young friend" in the Second Part of *Either/Or*. This in fact was the kind of despair he most obviously exhibited.

22 This word is enough to make a reader who knows S.K. alert to the fact that he is dealing here with his most intimate experience, which he often described mysteriously by this term.

23 Note that this (the offense, or scandal, or stumbling-block of faith) is a concept with which S.K. constantly deals. Cf. Appendix to the following chapter.

24 For the application to S.K.'s case see my *Kierkegaard*, pp. 124ff.

25 Precisely thus did S.K. understand himself, but before this book was written he had resolutely renounced the poetical and had published the *Three Godly Discourses on the Lilies and the Birds . . .* as poetry to end poetry.

26 This was exactly S.K.'s situation in 1848.

27 Perhaps I need not remark how intensely personal this whole paragraph is. It is not Anti-Climacus who is speaking here, but S.K. out of his own experience—as intimately as he talked with himself in his *Journal*, but with the assurance that no one would guess that he was talking here about himself.

28 From the days of the Reformers. Cf. *Apologia Confessionis Augustanae*, 7ff.

29 The notion that sin is qualified by being "before God" was implicitly discarded when Kant declined to recognize God's will as determining the moral law, but S.K. doubtless is thinking of theologians of his own time who, under

the influence of the Kantian philosophy, generally ignored this definition.

30 For the distinction which S.K. made between guilt and sin cf. *Postscript*, pp. 468ff.

31 Ephes. 2:12.

32 This was precisely S.K.'s own case.

33 These important concepts first emerged in the *Fragments* and were dealt with more fully in the *Postscript*.

34 *Kjøbstad*, a word which S.K. often applied scornfully to the Capital of Denmark, playing upon the name Kjøbenhavn, which means Market-Harbor. He makes the application plain in this case by mentioning the number of inhabitants it could boast of at that time, 500,000.

35 The allusion is to the well known ode of Horace (2, 10, 5) which extolls the golden mean.

36 *Adriennen paa* is an expression S.K. several times quoted from a popular play.

37 S.K. frequently recurs to the analogy of knotting the thread before beginning to sew. Subsequently he reflected that the only way to make the end thoroughly fast was by the martyrdom of the "witness to the truth."

38 This passage is aimed expressly at Martensen, then the Professor of Theology, and later (when S.K. attacked him more violently) Bishop Primate of Denmark.

39 A "position" means something posited affirmatively.

40 Only a year before this book was published did S.K. apprehend in the deep religious experience of 1848 that his sins were "not only forgiven by God but forgotten." See my *Kierkegaard*, pp. 391ff.

41 In 1854 S.K. wrote in his *Journal*, "Truly it was an injustice to Columbus that America was not named after him, but it is a very much greater injustice to Jesus Christ that Christendom was named after Him."

42 In fact Mephistopheles in *Faust* is the absolutely discontinuous, the sudden.

43 "Works sprung from sin acquire only through sin their strength and power." S.K. of course quoted Shakespeare in German, and I leave the passage as he read it, for this is one of the instances to which a German might appeal in support of the boast that Schlegel and Tieck's translation is an improvement upon the English. For all Mac-

beth said was: "Things bad begun make strong themselves by ill."

44 I, 3116.

45 See e.g. Tauler's *Sermons* (ed. of 1842), Vol. III, pp. 36f.

46 Note 1 calls attention to the fact that "willing to be one's own self, or not willing to be oneself" expresses strongly the wilfulness of the attitude. Here the formula is altered (involving in the translation a change from the present participle to the infinitive) because in the context of this chapter the wilfulness is still more evident and should be more strongly expressed. "Not to will to be oneself" is here equivalent to "to will not to be oneself."

47 Both are Roman military terms: the first (derived from *con manus*) means hand-to-hand; the second (derived from *e manus*) means at a distance, so that missiles can be used.

48 This passage cannot be translated adequately, for the reason that it plays upon the word *naergaaende* (literally, near-going), which is the picturesque Danish term for forwardness or insolence.

49 Perhaps this refers to *Politics*, III. cap. 11, where it is said that the argument that the multitude is better than all the clever people does not apply in all cases, for the same argument might be applied to the beasts. It is certain that what follows in this paragraph is aimed at the doctrine of David Strauss, according to which the God-Man is mankind. Cf. his *Leben Jesu*, II. §147, pp. 734ff. (of the 1st ed. 1836); *Dogmatic*, II. pp. 214f.

50 It is to be remembered that this book was written in the year 1848 when in Denmark, as all over Europe, the people demanded and obtained from absolute monarchs a constitutional government.

50a *Via negationis, via eminentia* = by way of negation, by way of idealization. Perhaps we may be permitted to borrow the brief and clear explanation given by Professor Swenson to these terms where they appear in *Philosophical Fragments*. These, he says, are "scholastic expressions describing two different methods of determining the divine attributes, as by denying of God some human trait, e.g., finitude, or by affirming of him some human trait in its ideal perfection, e.g., perfect justice, perfect love, etc."

51 A reference to an illustration in Plato's Apology.
52 In those days the telegraph was the newest miracle, and hence S.K. made much of it.
53 *Modo ponendo* means positively, in positive form.
54 S.K. frequently uses these words of Luther at the Die of Worms.
55 By this introduction one who is acquainted with S.K. will be apprised that he is about to speak out of his own experience. In fact it is evident that in this paragraph he has in mind the sacrifice he made for the sake of Regina Olsen. When he wrote this book he was already thinking of the possibility of establishing "a sisterly relationship" with her who was now Madame Schlegel. We can infer this from the fact that just when he was on the point of sending the manuscript to the printer her father, his inveterate enemy, died and made this seem a possibility. Then for fear that so trenchant a book as this might hinder the desired *rapprochement* he was in a torment of indecision whether to publish it or no. One of the strangest episodes in his life was the auditory hallucination which finally brought him to a decision. See my Kierkegaard, pp. 246ff.
56 Plutarch, *De garrulitate*, cap. 8.